A WILLINGNESS TO DIE

MEMORIES FROM FIGHTER COMMAND

A WILLINGNESS TO DIE

MEMORIES FROM FIGHTER COMMAND

BRIAN KINGCOME

Frontispiece: Brian Kingcome, by Cuthbert Orde

First published in 1999 by Tempus Publishing
This edition published in 2006

Reprinted in 2008 by
The History Press
The Mill, Brimscombe Port,
Stroud, Gloucestershire, GL5 2QG
www.thehistorypress.co.uk

Reprinted 2013

British Library Cataloguing in Publication Data.
A catalogue record for this book is available from the British Library.

ISBN 978 0 7524 4024 8

Typesetting and origination by
Tempus Publishing Limited.
Printed and bound in England.

CONTENTS

TO MY MINDER

AUTHOR'S NOTE

Anyone looking for a chronological sequence of events won't find it here. I'm no diarist, have no notes and a fading memory which at its best was never strong. I wanted to call this book 'The Ramblings of a Geriatric Ex-Fighter Pilot'. I was restrained, mainly by my wife whose benevolent terrorism, thank God, controls my life. Nonetheless the title would have been apt, for that's what it's really all about. There's a vague chronological thread where time seemed the most logical link, but in many instances it isn't and indeed is often an irrelevance.

In my mind events are linked by many factors often transcending the barriers of time, sometimes by a similarity of the events themselves, sometimes by the atmosphere they evoked, often by the sounds, the smells, the emotions, the fears, the passions they triggered. These are the paths down which my memory led me and which I've cheerfully followed when they seemed more natural than those dictated by a slavish subservience to calendar and clock.

This book is no more and no less than a brief glimpse into 'long ago' times and places by an eyewitness who considers himself lucky to have been born into that era. Interest in them may now have waned. If so, or if my chronological untidiness proves too confusing, I shall of course be disappointed but ritual suicide will remain low on my list of priorities.

I've enjoyed reviving memories I'd thought long dead.

And worse things happen at sea.

Brian Kingcome, DSO, DFC,
Erstwhile Group Captain RAF, Devon.

FOREWORD
BY GEOFFREY WELLUM

In early June 1940 and as a newly trained, very young and junior pilot officer, I was posted to and joined 92 Squadron. I immediately became aware of a tall rather nonchalant Flt Lt with a captivating personality. He was introduced to me as my Flight Commander, Flt Lt Brian Kingcome. Immediately, on first acquaintance, he commanded my greatest respect and during my time with 92 Squadron, from June 1940 until August/September 1941, I bent the knee to only one person, one Brian Kingcome.

During the Battle of Britain we lost four Commanding Officers but the squadron was led and indeed held together, during Fighter Command's most testing time in September 1940 and during its greatest days, by Brian.

He led from the front. He was a 'come-oner' and not a 'go-oner' and as a result earned the deepest respect and affection from all those who were fortunate enough to follow him into battle. Brian Kingcome was 92 Squadron.

This book makes for compelling reading and portrays a man, fighter pilot and leader of the highest quality, a man who could look any other man straight in the eye.

Sqn Ldr Geoffrey H.A. Wellum, DFC

First Light by Geoffrey Wellum is published by Penguin.

INTRODUCTION

I corresponded with Brian Kingcome only once. He was then about two thirds of the way through drafting the story of his early life and his wartime service as a fighter pilot, and he wanted an opinion on how he was getting on with it. To enable himself to write it he had bought an already venerable second word processor and was knocking out his memoirs on a basis of association as thoughts occurred to him – one recollection leading to the next.

The result was a text with problems for which solutions would need to be found. On the other hand, it was a manuscript with personality and charm that had points to make, and it was saying them in a way that made their tone quite distinct from that of much other wartime reminiscence. There was a powerful aversion in its viewpoint to the clichés of writing about war in general and of the experiences of Second World War battle pilots in particular.

A Willingness to Die was clearly a book with the potential to be published, especially since it came from someone whose name was a legend among the airmen of his generation. Kingcome was writing it, as he said, in the only way he could think of, off the top of his head. This being so, it seemed important not to stem the flow by putting forward ideas about editorial discipline. At that stage the priority was to urge him to continue and to make sure he was getting down everything he had it in mind to say. Tactful advice with editorial technicalities could follow when there was a completed manuscript draft. Some months later, on 14 February 1994, Brian Kingcome died suddenly.

He was still working on his text, and no one can say how much more he might have written. Nor can anyone say how the book might have turned out if he had been able to work on his draft armed with editorial comment and his own second thoughts. At a guess he might have added another thirty or forty pages to give more details of his time in Italy during the last stages of the war (particularly of his atypical experiences with 205 Bomber Group) and the early months of peace in the Middle East and Austria. The text has had to be shaped from the material he did produce. The last, post-war part of his RAF career was covered by little more than synopsis notes.

The editing has involved breaking down the text and rebuilding it to allow the emergence of a narrative thread (which happens to be broadly chronological, whether or not this would have appealed to Kingcome). Inevitably there has been rewriting as well as some writing in to provide links. In this case I have, in the role of editor, had to be more of a *locum tenens* for the author than usual. At every stage there has been the need to preserve, sometimes to enhance, Kingcome's 'voice', and to avoid putting words in his mouth that might ring false. This has been the basic challenge of the manuscript as he left it.

★ ★ ★

Brian Kingcome belonged to a generation for which the romance of the air was still pristine, before the growth of air travel had made flying a commonplace. It was still possible in the 1930s for the aspiring pilot to feel he was joining the ranks of the frontiers men, pushing back the barriers of the element of air and exploring where men had never been before while gaining an entirely new perspective on the world stretched out below. The novelist David Garnett, author of *Lady into Fox* and *The Sailor's Return*, described this freshness and exhilaration vividly in *A Rabbit in the Air* (1931), the diary he published about his civilian adventure in learning to fly in a Bluebird Mark III and a Tiger Moth between 1929 and 1931 as a 'mature student' in his late twenties.

I took her in and landed. I was drunk with air. I was wild, and driving home sang and shouted, full of realisation that we have found a new freedom — a new Ocean. For thousands of years we have crawled or run on the earth, or paddled across the seas, and all the while there has been this great ocean just above us in which at last we sail with joy. The longing for the sea: the call of the sea, one has heard of that, and that was the natural adventure in the past. But now it is a longing for the air, to go up.

Brian Kingcome came under this same spell while he was still at school, and all his early years may be seen as providing a background to the story of an airman in the making. It seems a natural outcome when, after leaving school in 1936, he goes to Cranwell RAF College as a flight cadet. Combined with this was another romantic conviction: pilots were going to be needed, since Europe was inevitably moving towards a Second World War despite the illusions of the appeasers; and when war came the fighter pilot would be uniquely placed to conduct his part in it. The skies were destined to be the last bastion of individual chivalry.

Within only a few short years the realities of war would provide sharp correctives to such a naïve notion, as we shall see. Kingcome's friend and colleague, Sir Hugh 'Cocky' Dundas, gave a graphic description in his own memoirs, *Flying Start* (1988), of what it felt like to be alone in the cockpit of an aeroplane, engaging the enemy for the first time. Above the seas at Dunkirk during Operation Dynamo Cocky had discovered in himself little but panic, confusion, an instinct to live and the draining away from his mind of everything he had been taught. As he came back to land at Rochford airfield, behind Southend, however, he found that 'a sense of jubilation replaced the cravenness of a few minutes earlier'.

I was transformed, Walter Mitty-like: now a debonair young fighter pilot, rising twenty, proud and delighted that he had fired his guns in a real dog-fight, even though he had not hit anything, sat in the cockpit which had so recently been occupied by a frightened child...

As an operator in combat Kingcome soon gave proof of his natural aptitude. By Dunkirk he was serving with 92 Squadron, which then went for a time to South Wales before moving to Biggin Hill at the height of the Battle of Britain. The official score for the 'kills' he made was always thought to be an underestimate by his fellow airmen as well as by later historians. The final figure at the end of his active service stood at eighteen enemy aircraft and included a number of German bombers. In part the uncertainty surrounding this figure may be attributed to the scorn he felt for the idea of keeping a precise tally. 'Of course I used up a lot of ammunition on 109s in the Battle of Britain – who didn't – but I don't remember claiming many kills', he wrote. 'In my experience there was usually too much going on upstairs to spend time following victims down to the ground for confirmation of a kill.' The need to follow a stricken plane down to be sure of a 'kill' in turn made a pilot vulnerable and left other possible targets free to attack again or escape. As Kingcome's obituarist in *The Times* suggested, 'He was without that sometimes fatal curiosity, and perhaps his relaxed attitude to combat statistics was, in the long run, his salvation'.

In Brian Kingcome's view, any attempts to draw comparisons between pilots was invidious. Those who stood outside the circle may have seen personal scores as a reliable yardstick, but the pilots themselves knew it was a grey area. Such claims were never likely to be able to bear too close a scrutiny. There was no such thing as a typical pilot personality. The warriors of the air were made up from a cross-section of people whose aspirations and reactions varied as widely as they would in a cross-section from any other walk in life. Some pilots saw big personal scores as an ultimate aim, but others were indifferent to trophies. Some loathed the limelight and avoided publicity while others were hungry for the spotlight and applause. There were also those who were natural hunters, stalking their prey and closing in for the kill, and among the leaders were those who ruthlessly put their own interests first and those who selflessly thought first of the men they were leading. In an aside trimmed from the present text Kingcome wrote:

> The controversial claims in the Battle of Britain were the sum total of many factors, but I suspect were mainly the results of duplication. No one without personal experience of being centre stage in a sky literally a maelstrom of aircraft in all attitudes, diving, climbing, spinning, some on fire, some smoking, some breaking up, dodging, ducking, weaving, searching frantically for targets, can understand how simple it would be in the heat of battle, with adrenaline racing, for two or more pilots to believe quite genuinely they had each destroyed the same aircraft. But to me, and to the majority of the pilots involved, these are all irrelevancies. The Battle of Britain and the battles that followed weren't numbers games, except for an insignificant majority. Who cared whether Smith claimed five and Jones fifty-five? We had a job. It wasn't about personalities or personal achievement. In 1940 it was about fighting-off invading hordes, about freedom and subjugation, and between them the Smiths and Jones's, their colleagues and friends, defeated their own fears and, in so doing, the enemy. That's all that history needs to know.

He was repelled by derring-do accounts of aerial battle, and the idea that the situation had produced men who could be singled out as heroes or that the job they did was in any way heroic was an anathema to him for similar reasons. At a ball given at the Savoy Hotel in 1990 to mark the fiftieth anniversary of the Battle of Britain he reacted brusquely to a conversational remark made by the columnist Barbara Amiel to the effect that, 'To us you were all heroes.' Later, fearing he may have overdone it, he wrote her a letter of 'apologia' to clarify his feelings:

> I think it quite wrong that, because the B of B turned out to be quite an important event in retrospect, the participants should be automatically classed as 'heroes'. Why can't they just talk about B of B pilots? Why does it always have to be heroes? I think it devalues

the word and denigrates all those others who were called on to face just as great odds and whose contribution and sacrifices are just as great, but whose exploits hadn't been pushed into the public eye by Churchill's splendid oratory. Dying is what's important, not the time and place you did it. If we're not very careful we'll start believing our own publicity, and I see a time when we'll start wearing our medals on our pyjamas.

Brian Kingcome's diffidence in these matters went back to the very beginning of the war. He was notorious for never having maintained or kept his flight logbooks, and when it came to souvenirs of any kind was determinedly unsentimental. No material of this sort therefore survives and the loss is ours. On the other hand, he wrote his draft for *A Willingness to Die* with no prompts at his elbow except his memory. What he put into the manuscript is what he wished to put in and what he wished to survive of his story. This gives us his human quality. To try to reconstruct the frantic minutes or seconds of long-ago air battles in mock-up recollections would have been to his mind a false and purposeless exercise.

We can see that he had his point about 'heroes' when we consider how wartime pilots like Richard Hillary and Guy Gibson have, in recent studies, been put through the mill of deconstruction and brought down to earth as flawed personalities. Heroes come into being only because society has a need for them. These figures do not, on the whole, pin the label on themselves and it may be unfair to their memory to pass them the blame, whatever their other failings. Hillary certainly stands reproached for contributing to the mythologizing of the fighter-pilot experience, even though it was his stated intention in *The Last Enemy* (1942) to strip away much that was 'untrue and misleading… written on the pilot in this war'. The author and critic John Lehmann, writing in the second volume of his autobiography, *I Am My Brother* (1960), felt that; 'the *mystique* that surrounded Hillary, and the doom that seemed to pursue that brave and tortured young man like a lover, cast a glamour over the prose expression that was not, I believe, inherent in it'. Even so, *The Last Enemy* was 'a classic description of the discovery by an apparently disaffected young English cynic that when it came to the point, he was neither disaffected nor cynical but braver and with a deeper feeling for what his country stood for than most of the patriotic tub thumpers. I shall never forget the sight of his smiling, mask-like, re-made face at a party of Sybil Colefax's not long before his death'.

Hillary died crashing an aged Blenheim bomber on a night-training flight. His first biographer, Lovat Dickson, cited the last will and testament found in his locker as his 'authentic voice' in *Richard Hillary* (1950):

> I want no one to go into mourning for me. As to whether I am buried
> or cremated, it is immaterial to me, but as the flames have had one
> try, I suggest they might get their man in the end.

There is in this a rhetorical hint of measuring up to spar with destiny, but as Brian Kingcome might have responded, wartime is full of these sorts of individual tragedy and for the most part they are never chronicled or noted. We also have to recognise the uniqueness of these experiences for those who went through them and survived. It is a notable feeling among survivors that only those who shared an existence on the edge can truly understand how it was for them and that ultimately this can never be fully communicated to another soul. The phenomenon applies to many groups as much as to the fighter pilot: to the men who fought in the Western Desert, for instance; to the shamefully unsung merchant seamen of the North Atlantic convoys; to the prisoners of war in Germany and the Far East; to the relative handful of persecuted humanity that emerged from the Nazis' labour and ex-termination camps.

Another aspect of the specific experience of the airmen that set them apart, especially during the battle on the Home Front, was the extreme contrast between being one moment high in the air in a life-or-death situation and the next, back on the ground, in the total 'normality' of the village pub among people who did not fly. At a time when life was uncertain, when the example of sudden, violent death was something that in some way or other touched everyone you knew, it became necessary to cultivate a distance and an apparent invulnerability to emotion. There was no time for the luxury of the 'stages of grief' in response to the loss of comrades, and relationships with the opposite sex held no guarantee of having a future. The prevailing self-protective style, which aimed to take these things lightly, concealed complexities that were rarely explored in British films of the war period. The 'stiff upper lip' syndrome was thus by the early 1960s a ripe target for parody in the *Beyond the Fringe* revue. Yet the mask had been necessary and it did not detract from a determination to enjoy life, since that aspect too was intensified and the old habits of mind remained in place once the war was over.

The only WAAF officer in the British Zone in Austria in 1946 recollected how it was when Brian Kingcome arrived to take over as the CO of 324 Wing at Zeltweg. Initially she was apprehensive that she might no longer be asked for weekends to 'Snobs' Corner' as the house in which the CO lived with his support officers was known. Before long an invitation arrived.

At first I didn't really take to Brian Kingcome, although I could see that here was the prototype – the person that all the young pilots wished to emulate. A cat that walked by his lone, one of the 'over-promoted, over-decorated young men' as someone has described them, who were the heroes in the RAF. The glamour was real, so also the charm and the strong personality, the quick decisions. 'Daggers' Rees, his Squadron Leader Admin. [Lord Rees, who as Merlyn Rees the Labour MP for Morley and Leeds South and Secretary of State for Northern Ireland], once told me that Kingcome was a very efficient Commanding Officer, who knew everything that was going on in his wing, despite his rather aloof manner and apparent lack of interest in anything other than having a good party as often as possible. I grew to enjoy Brian's quickness of mind and instant understanding of anything one said and luckily he found me amusing and invited me to continue my weekend visits. Often there would be a party – sometimes we'd sit around at Snobs' Corner, then go over to the officers' mess on the airfield for a while and spend a quiet evening. A 'snapshot' of memory comes to mind of Brian stalking into the mess one evening, his two large dogs at his heels – Melly, an Alsatian bitch, and Wilma, a young Great Dane and me a couple of paces behind. He was tall and walked faster than I did, but it was also that he couldn't bear to feel that he was encumbered by any girl. He liked women, and being very attractive had always had decorative female companions, but they must not become in any way possessive or dependent. This amused and suited me then as I was equally determined not to belong to only one person whilst I was one of the very few girls in an almost all-male world. To be labelled as so- and-so's girlfriend was not my line. Luckily the pilots liked having me around as a person. The lovely Austrian spring and early summer of 1946 remain forever in my mind as a time of pure happiness. An island in one's life, a summer's lease of all too short a date. When Barney Beresford [Brian Kingcome's predecessor at 324 Wing] flew in for a week's leave my happiness was complete. Brian and Barney and a couple of the squadron commanders drove down to Venice, taking me with them and we were allotted rooms in the Daniele by the Town Major at 25c. a night. During one lunch party at Harry's Bar Brian became convinced that the steaks were made of horse meat and got me to ask in Italian if they ever had beef. This caused quite an angry exchange – but we ate the meat anyway. Brian loved Venice and had an idea that some of his American ancestors had come from there.

In the opinion of many of Kingcome's colleagues, including P. B. 'Laddie' Lucas, the only factor that stopped Brian Kingcome going all the way to the top in the RAF after the war was the breakdown in health that led to his resignation from the service when he was still only in his early thirties. Lucas added one other qualification: that Kingcome would have needed to modify some of his attitudes to seniority and hierarchy. In the funeral address he gave for Kingcome, Cocky Dundas told a story from the brief period when he was in partnership in a luxury car-hire business with his former RAF colleague and friend, Wing Commander Paddy Barthropp. Barthropp happened to overhear a conversation that Kingcome was having with one of their regular clients, the Duke of Beaufort, who needed a car to meet him in London at Paddington Station and gave warning that he would be carrying a particularly long fishing rod. 'What a lucky duke you are,' Kingcome responded. 'We have a particularly long car for you.'

An aspect of his post-war career that Kingcome would certainly have told us more about if he had lived was the time he spent flirting with the film industry. The references he makes to it are frustratingly brief and incomplete, though we do also know that he worked on a script for a film version of Bruce Marshall's *The White Rabbit*, a book that was a best-seller in its day, despite being a broken-backed telling of the story of Wing Commander 'Tommy' Yeo-Thomas, the SOE agent who was captured in France and withstood the most horrific tortures of the Gestapo before being sent to Buchenwald, which he survived. Among others who worked on the script was the novelist Jack Trevor Story, and at one stage Twentieth Century-Fox were seeking to produce it. Kenneth More was front runner to play Yeo-Thomas, and the actor delayed other lucrative commitments for a year in the hope of the film being made. Unfortunately complexities over copyright proved insurmountable and the project was abandoned, though More did not let his personal ambition disappear from view. Later in the 1960s, on the crest of the acclaim he received for his playing of Young Jolyon in *The Forsyte Saga* television series, he took the book to David Attenborough, who was then head of Features at the BBC. By the terms of its charter the BBC could get round the rights difficulties, but only on condition that the production would never be repeated or sold. The result was a four-part series that had one transmission. Afterwards the tapes were destroyed.

There seems to be no doubt that Kingcome extracted enormous enjoyment from his fringe involvements with the film industry, though he also realised that its brittleness and tendency to self-admiration went against his personal grain. Integrity was something fundamental to him at every level, and this in itself created difficulties for him as he sought to find his way within a civilian existence. He found himself going through a very hard period of adjustment, made even harder by the lack of an emotional centre and the apparent blindness of the business world to what his personal qualities had to offer. 'A job for life' was still regarded as an ideal to be aimed for; people in management stayed put, and often stagnated where they happened to be. Indeed, a poor quality of management was one of the root causes of Britain's post-war industrial troubles. Ideas about flexibility of employment and the transferability of technical and management skills between various areas of activity would have to wait many years before they came to be seen as something that was socially desirable besides offering potential scope for the creativity and fulfilment of the individual.

In time the years of struggle led towards a personal resolution. He married Lesley Shute, a granddaughter of Sir Hector Macneal and the daughter of a squadron leader who had died in the war, and he became a family man. Together he and his wife eventually founded and built up a successful company called Kingcome Sofas, a design manufacture business widely recognised for the hand-crafted qualities of its furniture. To this he was able to apply the same principles and standards that had marked out his service career. At his funeral Cocky Dundas singled out the 'four key attributes that made him the man he was and enabled him to do the things he did. They were courage, determination, a total lack of pomposity or self-importance and an everlasting lightness of heart and touch.' These values governed his dealings with others on a personal and business level in the same way that they had gone to create the extraordinary leadership qualities which made him such an outstanding squadron leader during the crisis of the Battle of Britain. More than fifty years later one of the survivors who had served with him in 92 Squadron commented after he died, 'He really was 92 Squadron and all its spirit'.

★ ★ ★

The Epilogue was originally published in *Air Fair Biggin Hill* and the *Independent on Sunday*, and both I and Kingcome's family are grateful to the respective editors for permission to reprint it here.

★ ★ ★

For advice with preparing the text of *A Willingness to Die* for publication, I would like to record a debt to the late Wing Commander P.B. 'Laddie' Lucas, who kindly read through all the chapters concerning the war years and made several valuable points and corrections. I am also grateful to Sebastian Cox, Head of Air Historical Branch (RAF) at the Ministry of Defence, for giving Chapter 9, on the Morlaix raid, a detailed check to help with clarifying the squadrons that took part and also to correct several errors which might otherwise have slipped by. (It should perhaps be noted that Kingcome's memories of this abortive venture and his theories about the reasons for its failure do not necessarily coincide at every point with the conclusions of the original official investigation; but since he was a major protagonist in the operation it seems right that his eyewitness account should stand as a valid contribution to the record.) Above all I am indebted to Lesley Kingcome, the 'minder' of Brian's dedication, whose 'benevolent terrorism', he said, 'thank the Lord, controls my life'. She has given her support patiently throughout and has reassured me on numerous occasions that the editorial treatment was managing to catch and hold Brian Kingcome's authentic style and tone of voice.

Peter Ford
Orkney
January 1999

PROLOGUE

RAF HORNCHURCH, 1939

There are occasions so momentous, like the assassination of President Kennedy, that they become proverbial for all those who heard the news, who remember for ever after where they were at the time. An earlier such moment came at fifteen minutes past eleven o'clock on the Sunday morning of 3 September 1939. The indelible scene in my memory is of a dozen or so of us, young men in our late teens and early twenties, sitting, sprawling or leaning against the walls in the flight office of 65 Fighter Squadron, based at Royal Air Force Hornchurch on the eastern edge of London and therefore strategically placed at the forefront of our country's air defences. The volume of the wireless has been turned up as the doom-filled voice of Neville Chamberlain, the British Prime Minister, falteringly informs us that 'a state of war now exists between Great Britain and Germany'.

As I glance around at my fellow-pilots I wonder how they feel as the Prime Minister's voice, broken with sorrow and despair, crushed by an ultimate failure to avoid tragedy, announces the onset of this new era of death and destruction to a listening public not yet free from memories of the horrors and bereavements of the slaughter in the trenches of the Western Front only twenty years before. The same public is no doubt expecting and hoping for a rousing call to arms, something to help it forget its recent tragedies and to gird its loins anew for the future struggle, yet this is not it, most certainly. My own strongest feeling is one of unreality. We ought to be spellbound, gripped by an overpowering sense of history in the making, of epic upheaval, change and challenge. Instead the words ring hollow. It is as if we are all actors in a poorly scripted play.

Surely this grey, defeated voice coming over the airwaves cannot be that of the leader of the greatest empire the world has known? Where are the ringing phrases to kindle a fire in the belly, the inspired leadership, the confidence, the unswerving belief in an ultimate victory, however hard and long the road?

Only with difficulty do I shrug off the sense of unreality. Yet, if this is the real world, what does the future hold for us, a group of youthful airmen at the sharp edge of our country's defences? The Royal Air Force is a new, young service, hardly more than twenty years old, and it has no historical yardstick to assess the future other than the aerial battles of the First World War. If those were anything to go by, then the life expectancy of a fighter pilot in wartime might be measured in hours, perhaps in days, maybe even in weeks, but rarely in months. Under the onslaught of these darting thoughts, the sense of unreality returns and deepens as I try to absorb the unavoidable implications. All of these around me, my good friends, and I myself, will be dead by Christmas. What common denominator can it be that has brought us together at this time, young men from every corner of empire and all walks of life, to face extinction on the threshold of our destinies?

There were, of course, the obvious reasons, the very arguments we had used to convince ourselves and our families when we decided to become fighter pilots, the hack stuff repeated endlessly and parrot-like: the challenge of elements to be conquered, new worlds to be explored, new frontiers to be crossed; a recognition of the dangers ahead and the penalties there would be for failing to confront them; a fatalistic belief instilled in our pre-nuclear generation of the recurring certainty of war in history; an instinctive chivalrous reaction to the bully and the jackboot. These rationalisations were all very plausible and, properly dressed up, they gave a satisfying impression of self-sacrifice and selflessness. Yet, when it came to it, did they reflect a reality – a truth?

There were those in the era of appeasement who believed, or so they argued, that talk and reason were the ultimate defences and that the wave of arrogant nationalism sweeping across Europe could be contained by words. Among those of us who had taken the 'king's shilling', on the other hand, all patience with such cerebral elasticity had long ago been lost. Our plain pragmatism cut through the soothing smokescreen of words to what we saw as the stark reality beyond. In this imperfect world tyrants laughed at words seeing their use merely as a delaying tactic to be used for ruthless advantage. While diplomats debated, despots acted. In the meantime, a lust for power and physical domination had reached bursting point in the hearts and minds of new national leaders who had lived too long in the shadow of defeat. This was something never to be dissolved or deflected by persuasion or reasoning. There was one thing, and one thing only, that would stop them: Force.

At this point a doubt enters into my line of thought. Am I trying too hard to make crusaders out of us, ascribing a high-mindedness that simply did not exist? Perhaps we were motivated by nothing nobler than a mixture of boredom and bloody-mindedness. The latter is a wearisome weakness as a rule, though it can also be sublime in the right context, as I learnt years later when, after the war, I came across it at its most inspirational in the person of 'Tommy' Yeo-Thomas. He was arguably among the bravest of the brave in the Second World War, an Anglo Welshman born and brought up in France who became a manager to the Paris fashion house of the couturier Edward Molyneux. As soon as war broke out he volunteered for the RAF, but was too old for flying duties and instead was recruited, with his bilingual background to the Special Operations Executive (SOE), which co-ordinated undercover operations in Europe. Soon frustrated at being stuck in a desk job, he volunteered to train as an active agent and was dropped into occupied France on three occasions, and under the code-name 'White Rabbit' became a key element in the French Resistance.

Eventually the inevitable happened and he was captured by the Gestapo, who subjected him to almost three months of unrelenting, unspeakable torture and beatings. Entombed in solitary confinement, where the temptation to surrender is strongest, with no one to bear witness to acts of courage and day-by-day survival, no one to comfort or applaud, no contacts except for his inhuman tormentors, no break from the routine of hearing the rattle of keys in the lock before being dragged from a bare and freezing cell to endure more beatings and worse, he somehow summoned up extraordinary reserves of strength and never divulged a word. If he had been less valuable, the Germans would have killed him at an earlier stage, but the Gestapo badly wanted to keep him alive while they still hoped to wring a morsel of his priceless knowledge out of him. In the end, even, those master torturers had to admit defeat with grudging admiration. They packed him off to Buchenwald for extermination, and yet again underrated his indomitable will. Physically shattered he may have been, but in that desolate community of lost souls, among the doomed and dying for whom 'hope' and 'future' were forgotten words, his spirit triumphed over his broken body. Driving himself beyond conceivable limits, he once more contrived the impossible and escaped, making his way to the Allied lines as the Third Reich collapsed around him.

When I knew him after the war I asked him how on earth he had managed to resist the most crippling, agonising torture for hour after hour, day after day, week after week, when so few had been able to hold out for even the forty-eight hours needed to allow their contacts to disperse. What was this amazing force that he had been able to summon up, to give him a strength inconceivable to an ordinary mortal? 'Well,' he replied, 'I was often on the point of giving them everything they wanted. But no one said please.'

I would never presume to compare our watered-down version with the unique, heroic brand of a 'White Rabbit', but was that what it boiled down to in our case too: bloody-mindedness? Is all this philosophising nothing more than an attempt by me to create a highfalutin image of us as an elite band of Arthurian knights of the air, hanging on to our haloes as we took off in defence of the realm? – pretentious poppycock and a flight of fancy? It would seem so, and perhaps it is just as well. Sainthood would have been a heavy burden to us. At our time of life it was a comfort to be down to earth, accepting that we were nothing more than a bunch of normal healthy young men, motivated by the normal healthy qualities of the young in every generation – an un-dramatic mix of patriotism, bloody-mindedness and the spirit of ad venture.

Since war was inevitable, then let any would-be foreign invader attempt to set foot in our country at his peril! We had seen the pattern forming in Europe and felt our hackles rise. We knew, even if the politicians and prattlers appeared not to, that the time for words was coming to an end, that only fighting back would break the emerging pattern, and that the consequence of not breaking it would be for our world as we knew it to be lost for ever. As a nation, we would lose our freedom and our dignity. We should be humbled, our pride extinguished, a conquered subject people.

And no one would ever again say, 'Please'.

There was one other small but important ingredient, the link that completed the chain which bound us – too embarrassing ever to talk about, even to formulate into words, and most likely quite forgotten in a conscious sense. Yet at some stage it must have been recognised by each one of us, and become a chosen option, accepted before being dismissed and buried deep in the recesses of the mind. Without it none of us could have been in that room on that day, listening to the sombre, thin, defeated voice of Neville Chamberlain. It was the ingredient that gave reality to our unreal world, the positive bond – a very simple thing. It was a willingness to die.

ONE

A MINGLED EDUCATION

'What are you going to do when you grow up my boy?'

The question was predictable enough, the standard opening conversational gambit of my parents' friends whenever, as a schoolboy, I was introduced to them.

Among friends such a question was acceptable but asking about occupation was not the sort of approach you would take with a stranger. Nowadays it is a usual and convenient tactic for starting a conversational ball rolling when meeting someone for the first time, but in those more socially sensitive pre-war days it was a question to be avoided. A substantial portion of the public still had independent means from inherited wealth, and they would have been affronted by any suggestion that they needed to work for a living. My only problem with replying was that I had not the slightest clue what I should like to do, nor had I given the subject much thought. My fairly spasmodic upbringing had not steered me in any particular direction.

My father, Charles Kingcome, a Devonian whose family came from the then remote, unspoilt villages of Newton Ferrers and Noss Mayo, which sat astride the tidal waters of the River Yealm off Plymouth Sound and were linked by a foss that only surfaced at low water, had gone to India as a young man to work for a firm concerned with growing and exporting hemp. My mother, a most remarkable woman with a glorious independence of spirit, had been born as Ruby Fabris to peripatetic missionary parents, American citizens of English and Welsh origins, with a dash of ancient Italian blood to add piquancy to the mixture. They had taken off for China in the 1880s, and there Mother was born and continued to live until her early twenties. In that era when young ladies were expected to learn nothing more serious than household crafts and social graces, she felt bored by the prospect of such inactivity and limited horizons and studied shorthand and typing. She then landed a job working for a remote cousin, Colonel Sam Browne, best known for having designed the 'Sam Brown' belt, worn to this day by army officers.

The Boxer Rebellion having left her unscathed, she decided China had nothing more to offer within the limitations of the expatriate community and took off back to the United States on her own. She stayed in Boston for a time, supporting herself by her secretarial skills, then moved to Jersey in the Channel Islands for two or three further years, and afterwards went to Paris. There she met a young Frenchwoman, also of independent spirit, who became a life-long friend and whom I would meet years later and know as 'Tante Jeanne'. They joined forces to set up an English-style tea shop, which, despite its ultra-respectability, represented an outrage to convention. Unperturbed, they ran it with great success for several years, until Mother's feet began to itch again. She decided to give India a try, and it was on the boat sailing east that she met my father. He was returning from one of the six-month spells of home leave he was granted every two years.

He must have been mesmerised by the unheard-of independence of this attractive young woman, Miss Fabris, travelling alone with no parents, no chaperone, no fixed address and no particular destination in view. It sounds fairly routine by the standards of today, when television travelogues, jumbo jets and package holidays have taken the excitement and mystery out of foreign travel; but in my mother's time all travellers were still adventurers, challenging the unknown, revelling in the sheer romance of discovering, exploring and developing strange new worlds and lifestyles, each fresh place magically cocooned in its untouched culture and time warp.

My father, entranced and intrigued by this self-possessed young woman, whose disarming femininity barely concealed a daunting independence of spirit that boldly defied convention's iron discipline, was himself an attractive man — tall, pleasant looking and athletic. And as the outward bound P&O liner ploughed its long and leisurely way eastward, and as the nights grew warmer, the sea calmer, the moon larger, a romance was born and soon began to blossom. Before the ship docked at Bombay, my father had proposed and been accepted.

My mother was by then in her early thirties, unusually late in life in those days to marry and start a family. But she had never been one to count the cost and would have been motivated by the old-fashioned notion that she had a duty to her husband that went side by side with her own natural desire to have children. After the conventional year or so of child-free marriage, my elder sister, Patricia, was born, followed two and half years later by my self, and finally, four years after that, by my younger sister, Ione. By the time I was born Mother was in her mid-thirties/early forties, and was to be in her forties when sister Ione arrived. Childbirth was then, of course, a highly hazardous medical experience for women in their later fertile years.

My father was stationed in Calcutta, with a house full of indoor and outdoor servants — par for the course in those leisurely days. We children were looked after by an ayah, one of the lovely Indian nannies famous for their intense loyalty and the loving care they lavished on their charges. English children in India were lucky indeed to be placed in such caring hands. Each year during the hot season my mother took Patricia and myself, together with our ayah, up into the cool foothills of the Himalayas to escape the heat of the plains. Sadly I retain no memories of my infancy in India, the only legacy of those far-off times being a few faded and yellowed photographs.

At that time of a busy and developing empire, many English families spent their working years abroad and many children were born overseas, but it was generally unthinkable that they should be educated anywhere except England. So it was fairly normal practice for colonial children to be sent 'home' at a tender age. In my case I was two and a half, and my elder sister five, when we were dispatched together back to England to stay with our widowed paternal grandmother and our Aunt Madge in Plymouth. Sister Pat was presumably sent home because at five she was deemed to be ready to be fed into the English educational system. I can only assume that I was sent at the same time to keep her company. Be that as it may, sister Pat was promptly packed off to a boarding school at Launceston in Cornwall, where two years later, at the age of four and a half, I joined her.

It is here that my memories begin, albeit hazily. I remember that we had to make our own beds, and also my terrible frustration at not being able to reach high enough to straighten the bed clothes, and Pat coming to the rescue. I remember no feelings of homesickness, undoubtedly because of the colossal comfort of being under the wing of a fiercely protective elder sister. How she must have felt when first sent to the school on her own, with no shoulder to cry on, one can only despair to imagine, but already she had the stoicism and reserves of strength that were to characterise her throughout her life.

One particularly vivid memory was of the 'great escape', in which sister Pat was ringleader, needless to say. She must have been all of seven at the time. Even then she carried considerable clout, since somehow she managed to persuade her co-conspirators to include me in the escape plan. In the light of my age and general uselessness, this alone paid tribute to a formidable personality. In all we were a group of about half a dozen, and sister Pat and two of her older cronies formed our escape committee. I suspect that the 'old cronies' were included in the top brass simply to encourage loyalty and bolster flagging resolve. It seems doubtful whether sister Pat ever intended to delegate any real authority.

It was snowing heavily when we made our break. Whether this was a cunning ploy to foil pursuit or whether the escape commit tee had simply forgotten to look out of the window must eternally remain a mystery. The fact remains that, once we had reached the edge of the school's confines, we were left with no alternative but to ignore the weather and head for freedom as fast as we could. So we walked, and we walked. And we walked. And after what seemed for ever the committee convened an emergency meeting to decide on the next move. It was agreed we must by now be quite close to London. Since I'd never been there, I thought we were more likely closer to Calcutta, but was outvoted on the issue.

We were in fact in a well-to-do road flanked by houses, and because we were all beginning to feel very cold and hungry, the committee judged it expedient for us to knock on the nearest front door and offer to clear the snow from the path in return for food. This motion being proposed and carried, we approached the house and stood in a frozen huddle on the doorstep, shuffling nervously while sister Pat knocked. Eventually the door was opened by a lady who listened gravely to our offer. 'What a good idea,' she said. 'Why don't you come in and sit down in front of the fire and I'll make you a cup of tea before you begin work?'

She disappeared into another room as we all crouched gratefully in front of the fire. Five or ten minutes later a car drew up outside and out of it stepped the school matron. It hadn't taken the kind lady who invited us in many moments to realise where we were from and what we were up to. Under the pretext of making us tea, she had therefore telephoned the school to report her find. Telephones were still quite a rarity in those days, and it was our luck to have picked one of the few houses in Launceston that had one installed.

We were bundled into the car and driven back to school – a journey that took all of ten minutes. My clearest memory of that inglorious episode was the chastening realisation that after all our globe-trotting and the endless miles we knew we had covered, we had ended up virtually just round the corner.

Some two or three years later my mother returned to England with Ione, leaving my father on his own in India. From then until the start of the war we saw him only once every two and a half years, when he arrived back in England for his six months' home leave. Since I was away at various boarding schools during those periods, I saw very little of him even then.

★ ★ ★

My schooling was marginally eccentric, which was only to be expected, organised as it was by my more than marginally eccentric mother. There were at least nine different schools that I went to, and I dare say one or two others have slipped through memory's ragged net. I do not think I was at any one of these institutions for more than a year or eighteen months, and it seems amazing that I was left with any shreds of sanity. No sooner had I established my place in the pecking order at the latest school, than Mother would take tea with a friend who had recently heard how someone else's son or nephew was doing very well at some school elsewhere. Or else she would decide, at the beginning of the school holidays, that my toenails were far too long. Here was a sure sign that whatever school I then was attending was deplorably lax in its attitudes – an indication of an unacceptably poor standard of supervision. Off I would be whisked the following term to yet another establishment.

One hears a lot nowadays about brutality and sadism in the pre-war educational system, particularly in boys' public schools. Personally I never came across it. Certainly corporal punishment was the accepted penalty for breaking rules, but being the norm it excited no interest or comment. The important thing was that there were clear-cut rules with clear-cut punishments for their infringement. Consequently boys knew exactly where they stood. They didn't have to break the rules, but if they did they took a calculated risk, and if they were found out they accepted the punishment as a matter of course without fuss or rancour.

One of the most enjoyable schools I sojourned briefly at during my labyrinthine journey through the educational system was a minor public school called Allhallows, then at Honiton in

Devon, though it subsequently moved to an equally enviable site on the Dorset coast at Lyme Regis. In my day it was situated in a beautiful valley, then unspoilt but subsequently vandalised by those hideous monuments to progress, massive electricity pylons that clod-hopped across the hitherto magical countryside. At weekends we had complete freedom to wander the valley, and one day I discovered a quarry inhabited by jackdaws. I stole a couple of nestlings, took them back to school and housed them in a disused shed. There I fed them on scraps smuggled from the table after mealtimes, always making the same call as I approached them. They soon adopted me as their parent, and when they were old enough I taught them to fly by perching them on my wrist and running like a hare into the wind until they had lift-off. The door of their shed was left constantly open, and they were allowed to fly free, but although, when they were older, they eventually joined the local flock, they would still detach themselves and fly down to me if ever I called them. Their one bad habit was to fly into my dormitory and help themselves to anything which glittered. Apart from this genetic shortcoming, our relationship was good and trusting and I was heartbroken to have to say goodbye to them when my time there came to an end.

Allhallows was one of my few earlier schools to leave me with any concrete memories, and these were largely confined to countryside explorations, my jackdaws and the various sports in which I represented the school in the Under XIV Colts. I do vividly remember cold showers each morning in cubicles lining an open courtyard, and the bitter shock to the system these had in deep winter. On the scholastic side, the sole memory I retain is of turning in a blank paper for a chemistry exam, for which I was half-heartedly beaten by the chemistry master, a charming man who used to call me 'Dosey'. He was one of the few who realised that, behind my fixed expression of intense interest, I was fast asleep. Perhaps if he had beaten me with more enthusiasm, he might have cured me. He was too nice; he didn't; I never was cured.

The school had a very good choir, of which it was justly proud, and members were rewarded with their own special half-holiday once a term. Achieving eligibility for the choir half-holiday was one of my more spectacular successes. Music I love, and a note off-key jars with me instantly. To my intense frustration, however, I never was able to sing in tune. Perfectly aware of this formidable obstacle, I somehow infiltrated myself into the choir, where I remained undetected for several weeks. My comeuppance was inevitable. One day our slightly dreamy choirmaster was away sick and another master stood in for him at choir practice. As we let forth with an anthem the stand-in circulated among us, listening to each singer in turn. My heart sank ever lower as he came ever closer to where I stood. Finally he arrived on the spot, bent forward to listen and discovered that, while my mouth might be opening and shutting with a vigour to outshine the rest, not a sound emerged. I was unmasked; I was also fired.

All was not lost, however. The chapel organ was operated by a bellows which needed to be pumped by hand, and the pumper too qualified for the choir half-holiday. I was on to this dodge like a rat up a drain. The one drawback was the sheer monotony of the job, which made it easy for the mind to wander and lose concentration, especially if the mind concerned was anything like mine. Whenever this happened I would be roused from a day dream with a violent start by the organ's coughing and wheezing as it gasped for breath. Then I had to begin pumping frenziedly to restore the situation. Somehow, despite these moments of crisis, I managed to hold the job down and to win the coveted privilege of the extra holiday.

Alas, I was only at Allhallows for eighteen months before Mother decided my toenails were below par. Off I went again, this time to the most bizarre school of the bunch. Mother had a few years previously become a Christian Scientist, a religion she embraced fervently, albeit without in any way becoming a bore about the teachings of Mrs Eddy, and which brought her great comfort. Word reached her of a new Christian Science school called Paxton Park in Huntingdonshire – a co-educational school, of all things, and luckily an extremely rare phenomenon in those civilised days. To my shock and horror I found myself there, ill-cut toenails and all. It proved to be a deeply traumatic experience.

One effect Paxton Park had on me was to leave me with the unshakeable conviction that co-education is a disaster as an ingredient to learning. Pubescent youth has enough uneasy, inexplicable mental and physical stirrings to make the teens a confusing time of life, without adding sex to the mixture. At this period of development especially, living should be kept to its simplest form and distractions minimised. To mix the sexes at this time is simply to add yet another confusing distraction and place quite an unnecessary obstacle in the already painful path of learning. Certainly the cause of furthering my education slipped all the way to the bottom of my list of priorities from the moment I arrived at that extraordinary establishment, and I was not alone.

After the initial numbness had worn off, life on the other hand, took an upward turn, if not in the academic field. As a seat of learning Paxton Park may have been a dead duck, but as a school of life it turned out to be full of surprises. The establishment was run by Mr and Mrs Boardman, Mrs Boardman having a title which she did not use. I formed a vague impression that the handsome Georgian manor in which the school was housed, with its beautiful park and adjoining home farm, had originally belonged to her family. She was perhaps in her sixties, dedicated, principled and fervently sincere. Mr Boardman was perhaps ten years or so his wife's junior, though it may have been that he looked more youthful than he was. The lines and wrinkles of encroaching age had been smoothed out by superfluous flesh, the blessed result of years of good living and no exercise. He was a large, booming, expansive man with a fruity presence, a shiny bald pate fringed with white hair, and a resonant voice. Outwardly Mr Boardman's massive personality dominated his wife's, though one sensed that her hidden strength was the true driving force of the relationship, and that without her he would have deflated like a punctured tyre. Their partnership certainly worked. They were a happy and devoted couple and I remember them with affection.

In a way, Mr Boardman might be described as an English version of the archetypal American evangelical preacher, and even at the time he seemed to me too good to be true; but whether or not he was play-acting, he always treated me with great kindness, almost to an absurd degree. Even had he not been such a memorable character, the extraordinarily benevolent eccentricity with which he treated me would have made him unforgettable. I would like to think that his astonishing indulgence was prompted by the impression I had made on him with my electric personality, but out of modesty I have to admit that it was more likely triggered by a visit to Paxton Park from Philip Gordon-Marshall, a friend from Allhallows.

Philip was four years my senior, and our paths had barely crossed, but he had met my sister Pat when she visited me with my mother for a school function and I think was rather taken with her. He kept in touch, at all events, and in fact remained a much-loved family friend for the rest of his relatively long life. When he left Allhallows he had tried for the Royal Air Force, but had failed his medical. This was a devastating blow to him. All his life till then he had known, without a shadow of doubt, that the RAF was to be his entrée to a career in the sky. As one of the school's top cross-country runners, moreover, he had taken his physical fitness for granted. But Philip was never one to subside into moping. Once he had picked himself up, dusted himself down, he decided to go for civil aviation as the only alternative way to satisfy his urge to fly.

One sunny afternoon early in my first term, while I was still bemused by my new habitat, there came the drone of an aero engine overhead − not a common sound in the mid-1930s − and a small aircraft circled the school a couple of times at roof-top height. The whole school rushed out to watch spellbound as the tiny machine throttled back and, in that lovely burbling, swooshing silence that follows the throttling back of an old-fashioned aero engine, glided in to land in the park in the front of the house. Out of the aircraft stepped Philip Gordon-Marshall, nonchalant in flying helmet and silk scarf, cutting every bit as romantic a figure as Errol Flynn in *Dawn Patrol*. 'Is there a Brian Kingcome here?' he asked. 'Have I come to the right place?'

He had, and there was. My stock soared. Out from the house rolled Mr Boardman, as beside himself with excitement as any one. I introduced him to Philip, who asked permission to take me up for a spin. Basking in the gaze of many envious eyes, I climbed aboard and a moment later found myself for the first time in a world I had never dreamed could exist – a world free from the drag of earth's umbilical cord, free to climb, swoop and dive, free of boundaries, free of gravity, free of ties, free to do anything except stand still.

At that moment, in an instant, I understood Philip's passion for flying. It had nothing to do with mechanical or engineering wizardry, though the trappings for that were there aplenty. Much more was it about stepping into a new dimension, an intoxicating new world with no limits to the opportunities for exploration, innovation, travel: a world still small enough to be a club where everyone knew everyone else, in which there existed a special unexpressed camaraderie, where bureaucracy, with its stifling regulations and heavy-handed restrictions, was as yet unknown. From that day onwards, ideas began to take shape about my own future direction in life.

Not long after Philip's visit Mr Boardman summoned me to his office. Among his consuming passions was a large rockery which he had designed and built entirely with his own hands and where he spent all his spare time. It incorporated small meandering streams that fed two or three pools stocked with brown trout. Unhappily for him and the trout the local herons had stumbled on this handy larder and would carry out dawn raids from time to time, sorely depleting his treasured fish population. On the morning he sent for me the herons had achieved a particularly successful raid, and on his desk lay a double-barrelled twelve-bore shotgun. Would I be prepared, he asked, to mount an anti-heron dawn patrol and destroy the marauding predators? In return he would pay me ten shillings (50p) for every heron I shot – a princely sum indeed when £2 or £3 was an average weekly wage. And while I was about it, he wondered, might I also be prepared to man an armed nightly anti-poacher patrol, to wander the grounds after dark to scare off unwelcome intruders? Poaching had lately become a bit of a problem, it being known locally that he employed no gamekeeper.

Here was an unheard-of offer, and naturally I leapt at it. Indeed, I would cheerfully have given back to Mr Boardman any ten shillings I might earn, seeing it as a small price to pay for the excitement and individual freedom he was putting on offer. In the event, I never got to shoot a heron. Somehow the birds always sensed my presence, however craftily I hid myself, and steered clear. But at least they abandoned raiding the trout, so Mr Boardman kept his money and my hands remained unstained with herons' blood. Come to that I never shot a poacher either. Perhaps the sight of a flickering torch beam and the word going about that the grounds were now being patrolled at night were enough to act as effective deterrents.

In those days, after all, poachers were not the dangerous gangs of professionally organised criminals they have often since become, but merely locals scouting for the odd rabbit or pheasant for the pot. Moreover, they were not to know that the 'patrols' consisted of just one nervous schoolboy groping his way through dark and sinister woods as he struggled to convince himself that the small rustling noises which seemed to be stalking him were nothing more than imagination; and that he would probably have fled like a startled hare had he bumped into a real poacher. Or perhaps they did know, and wisely considered that one jumpy schoolboy, armed to the teeth and liable to blast off in panic reaction at the first thing to move, was more to be feared than any professional keeper with his controlled, predictable response. Whatever the reason, the poaching did seem to lessen, and I felt I had kept my side of this part of the bargain as well, even if I had no scalps to show for it.

In a different context I did pick up a few sad little scalps in a way that appals me to think back on. It shows, on the other hand, that I was no better or worse than the average unthinking schoolboy. As I wandered through the woods at night, I was constantly impressed by the numbers of birds I saw roosting in the lower branches of the trees, and noticed how they became mesmerised and motionless in the light of my torch, so allowing me to get close enough almost to touch them. Taxidermy, very widely practised in those pre-conservation days of trophy collection and display, had always held a sort of morbid fascination for me, and now, as I stumbled through an inexhaustible reservoir of subjects to work on, it seemed a heaven-sent opportunity to try my hand at the craft. On my night-time prowls I therefore took to shooting, with thoughtless callousness, suitable specimens of various breeds. These I dismembered, cleaning out the skulls and filling them with a dreadful embalming concoction of my own devising before mounting the heads, wings and tails artistically – as I thought – on pieces of bark.

My creations were ghastly, of course, and luckily it did not take me long to realise it. The concept was appalling, my taste was execrable; and I was disenchanted to discover that what is beautiful in life may become merely ugly in death, however carefully dressed. At least I was now able to cross taxidermy off my list of possible careers, but the fact that, as I progressed through my teens, I developed a squeamishness about killing birds and animals may seem a strange quirk in someone who would eventually become a trained assassin. The lack of logic in the situation never struck me till later. I am the sort of hypocrite who will eat and enjoy the pheasant someone else shoots, or the lamb someone else slaughters, but would not care to do the dirty work himself. Yet, when it came to it, killing people never troubled me at all.

Perhaps my squeamishness about the animal kingdom was set off by my squalid venture into taxidermy, but it was finally brought to a head by two incidents in particular. The first happened at Biggin Hill, the RAF fighter station where I spent two of my most enjoyable war years. It was the summer of 1940, and the Battle of Britain was in full swing, when someone had the idea that it might help fighter pilots to keep their eyes in when not flying if they were given clay pigeons with traps and guns to practise shooting between sorties. One day, as I was awaiting the call to 'scramble' and killing time by idly banging away at some clays on the airfield behind the dispersal hut, a flock of rooks flew overhead. Without conscious thought, I swung the gun round and picked off one of the birds. No sooner had it hit the ground than the rest of the flock turned back and, with a deafening cacophony of cawing, began to circle the sorry little corpse. I did not have much time to watch, horror-struck, for at that point we were scrambled.

When I landed back an hour or so later I was disconcerted to notice the flock still there, still endlessly orbiting the pathetic crumpled bundle of feathers on the ground. It was approaching twilight before finally, in ones and twos, the circling birds began to leave, until at last only one was left, presumably the victim's mate, a forlorn creature that continued to circle its partner's body, cawing desolately, until dark.

I have never shot a bird since.

The second incident happened a year or so later, in the autumn of 1941, when I had taken a few days' leave and was staying in a pub at Luss, a tiny village on the edge of Loch Lomond. No doubt there have been many changes in the locality since, but in 1941, apart from the village pub, the 'big house' on one of the islands which dotted the loch, and the scattered dwellings of crofters, there was virtually no habitation. The village lay deep in Colquhoun country, the Colquhoun himself being away at the time, so that the big house was empty. But there was scarcely a soul in the place who was not kin to the clan. The pub, the

Colquhoun Arms (naturally), was run by a splendid couple called Sinclair and Cecile Colquhoun (what else?), and in the evenings its bar filled up with Colquhouns of every shape, age and size. I had the privilege of getting roaring drunk with them, and was deeply honoured to be made an honorary clan member and allowed to wear the clan kilt during my stay.

During the hours of daylight I took a boat out on to the loch to explore the islands, usually with a gun loaned to me by Sinclair Colquhoun, who added instructions to bring back a deer if ever I should come across one. In the fullness of time I did. As I was pushing my way through chest-high bracken in a wood, there came a crashing in the undergrowth and a brown shape was momentarily visible as it plunged through the dense cover. I took a quick shot, and the crashing came to a sudden halt. Following the track through the bracken, I came upon my victim, a young hind, not half-grown and still alive. I knelt beside it, and as it looked up at me with huge, melting bambi eyes, experienced an overwhelming feeling of self-disgust. Although it was now a kindness for me to finish its life, I felt like the murderer I was. But being also a self-confessed hypocrite, I lugged the carcass back to the pub and we ate it. Yet the memory remained indelible, and apart from human beings the hind was the last living creature I ever slaughtered.

★ ★ ★

The other discovery I made at Paxton Park had to do with girls. Up to that point they had been creatures from another planet, neither admired nor scorned but simply ignored. There was no reason for contact because there was no common ground. They had their ways, their habits, their interests, and at no point did ours converge with theirs. The only puzzling thing was why they should be there at all. They couldn't play rugby or any other decent game, and what else was there? I had sisters, of course, but somehow they didn't figure in the picture.

Now, however, I suddenly found myself looking at the opposite sex in a different light. Good heavens! Girls were actually human beings. You could communicate with them. Perhaps there might be a reason for them after all. I'd heard extraordinary rumours which, of course, simply couldn't be true, but nonetheless I became aware of certain looks, sideways glances, eye contacts that set off unfamiliar feelings, inexplicable stirrings of excitement and curiosity. It all made me realise that a door into a new world was slowly opening. Maybe it sounds unbelievably naïve in this knowing, crude and explicit age, when condoms seem the most popular subject for public debate, that someone in his teens should still have found sex a mystery. But I did, and I'm glad I did.

Indeed, I sigh for the young of the post-1960s and post-pill generations, for whom the magic, the mystery and the fascination of sex have been relentlessly trivialised by over-exposure and over-familiarity. Sometimes I compare the only 'blue' film I ever saw with the explicit sex scenes that now seem obligatory in so many films and TV dramas, however irrelevant they may be to the plot. I find it hard to resist the thought that these scenes must be one of the reasons for the recent falling off of the birth-rate in the West, since there can be no greater sexual turn-off than the sight of two strangers locked in a graceless, grunting grapple. Be that as it may, my blue film experience came about in early 1941, and I doubt whether the film in question would now be considered shocking enough to be banned from prime television time for children. In those days anything in the 'blue' category was strictly illegal and shown only in great secrecy to carefully selected audiences. The mere mention of the word 'blue' was enough to set people off looking furtively over their shoulders.

The Battle of Britain had been fought and won three months earlier, and Leslie Howard, the country's best-loved, best-known film actor, was directing and acting in his film *The First of the Few*, based on the life of R.J. Mitchell, the designer of the Spitfire. He himself played Mitchell, with David Niven taking the part of a fictional character called Wing Commander Crisp, who was a composite portrait of the test pilots who nursed and developed the Spitfire from its cradle, including the great Jeffrey Quill. All the important roles were taken by professional actors, but Howard felt that a little authenticity might rub off if a few Battle of Britain pilots were to play themselves. That, at least, was the official reason, though it proved to be a piece of misplaced optimism and the actors came over far more convincingly than the genuine airmen. Howard's main concern was his budget, I suspect. Serving officers could not be paid.

I was one of the fortunate half-dozen or so pilots whose names came out of the hat, and the whole enterprise was the greatest fun. Our roles called for little more demanding than lolling about in flying clothes in a fake dispersal hut, going outside to look sombrely skywards from time and time, and delivering such daft lines as, 'Good luck – they'll need it,' to cue in stock shots of Spitfires and German bombers flying overhead. Most of the stock shots in Second World War flying films include rapid frames of the interior of a Spitfire cockpit with a close-up of the pilot's gloved hand holding the control column, thumb on gun button in readiness for the decisive burst before the montage cuts away to an external shot of an enemy aircraft being brought to grief. The same stock shots are wheeled out regularly to support documentary and news items to do with the battles in the air of the Second World War. That thumb on the firing button, which must have been seen by more people than any thumb in history, is my claim to immortality. Reader, the thumb is mine.

The film-making episode with Leslie Howard was a joyous interlude and a marvellous break from airfield routine. I hardly remember when I enjoyed myself more. To make up for the fact that we were giving our services free, we were put up at the Savoy Hotel for the three or four weeks we were needed. What was more, a PR representative of the production company was placed at our disposal to make sure we were properly looked after once each day's shooting was over. This meant an endless nightly round of London's best clubs and pubs, no expense spared, all paid for by an apparently grateful movie management.

The word soon got round, as words do. It was remarkable how many off-duty members of various RAF units 'just happened' to be passing the Savoy whenever we were setting forth on our nightly expeditions. To ask friends to join us was a handy, painless way of returning earlier hospitality. The clubs we frequented most were the Four Hundred, whose dimly lit dance floor and seductive music were excellent backdrops for young men in uniform trying their luck with the 'I'm off to war tomorrow and may never come back' routine; and the down-to-earth Bag o' Nails, a far more raucous affair where serious boozing took priority. We would then all finish up back at the Savoy, revelling in the music of the great Carroll Gibbons, that lovely man, pianist and bandleader, and his Savoy Orpheans. All in all, we fared extraordinarily well, and considered ourselves to be more than amply rewarded for our meagre, amateur contribution to the film. Apparently Leslie Howard disagreed and thought we deserved yet more. Amid much sly nudge-nudging and wink-winking and many taps to the nose, we were informed that a special treat had been laid on for us – one of 'those' films. It required to be shown in great secrecy after the studio had finished the day's work and everyone else had gone home.

At the appointed hour we crept with laboured self-conscious jokes into the private projection room, led by Leslie Howard, who seemed in the greatest state of excitement of any of us. We then settled into the deeply comfortable armchairs of the small cinema and awaited our treat; and treat it was, though not in the way we had anticipated. Those who had expected titillation encountered a rude though not unpleasant shock, for the film was hilarious. It looked as if it had been shot in the 1920s – silent and in black and white – and the title alone, *A Walk in the Woods*, must have given its creator much satisfaction. The action began with a car being driven along a woodland track by two pretty young women, who very soon decided to stop and take a walk in the woods – so justifying the title; though from this point on, justifying the title ceased to be any central concern. The young women pointed upwards at the sun and, with suitably histrionic gestures, indicated how hot it was today. This gave the cue for them to begin to take off their clothes. Edge of seat stuff!

Meanwhile, visible to the audience but unbeknown to the girls, a shady-looking young bounder lurked amid the trees. One glance at his waxed *moustachios* and sleekly oiled hair had been enough to make us suspect that he was not there just to study botany, and we were right. As soon as he spied the girls he whipped off his own clothes, with much twirling of *moustachios* and lewd rolling of eyes, and then began to close in on his prey, leaping from the cover of one tree to the next as the twirling and eyeball rolling built up to a blur of speed and frenzy.

The girls in the meantime had decided on a little light exercise, only to find, in the midst of their innocent pastime, that the rotter had sprung among them, roaring lasciviously. Aghast to begin with, they flapped their hands in helpless gestures of modesty, until they evidently remembered that it is rude to say no and decided to submit to the amorous antics. From then on it was all go, but projected, as it was, with a jerky speeded-up action to match the wildly exaggerated gestures and expressions which passed for acting in early movies, the effect was achingly funny. I can only hope that, as we split our sides, we did not cause offence to our kindly host. It came across as more of an energetic parlour game than a sex romp and I feel sure that this blue movie, at any rate, would slip past today's watchdogs, not excluding Mrs Whitehouse, as an item fit for family entertainment.

TWO

THE CALL OF THE AIR

In many ways I was loath to give up the marvellous niche fate had carved out for me at Paxton Park, but I was beginning to realise that the lotus life there was unlikely to prepare me for school certificate or matriculation — essential passports to any decent career. I was also becoming increasingly embarrassed during school holidays by the inevitable question from other school children, 'What school do you go to?' To have to admit I was at an 'advanced' co-educational establishment seemed like making a confession to being an exhibit in a freak show. This time, when I put the problem to my mother during the school holidays I found her instantly sympathetic. Perhaps my education really should be rounded off on a more conventional note. In that case, where would *I* like to go?

It was no easy decision. In those days few schools had waiting lists, which meant the choice was wide. There were several where they played soccer instead of rugby — Charterhouse and Lancing, for instance — and this ruled them out for me. A few others, like Ampleforth and Downside, were Catholic and therefore would not have considered me even as they would have come in for Mother's stern disapproval. Scotland and the far west of England had some good schools, but by this stage my ever-restless mother had moved to London and they seemed too far away for convenient contact. Bedford, on the other hand, was almost in the same stretch of country as Paxton Park and Bedford School had an excellent reputation for rugby and rowing. Why search further?

Mother agreed, the school was approached and the head master, Mr Grose-Hodge, intimated that he personally would call on me the following term at Paxton Park to interview me himself. This at once struck me as over and above the call of duty, but looking back it seems more likely he was prompted not so much by duty as curiosity. Doubtless he had heard rumours of the weird, unconventional school run by the Bowdens and was unwilling to pass up a pretext for giving it the once-over. Whatever his motive, he arrived in an imposing chauffeur-driven car and I was ushered into his presence.

The way in which small, insignificant incidents tend to stick in the mind while more important ones fade into oblivion is one of life's curiosities. From the interview I recall only one small item, which came up as the subject of French was broached. This was no doubt because of the lasting impression created by the French master, Mr Poynter, who, other than the Boardmans themselves, was one of only three Paxton Park members of staff I found in any way memorable.

The other two were the sons of Mrs Boardman by a previous marriage: the younger brisk, bright and ambitious, a positive force in running the school, but more, one felt, out of reasons of personal ambition than religious principle or loyalty to his mother. The other, his elder brother, huge, shambling, genial and likeable, but perpetually subject to epileptic fits. So frequent were these attacks that it was commonplace in his classes for pupils to have to wait several minutes once or sometimes two or three times in a lesson as he lay writhing and foaming on the floor. After each occasion he would recover suddenly, climb unaided to his feet and carry on as though nothing had happened.

And then there was Mr Poynter, the French teacher, unique in his time but retrospectively recognisable as a prototype for today's socks and sandals brigade: tall, thin, austere, possessing a bicycle plus bicycle clips, which he seldom took off and, most unusual of all in those far-off days, a beard. Perhaps it was a reaction to the then not so distant Victorian and Edwardian times, when beards were normal wear for adult males, but in the 1930s they were almost unheard of – so rare, in fact, that small boys would follow their owners in the streets, shouting out, 'Beaver!' They were occasionally to be seen on officers and ratings of the Royal Navy, since the Senior Service alone of the three fighting services allowed its personnel to wear them as a concession to the long sea voyages and cramped conditions that were often the lot of naval personnel, especially submariners; but the rule was that they had to be full beards with no part of the face shaved. The army and air force allowed moustaches, but these also had to be full, with no part of the upper lip touched by a razor.

I had become a great fan of Mr Poynter and enjoyed his classes, though the factor that made them unlike anything else was his insistence that teacher and students speak nothing but French. This was an unheard-of departure from the then standard method of conducting all language instruction in English with exclusive concentration on grammar and the written word. When I mentioned Mr Poynter's way of teaching to Mr Grose-Hodge during the course of the interview, it instantly caught his interest. Switching into a French that I seem to remember was little better than my own, he asked what had influenced my choice of schools and why I had my sites on Bedford. I replied that, among other things, I happened to know one or two of the boys who were there already.

After the interview was finished and I was going over it in my mind, I realised to my dismay that I had, in my reply, inadvertently used the verb *savoir* instead of *connaître* for 'to know'. For several days I agonised over whether this might have lost me the interview. I need not have worried. Either Grose-Hodge himself was unaware of the difference or else he let it pass as a slip of the tongue. My letter of acceptance arrived and the following term I reported to what would mercifully be my last school.

Again, however, events were to conspire to make my stay there shorter than planned. One day my attention was drawn to an announcement in *The Times* – for the life of me I cannot think how since I was never a *Times* reader – stating that applications for permanent commissions in the army and General Duties branch of the Royal Air Force must be received by such and such a date in time for entry to the relevant cadet colleges by the start of the academic year in September. The advertisement gave little or no further information, but subsequent inquiries produced several thought-provoking facts.

Candidates, who had to be between the ages of seventeen and a half and nineteen and a half, were required to sit a written examination, attend an interview and be found medically fit. Failure to pass either the interview or the medical would not only nullify a candidate's current application, but would disqualify him from applying again at any time in the future. The written examination would be competitive. Only the top twenty-five would be eligible for the Royal Air Force Cadet College at Cranwell; the first sixty for Woolwich, where candidates for specialist branches of the army, such as gunners and engineers, were trained; and the first 200 for Sandhurst, training ground for officers of the army's fighting branches. It sounded intimidating stuff, especially if your goal should be the air force, but it was also challenging enough to whet the appetite.

I was still completely ignorant of the Royal Air Force and its ways, all my flying interests having been directed towards civil aviation as a result of the influence of Philip Gordon-Marshall. A little more delving revealed that the General Duties branch of the RAF was the executive branch, the branch which in fact ran the whole show. Only General Duties (GD) officers were eligible for the highest command and the first prerequisite for eligibility was a pair of pilot's wings. The idea was that those in control of the operation and direction of the force's main weapon, the aeroplane, could only do their job properly if they had practical experience of its capabilities and limitations.

There were various branches to cater for the other disciplines, such as engineering, medical or signals. Specialist officers would command specialist units, but these would be slotted into an overall structure that would always be commanded by a GD officer. The latter would also receive enough training in the specialist disciplines to understand the problems and discuss and analyse them intelligently with the specialists concerned. The thinking was that only those with a balanced, overall training could take a balanced, overall view; that the judgement of a specialist, no matter what his field, would inevitably tend to be biased by his own particular discipline.

The Royal Air Force's recruiting strategy for commissioned officers was twofold. First, it needed a small nucleus of permanent career officers for its GD branch. These would undertake the two-year training course at Cranwell, which catered exclusively for the GD branch and ran a curriculum to include flying to 'wings' standard. Secondly, it needed a reservoir of pilots, young men who were not only trained to fly aeroplanes but were also suitable material to attain junior commissioned rank and who could be called upon in an emergency.

Certain minimal educational standards would be required for this second line of opportunity, but selection would be largely on the basis of interview and medical fitness. Those who were successful would be offered a 'short-service commission' of five years, which could be extended, if mutually desired, by another five years to a 'medium-service commission', or, in a few cases, converted to a permanent one. At the end of their commissioned service these officers would be placed on a reserve list. Thus it was hoped to create a large pool of trained pilots who could be called up quickly in the event of war and slotted effortlessly into front-line squadrons and other flying units.

These prospects excited my imagination but left me well and truly stuck between ambition and conscience. With reluctance I had promised Mother, understandably fearful for the safety of her only son, that I would not make aviation a career. But because of Philip's influence the only sort of aviation to have come into the discussion was the civil variety. Morally, of course, there was no argument. I was perfectly aware that it was flying in general that concerned Mother, who gave not a hoot for technical classifications. And even if she had, the military option would undoubtedly have filled her with even greater horror than the civil one.

It became a deeply upsetting time. Mother had always been so marvellous to me – so unbelievably accommodating – that I was desperate not to hurt her in any way. On the other hand, flying in the 1930s exerted an obsessive pull for the lucky few who came into direct contact with it, and I, for sure, was utterly under its spell. Among the other points to consider was the fact that I was coming up to eighteen and was otherwise uncertain about my future. The RAF offered not only a permanent career but a more exciting and rewarding one than I could have believed possible. *Actually to be paid to fly the best aeroplanes in the world* – it was a notion surpassing my wildest dreams. And since every generation before the age of the nuclear deterrent was raised to accept the inevitability of war and since there were enough rumblings in the late 1930s to suggest that the next one was not far off and since my age-group would among the first to be called up – then why wait for it? I might end up as a cook if I let things slide. Why not get in at once on the ground floor?

The short-service commission looked the likeliest solution, but still I had to think of my mother. If ever I were to persuade her to drop her objections to a flying career, then it would need to be for something permanent. That made it Cranwell or nothing. I was well within the age band, so had the choice of either going in for the forthcoming exam (the one *The Times* was currently advertising) or else taking the one in the following year and using the interim period for preparation. It was already the end of the spring holidays. Going for the first option would therefore leave me with only about eight weeks to prepare. But my juices were on the move and I wanted action. After further agonising I decided to put my name down but not to tell Mother just yet. The die was cast. Either I went ahead or I lost my chance for ever; but if I passed, and Mother was inconsolably distressed, then I could always cancel.

Time was certainly short, but the thought of failure never crossed my mind. I was one of those lucky people who never found exams a problem. This is a superficial facility, as I am the first to admit, for I perceived early how an ability to pass exams is a knack akin to the ability to solve crossword puzzles. Neither skill is much use outside its limited area, but such knacks come in handy enough at times, if, in the longer term, a few grains of hard common sense are far more valuable. Here was one occasion, at least, when I felt grateful to possess the knack.

When I sent off the application documents to the Air Ministry I told no one except my form master, who was wholly co-operative. Since I was the only Bedfordian to sit the exams that term, I needed his help to plot out a work programme. The prospect was quite formidable. Candidates had to sit five written papers, but could pick them from scientific and non-scientific subjects. Mathematics and all things related were always incomprehensible to me, so I zeroed in on the non-scientific range, only to discover to my dismay that elementary mathematics was compulsory for all non-scientific candidates. The scientific applicants did not have it all their own way, either; they landed the same deal with elementary English.

Worse was to follow. Candidates' final placings were to be decided by the total of their marks in all five subjects, but − and to me it looked like a huge 'but' − failure to reach the minimum mark of 25 per cent in either of the two compulsory subjects would mean failing the entire exam, however brilliant the results in the other four. My planned tactic had been to do well enough in the non-arithmetical subjects to make good on the unavoidable flop in the maths department, but now here was this unexpected and chilling proviso that introduced an alarming new hurdle which not only shifted the goal posts but called the bluff on my exam knack. It became clear that luck and a following wind were going to be the deciding factors.

With my application accepted there was nothing for it but to face up to reality and settle down to seven or eight weeks of a routine of boring slog. By arrangement with my form master I attended all the classes covering my five subjects and worked on my own for the rest. I managed to get hold of some old exam papers, to give me a feel for what was wanted and worked my way through them. No particular alarm bells sounded, except in the case of the maths paper, and since no amount of study was ever going to turn me into a mathematician there was no point in panicking.

The weeks rolled on and I sat the exam, afterwards feeling reasonably happy with my performance and even hopeful that I might have scraped by in maths. The result would not be published till mid-August and meanwhile there were the medical and the interview in London to be gone through. These were neither of them as gruelling as I had feared. In the medical, the doctors were mainly interested in eyes, hearts and lungs. Because it was a new experience, I found it intriguing rather than worrying, though looking back I realise that the tests were highly rigorous. Eyes were straightforward: either you had the perfect vision you needed without glasses or you did not have it. Heart and lung tests consisted mainly of jumping on and off chairs, holding your breath and supporting a column of mercury in a calibrated glass tube by lung power, pulse rates being monitored throughout.

So long as you were a healthy young man, you had no problem with these tests, though the tiniest deviation from the precisely defined medical parameters set by the Air Ministry would be quickly revealed and spell instant failure with no rights of appeal. Fortunately for us, and, I believe, for the RAF in that generation, there were none of today's psychological and aptitude tests, which would have failed a majority of candidates for short-service and permanent commissions and I suspect might have cost us the Battle of Britain.

When it came to the interview I felt fairly relaxed from the start. There were five or six interrogators, presumably a mixture of senior serving officers and civil servants, though since all were in mufti it was difficult to be sure. They were all highly civilised and went out of their way to be helpful. The thought of an interview is always more intimidating than the reality. There are only limited numbers and types of question that an interviewer can ask, so it is normally possible to anticipate many of these and plan the answers. Inevitable openers, for instance, are what you do in your spare time. If you then give reading as a favourite occupation, it being a fairly safe one, you need to anticipate the obvious follow-up, namely your preference in books. Here it became essential to strike a balance between seeming too egg-headed with citing Shakespeare and Tolstoy or too shallow to hold senior rank by proclaiming a taste for 'Sapper' and Edgar Wallace.

It was fortunate that I was able to name sailing as one of my hobbies, this being, along with hunting, one of the pastimes most favoured by the top brass of all the services at the time. The rationale for good horsemanship went back to the days of the Royal Flying Corps, ancestor to the RAF, when many of the first pilots were recruited from cavalry regiments − the thinking being that the sensitive hands which could coax the best from a horse would be those most suited to the delicate controls of a flying machine. The same rationale was later applied in the case of yachtsman, whose empathy with nature's moods and movements was believed to make them especially suitable for aviation. This placed them among those best able to understand and exploit the capricious upper elements, where responsiveness to natural forces was paramount and ham-fistedness the ultimate unforgivable sin.

My own sailing experience arose from a life-long friendship between my parents and Janet and Rowland Smith. Their two children, Daphne and Alec, were the same ages as sister Pat and myself (poor sister Ione being, as usual, the odd one out) and we had formed the habit of joining forces for summer holidays. During the last few years before the war, our regular holiday base each summer was St Mawes in Falmouth Bay, a small and then still undiscovered Cornish fishing village. Rowland Smith, later Sir Rowland and chairman of the Ford Motor Co. throughout the war and for several years thereafter (he was 100 when he died) was a keen yachtsman who always brought his boat to St Mawes for the summer. He changed his boats quite often, but the craft I best remember was a truly beautiful topsail cutter named *Leonid*. She had a lovely clipper bow and massive bowsprit and could sleep between six or eight. Her rig was the complicated old-fashioned type of her day, and with her main sail, topsail, foresail, jib and flying jib, plus a spinnaker that seemed the size of the Royal Albert Hall, she kept Rowland, Alec and I at full stretch whenever it came to handling her in serious weather.

Apart from having access to his father's yacht *Leonid*, Alec himself owned a 14ft International-class dinghy, which was probably among the loveliest and handiest of the small-class racing craft of the time. With its fragile carvel-built hull and rare turn of speed, it was designed to be crewed by a helmsman plus one. Alec was a natural and gifted helmsman, who after the war retired to Hamble on the south coast and started a successful sailing school. He had a passion for racing, and we entered for all the local regattas, of which there was at least one a week during the summer season. Generously he would share the helm with me, but I never could take competition racing as seriously as he did.

Sailing I loved as a relaxation but 'relaxation' is a foreign word to a racing yachtsman. Yachting comes high in the list of those pastimes which seem to drain their devotees of humour. Skippers in particular tend to fall prey to an obsession which transforms them from the charming, friendly types they are as a rule on dry land into blaspheming curmudgeonly caricatures of their normal selves. I always felt it was the spirit of competition taken one step too far, draining the enjoyment and thrill from what ought to be a glorious sport. Those pre-war experiences were enough to cure me of any urge to race yachts, though never of my love for the water and the matchless grace of sail and sea. When we were not sailing, Alec and I spent endless hours exploring that fascinating Cornish coast in his dinghy, and the strength of the pull of that untouched part of Cornwall, with its lonely estuaries hemmed in by steeply wooded banks, its tidal reaches and mud-flats alive with wildfowl, its haunting sounds and smells — above all, its solitude — was never to leave me.

★ ★ ★

The summer term swiftly came to a halt soon after I had sat the exam and been to London for the interview and medical. School terms were better organised then, with summer exams ending more or less in phase with the end of term, so that pupils had just a few days in which to revel in glorious anticipation of the arrival of the holidays. When Robert Louis Stevenson wrote that, 'To travel hopefully is a better thing than to arrive,' he must have been thinking of his school days. The only fly in my personal ointment was having to wait till *The Times*, in mid-August, published the names of the chosen few for places at the cadet colleges.

I never was one to allow tomorrow's possible storm-clouds to darken today's horizons, however, so put the whole thing out of my mind. When the day finally came, I sneaked off to the stationers and bought my copy of *The Times* and, with a dragging sense of dread, ruffled through to the appropriate page. Here I snatched a furtive glance. A profound wave of relief swept through my system. There was my name, twenty-first out of twenty-five. It was not a brilliant result, perhaps, but I felt that in the circumstances it was not a bad effort either. It was, after all, a pass. Later I discovered that in the all-important elementary maths I had scored 26 per cent, just 1 per cent above the disqualifying minimum. I had come uncomfortably close to failure, but what more did I want? I was in.

The remaining hurdle was to break the news to my mother. There was no subtle way of doing it. All I could do was come out with my confession, straight and bold, and hope for the best. It was a task I hated. Mother, great lady that she was, made things easy for me, as I suppose I had half-expected she would. There was no scene, no outward upset, no reproach. She would, she said, have preferred some other path for me but if I felt sufficiently strongly about a career in the air force then I must pursue it. Beneath her calm exterior, her stomach must have been churning, but as a practising Christian Scientist, her faith in God was strong. She relaxed in the knowledge that, so long as she kept her faith burning bright, then the error of evil could not prevail and God would see me safely along my chosen path. As, indeed, he did.

My father, when he received the cabled information in Calcutta, was equally compliant. In my preoccupation with the − to me − paramount problem of passing in, I had entirely overlooked the small matter of fees. The subject was never even mentioned between us. I think, poor chap, that his conscience was so uneasy about the way he had cut himself off from his family and been an absentee parent that he would have rubber-stamped any proposal from home, sight unseen.

THREE

LOSING FACE AND GAINING WINGS

In a crumpled Clyno car on a foggy night in 1936 I lay for a few dazed moments, trying to assess the situation from upside down as I rested on the top of my head. The ticking of contracting metal continued, but the hissing of fuel seemed to have stopped. There was no fire. My face felt strangely numb, but otherwise I seemed all in one piece. Where was Puker? I wriggled free and looked around for him. No sign of Puker. I tried to think how we had got here in the first place.

The Clyno was an open two-seater with a dicky, a popular style in the 1930s. The make is long extinct, and never was one to set the world on fire, but it was my first wholly owned car and it performed surprisingly well. What was more, it had cost me £5 – almost a month's pay for a flight cadet – and hence was a cherished investment. The road we had been travelling along was an old Roman one, straight as an arrow except for the occasional obtrusive bend. The night was one of those when occasional fog patches interrupt clear stretches of road, common enough in that part of Lincolnshire at that time of year. Even as we plunged in and out of fog patches with no reduction of speed, Puker had suggested mildly that perhaps we ought to slow down a little. Many years later my archetypal famous last words still rang in the corridors of memory: 'Don't worry, old chap. I know this road like the back of my hand.'

Hardly had I spoken before we hurtled into the next fog bank and a straying telegraph pole suddenly loomed in front of us. Here was one obtrusive corner I had overlooked. Not over-fussed, I spun the wheel and we drifted clear of the pole, but as I straightened out of the slide the rear wheels just clipped the grass verge. At the speed at which we were travelling it was enough to flip us over. We did two or three complete rolls before the car came to rest on its back in the middle of a field.

I was beginning to grow alarmed about Puker when all at once, on the other side of the road, I spotted two mini legs pointing skyward out of the ditch and wriggling frantically. I made my way across, grabbed hold of these lively limbs and heaved. Puker came free with a sucking noise. He had been thrown clear of the Clyno on its first roll and landed head-down in a ditch full of mud. Had I been knocked unconscious, as by all the laws of nature I should have been, or trapped in the wreckage, then poor Puker would have drowned. Alas, his lucky escape would win him only a few more short years of life. He was one of Cranwell's characters, remembered clearly even half a century later: a big heart in a diminutive body. How on earth he fiddled himself through the minimum-height regulations for aircrew no one could understand, but he was extraordinarily popular, respected and admired. The dice fell badly for him in the end and he died in a bomber raid over Germany.

On that particular cold and foggy night of 1936, and on that deserted stretch of road, there was little we could do except start trudging in the direction of Cranwell in the hope that sooner or later a car might pass us. There was very little traffic on any road in those days, and especially not on this one. Eventually a car did come by, however, and its kindly driver, eyeing us uneasily, gave us a lift to the sick quarters at Cranwell, where we waited for the duty medical officer to be dragged out of bed.

As we sat there I realised I must have damaged my face more than I had thought. There were some oranges in a bowl in the waiting room, and I thought I would eat one to while away the time. The deed was easier in theory than in practice. I was completely unable to open my mouth to get the segments past the barricades of my teeth. There was also a mirror in the room, and as I looked into it I observed that while I was able to move the top half of my face up and down, my lower jaw failed to move with it. To all appearances the lower jaw had become detached. I raised the upper teeth with my fingers and squeezed a segment of orange between my jaws, but still could not generate enough pressure to penetrate the pulp. When the duty MO finally arrived he pronounced Puker fit and well. Where I was concerned he could detect no damage except to my face. This had most of the bones in the nose, cheek and jaw crushed or broken. Obviously a course of extensive surgery lay ahead.

In those pre-war days it was an accepted fact that the services tended to provide a refuge for doctors and surgeons who were unable to earn a living in the competitive civilian world outside. The ones who now set to work on me were prime examples. They cobbled my face together within the limits of their dubious skills, which fell far short of those of Dr Frankenstein. Then they consigned me to the sick-bay for six weeks with my jaws wired together. There was no way I could eat, of course, but where two of my front teeth had broken off in the crash a gap was left through which a tube could be pushed for me to suck up soup and other liquids. For those six weeks I lived on liquids alone. Initially it was feared that I might lose all my top teeth, the jaw having been cracked right along the line of the top gums. Luckily this anxiety was never realised.

A few days after the operation my mother paid me a visit. She opened the door, peered around its edge and hurriedly backed out, apologising for having come to the wrong room. It took some while to convince her that the mangled face she had encountered really was that of her only son. Fellow-cadets meanwhile derived enormous pleasure from dropping by to chat in the evening after dinner, so that they might regale me with details of the food they had just enjoyed as I sucked morosely on my tube. Curiously I developed a passion for Horlicks and arrowroot, two of the main courses available to me, and came ever afterwards to think of those beverages with nostalgic fondness.

As my six-week sentence drew to an end, my imagination began to work overtime as I mentally drew up and discarded menu after menu for the first solid meal with which to celebrate the end of my forty days and forty nights of fasting. Gastronomic delights followed one another in slow procession though my imagination: hors d'oeuvre of fresh young English asparagus served cold with a subtle, quite gentle sauce vinaigrette; smoked salmon with Baluga caviar, sharpened slightly with fresh lime juice and finely chopped shallots; a succulent steak, done charcoal crisp on the outside, rare in the middle, sitting on a bed of fried bread and *foie gras a la Tornado Rossini* with really young, tiny broad beans fresh off the plant and Cornish new potatoes; fresh raspberries smothered in heavy Devonshire clotted cream; strong black coffee; and a savoury (in the 1930s it was usual to have cheese after lunch, savouries after dinner) to give bite to a glass or two of vintage port. It was nothing but daydreaming, but it passed the time and, whatever the menu might be, I awaited the unlocking of my jaws and my first solid meal with the excitement of a schoolboy taken out for a binge.

The great moment, when it finally arrived and they placed a meal in front of me, was the saddest anticlimax imaginable. The minute wires clamping my jaws were duly removed and I tried to open my mouth. I tried and I tried. Never a movement. I strained till my jaws ached. They remained tightly clenched. Even had they placed the menu of my dreams in front of me, rather than a washed-out tasteless meal cooked, one suspected, in the excess steam from the laundry room, I would still have been unable to eat it. After all their weeks of immobility, the jaw muscles simply refused to respond. Days were to pass before I could open my mouth wide enough to squeeze even a tiny portion of scrambled eggs between my teeth, by which time the idea of food had lost its magic.

Eating turned out to be the least of my worries, however. True to their reputation, the superannuated surgeons of the air force had more or less put my face together back to front. The sinuses were rendered useless, the nose was flattened and inoperative. Worst of all, my left eye had floated halfway down my face, leading to double vision. Unless this fault could be corrected, it was enough on its own to mean the end of my flying days, and hence of my RAF career, quite apart from any frightening effect I was liable to have on small children and dogs.

There was nothing more the air force could do for me, short of bringing in outside specialists, and it certainly was not going to spend that kind of money on a mere flight cadet hardly into his first term. Mother, on the other hand, sprang into action as soon as she perceived the situation, deciding the time had come to give the workings of Mrs Eddy's benevolent providence a helping hand. She took me to see one of the most eminent surgeons of the day, a New Zealander by the name of Harold Gillies (later Sir Harold), doyen and pioneer of the new science of plastic surgery, many of the techniques for which had been learnt from dealing with facial injuries during the First World War. Mr Gillies studied me intently, then asked to speak to my sister Patricia, who was waiting outside. 'Was brother's face like sister's?' he asked.

'Good heavens no,' said Pat with an indignation that startled me. 'My brother's nose was straight!'

Peering again at the battered blob somewhere about the middle of my asymmetric features, Mr Gillies masked his incredulity, doubtless marvelling at the strength of sibling loyalty. Then he declared that he would accept the challenge, obviously glad to come across a guinea pig to help him to extend knowledge within his field of speciality. He was assisted in the operation by his cousin, a rising young surgeon called Archie McIndoe (later Sir Archibald), who would become the founder of the world-famous Guinea Pig Club at East Grinstead, where the formidable skills of his powerful, almost stubby square hands and the force and warmth of his personality made miracles a daily routine as he rebuilt the shattered bodies and minds of the burned casualties of the Second World War.

After the war Archie made me an honorary 'Guinea Pig' and invited me to be his guest at one of their annual dinners. I went once, but never again. I felt like an interloper. Whenever those who have shared a common horrendous experience gather together, they have a special bond, an intimacy, an invisible but almost tangible barrier that outsiders can never penetrate, how ever warmly they may be welcomed. I have often sensed the same feeling among prisoners of war, whose suffering, in my view, has never been sufficiently appreciated by the public. To be incarcerated through sheer bad luck for an indeterminate time for doing your duty – quite possibly well beyond the call of duty – and laying your life on the line for your country, to be snatched from unit, colleagues and a war to which you were completely committed, must be witheringly frustrating. Those who were rounded up by the Japanese, and survived, have also had to carry the unimaginable burden of all which they saw and experienced of extremes of deprivation and cruelty. Whenever I have been among my many good friends who were both 'Guinea Pigs' and former PoWs, I have always been aware that, although I can be with them, I can never be of them.

I do not now remember where I was sent to have the operation on my face, but I do remember the convalescent home, Sister Agnes's, where I went to recuperate afterwards. It was situated in Grosvenor Crescent, the road connecting Hyde Park Corner with Belgrave Square. Sister Agnes had been one of Edward VII's mistresses, and after his death she involved herself in charitable work. She founded her convalescent home in Belgravia to cater in particular for serving and retired officers of all three services, and so popular did it become that, after her death, it was expanded and moved to a modern building in Cleveland Street, off Harley Street, and renamed King Edward's VII's Hospital for Officers. At the time when I was an inmate Sister Agnes was still alive. I have fond memories of exquisite food, superb service and a tiny bird-like creature, by then well into her eighties yet still upright and chipper, dressed in a flowing Victorian nursing garb of the style favoured by Florence Nightingale as she made a regal progress round the wards, accompanied by a band of faithful acolytes.

In the circumstances, from the functional if not the aes-thetic angle, Gillies and McIndoe made as good a job of my face as was possible. The nose certainly no longer resembled the handsomely straight proboscis my sister Pat had claimed for me. My left cheek bone was clamped together with wire, my left eye remained slightly lower and larger than the right, but the truly important detail was that I no longer suffered from double vision. From the flying point of view, nothing else mattered; the rest was vanity, and in the 1930s male vanity was seen as a deadly sin. It simply wasn't done for a man to be aware of his looks, and to be caught narcissistically examining yourself in a mirror other than to shave would have placed you quite beyond the pale.

The two surgeons were keen to round off the job with a spot of cosmetic tidying, mainly so as not to let pass any opportunity which came their way to hone their skills, but also partly, no doubt, to see if my sister hadn't exaggerated. I was sorely tempted to take them up on this. After all, I was still in my teens and was not finding it easy to come to terms with the idea of being saddled for the rest of my life with a distorted version of a face I had once been secretly rather pleased with. But, as I say, this was the 1930s. However unhappy I may have been privately over a loss of looks, publicly I had to appear indifferent.

My main worry, in any case, was that six months had gone by since the accident and it was becoming highly likely that the air force could grow disillusioned and fire me if I took more time off. So back I went, to the disappointment of my mother and sister and, I suspect, of Harold Gillies. The time out for facial repairs had left me well behind on the level of learning reached by my own intake at Cranwell, so I dropped into the term below. Those few seconds of over-confidence at the wheel of my Clyno had cost me six months' seniority and my original face. I was lucky, though. They could have cost me my career; even my life.

Apart from the hiccup of the car accident and the consequent loss of seniority, the Royal Air Force College Cranwell was everything I could have hoped for. Among the college staff I recollect four names only. Our commandant was Air Vice-Marshal Cave-Browne-Cave, a charming man whom I remember chiefly for his car, a Rolls-Royce Replica. In those days of personal service and style, Rolls-Royce did not make the bodies for their cars. Instead they only built the engines and chassis, which were then sold on to one or other of the established coach builders of the day – Park Ward, James Young, Thrupp & Maberley, Hoopers, Mulliners and so on – who went on to build special bodies for them, custom-made to the requirements and whims of the individual client. Rolls-Royce Replicas also built special bodies, but they mounted them on second-hand engines and chassis. These vehicles were indistinguishable from the new article, except for the 'Replica' motif on the bonnet, which took a little of the shine off the snob value. They were marvellous bargains even so: the hand-crafted Rolls-Royce engines of the day were not considered properly run in until they had done at least 50,000 miles.

The second name I remember from Cranwell is that of the riding master, Mr Penfold, an ex-cavalry instructor who was brilliant at his job. Riding was a voluntary extra on the course, and although I had never been keen on horses before, it seemed a good opportunity to learn what, if anything, I might have been missing. As I discovered, it was quite a lot. Soon I was an enthusiast, under the tough but under-standing tuition of Mr Penfold. He treated everyone as a novice, irrespective of experience, and put us through the same training hoops as he would have the raw recruits in a cavalry regiment.

Cranwell lay deep in Lincolnshire hunting country, and several well-known hunts would do the college the honour of meeting there from time to time, the Quorn and the Belvoir among them. But while I loved riding, hunting I never really enjoyed. My reser-vations had nothing to do with today's tiresome controversy over ethics, which were seldom in question in the 1930s. Even if they had been, my position would have been strictly neutral, then as later. The thing about hunting, as with any other pastime, is that it either catches your fancy or not as the case may be. In my case it didn't.

The third name I remember is that of our armaments officer, Flight Lieutenant Tindell-Carroll-Worseley, mainly, I am afraid, because it was hard to forget. This leaves, finally, our college adju-tant, the driving force of the college, who shall be nameless. With his powerful personality, powerful voice, beautiful wife and colossal self-esteem, he appeared without a shadow of doubt to be destined, certainly in his own mind and I am sure in the minds of many others, for a meteoric rise to the topmost rank. Without the intervention of the war his ambitions must surely have been realised. Sadly for him he was born ten years too late. His talents turned out to be tailor-made for peacetime service though not for the harsh realities of wartime. Early in the conflict he was given command of one of the Hurricane squadrons dispatched to France with the Expeditionary Force, he swiftly landed in a situation that required more than a loud voice and heroic posturing. From that point onwards his career went into a terminal decline.

So far as specific incidents at Cranwell go, surprisingly few have stuck in my mind, as often seems to be the case with me. Those that did stick are mostly mundane, and one of the most lingering concerns an aspect of total insignificance − breeches and puttees. When I first arrived at Cranwell these were regulation wear for officers up to the rank of flight lieutenant. It was a hangover from the days of the RFC, with its cavalry influence, and I have no doubt that it lasted as long as it did because senior officers, having themselves survived the exasperation and laborious impracticality of such a tedious garb, fancied themselves in the polished riding boots they were allowed to wear once they reached the rank of squadron leader and above.

The great challenge with puttees lay in getting the tension exactly right around the calf muscles. The puttees, wound from the ankle upwards, had to finish at exactly the right level, with the seam of each puttee precisely in line with the appropriate seam of the breeches. If they were wound too loosely, the layers of fabric would hang away from the swell of the calf muscle, and if too tightly, they would constrict the muscle and cause agonising cramps. On our early route marches, covering six or seven miles at a brisk stride, the extraordinary pain caused by over-tight puttees was a regular feature. They were the bane of our existence until suddenly, like learning to ride a bicycle, we found ourselves putting them on in seconds without even thinking about it. And exactly at that point, needless to say, the policy changed and we went into trousers – an early example of Sod's Law.

The college schedule was very civilised. Each day, including Saturday, began with an early morning parade, and there was a church parade on Sunday. Parades were followed by classes, including an hour or so a day of flying instruction. Wednesday and Saturday afternoons were set aside for sport. We dined formally in mess each night from Monday to Friday. From Monday to Thursday we wore mess kit consisting of leg-hugging mess-overalls strapped under half-Wellingtons, with black tie, blue waist coat, stiff shirt and butterfly collar. Refining my technique, I found I could leave the squash court eight minutes before dinner, shower, change and still arrive in mess on time. Friday nights were guest nights, when black tie and blue waistcoat were replaced with white. Dining in mess at weekends was optional, but if you did you wore a suit on a Saturday, tweed jacket and slacks on a Sunday.

On Saturdays and Sundays you were allowed an evening pass, but had to report back by midnight. A cadet's pay being six shillings (30p) a day, half of which was retained as a contribution towards his mess bill, it may be thought that this was academic, since he would be out of cash well before midnight, unless he had a private income. Far from it. There was precious little to spend money on in the mess, so pay for six weekdays spent in financial purdah netted around eighteen shillings (90p). A pint of beer or a glass of whisky each cost you no more than tenpence (the equivalent of 4p), so plenty of leeway remained.

Before Cranwell I had never had a drink or a cigarette – not out of any high-flown principles, but simply because the thought had never occurred to me. Mother had never drunk or smoked, even before she became a Christian Scientist – probably a result of her missionary upbringing. Father did smoke, but he never drank. This seemed quite astonishing in someone who spent so many years of his life abroad, where suns over yardarms and *chota* pegs were for many the *raison d'être* of living. He always said his reason for abstaining was in part because it was too easy to get a drinking habit in the artificial atmosphere in which expatriates lived with endless time, servants, and long tropical nights, so that socialising became the focus of existence. Anyway, he said, luckily he'd never really liked the stuff.

Cranwell started me on drinking, and it was one of the lecturers there who started me on smoking. In those days a non-smoker was a rarity, almost a curiosity, and one or two people from those times were memorable for no other reason than that they were non-smokers. There was, of course, no perceived health hazard, and cigarettes were affordable at a shilling (5p) for twenty (or 2.5p for the cheaper Woodbines). They also offered a handy social crutch, and gave you something to do with the hands; and if you ran out of conversational banter at a party, you could always offer a cigarette.

The lecturer in question was a heavy smoker who chain-smoked throughout his classes, and it fascinated me to watch how, after he had drawn on his cigarette, the smoke went on trickling from his mouth for several breaths as he continued talking, instead of coming out in a series of puffs, as I would have expected. I had never given much thought to the phenomenon before, assuming that smoke would be held in the mouth and having no idea that smokers actually drew it down into their lungs. Determined to unravel the mystery, I bought a packet of cigarettes, then another, and another. By the time I had unravelled the secret I was, of course, hooked on nicotine. It seems interesting that, while I clearly recall this instructor teaching me to smoke, I cannot for the life of me remember his class subject.

Learning to fly was wholly the joy I had anticipated. We each began on an Avro Tutor, a completely vice-free biplane trainer that stood up to the cruellest abuse with a happy smile. We then graduated to a Hawker Hart, a gentle general-purpose aircraft still in use in front-line squadrons: a two-seater biplane with two cockpits in tandem, the rear one for an observer/rear gunner/ wireless operator/bomb aimer − anything except a batman, it seemed. The final term was finished on Hawker Furies. This single-seater fighter, another biplane, was also still in operational squadrons and was another truly joyous machine without a vice. Before we could fly a Fury, however, we had to take on the Bristol Bulldog, a single-seater fighter that was an extremely brisk little aircraft just then being withdrawn from front-line service.

For the most part the Bristol Bulldog obeyed the laws of aerodynamics, though it could also develop ideas of its own that occasionally led it astray. Its least endearing habit was every so often to decline to recover from a spin − one of the earliest manoeuvres the trainee pilot has to master. A graphic illustration of the waywardness of this little plane, and also of the hazards of bailing out of it, was displayed by one of the cadets in my senior term, who walked with a pronounced limp. Spinning his Bulldog one day, he had failed to recover, had bailed out, and lost most of the calf muscle from one leg as it was struck by the tail.

A spin is an attitude adopted by an aircraft that has, for whatever reason − often but not necessarily pilot incompetence − ceased to fly through the air in the way it was designed to; whereupon the laws of aerodynamics give way to the less 'complicated law of gravity and it plunges uncontrollably out of the sky. There is little to choose between the flying characteristics of a stalled aircraft and a falling brick. Since an aircraft in a spin is the ultimate antic of aerodynamic instability, pilots must learn to cope with it. The out-of-control mode is deliberately induced by throttling back and raising the aircraft nose until the velocity falls off to stalling speed − a critical speed, varying with different aircraft, at which the air ceases to flow quickly enough over the wing surfaces to support the machine's weight. It then begins to sink, and as gravity takes over and it falls out of control, the pilot aggravates the situation on purpose, pushing the aircraft into a simulated death throe by pulling the stick hard back into his stomach and applying full rudder. The abused machine then drops earthward in the classic out-of-control spiral much favoured by special-effects stunt men in flying films. Recovery in a well-behaved aircraft is not difficult.

Flying involves an instinctive technique; it exerts no strain on the brain. This is one of the nicest things about it. You push or you pull the controls in whatever direction you wish to go. Pull the stick back: the aircraft's nose comes back towards you, irrespective of your position – on your back, on your side or right way up. Push the stick forward: you push the nose away. Recovering from a spin bends these rules marginally. As you are heading downwards towards a crazily whirling earth, your instincts tell you to pull the stick back, and quickly. You do no such thing. Resisting the temptation, you instead push it hard forward, meanwhile applying full rudder in the opposite direction to the spin. Any well-behaved aircraft will then respond quite quickly and straighten out, transforming the spin into a dive as the air ceases its directionless frothing around the wing surfaces and renews a smooth flow over them. Lift is restored, gravity defied, and aerodynamic law comes back into its own. Occasionally, however, as with the wayward Bulldog, the theory falls apart, the aircraft refuses to respond, and the pilot, provided he has left enough air space below him, takes recourse to his parachute.

There is one other situation in which it is essential for instincts to be made to take second place to scientific technology. This arises with learning to fly blind by relying solely on the instruments. The old adage about 'flying by the seat of your pants' can be fatally misleading when it comes to flying in cloud or other conditions of zero visibility. If you are to stay alive, you have to believe your instruments and ignore whatever messages your instincts may be screaming at you. You're in a dive, pull out, your instincts tell you; no, you're not, the instruments contradict, you're climbing. You're on your back, shout your senses; on the contrary, the instruments say, you're right way up. You positively know you are flying straight and level; no, the instruments coolly indicate, you are in a steep turn.

The basic lessons were taught in a 'Link Trainer', a primitive fore-runner of today's astonishingly clever flight simulators. Even these lessons we could not quite believe, and it was only by spinning a few times out of a real cloud that we finally became convinced that attention to our instruments was the top priority. The advantages of sophisticated instrumentation were also not yet available. We had only our dials and needles, and none of the artificial horizons or other gyroscopically operated instruments, whose moving images clearly and graphically indicate the aircraft's attitude in relation to the horizon, which pilots rely on today. With the introduction of these later instruments, blind flying became a walkover, though the first gyroscopic instruments, which began to appear just before the war and that we used throughout and for a time afterwards, had one dramatic drawback: any violent manoeuvre toppled their gyros and temporarily put them out of action. It then took fifteen minutes of straight and level flying to get them back in kilter. If in the meantime you needed to take temporary refuge in a cloud while being pursued by the ungodly, you crossed your fingers and hoped you could still remember how to retain control with only the primitive instruments you had been brought up on but now largely ignored – otherwise you were liable to give yourself as well as the enemy quite a surprise.

★ ★ ★

Two extracurricular events of note occurred during my two and a half years at Cranwell: the abdication of King Edward VIII in 1936 and the coronation of his younger brother as King George VI in the following year. The months leading up to the abdication aroused very mixed feelings in me. Like most of the general public of those days, I was a staunch royalist and had great affection and respect for Edward, both as Prince of Wales and later as king. He was an attractive, innovative and caring young man, with an endearing familiarity that came as a refreshing change after the strict adherence to protocol which had marked the manner of his father, George V. He was obviously genuinely moved by the poverty and hardship he saw around him when visiting some of the poorer areas of the country, and he constantly embarrassed the authorities by making spontaneous promises of help which the government was unable or unwilling to back up.

When Edward's affair with Mrs Wallis Simpson began, it was viewed benevolently and tolerantly by the public at large. Royalty, with its centuries-old tradition of arranged marriages, had always had its mistresses and its lovers, a tradition accepted as normal and followed unthinkingly by most of the great families of Europe. Mrs Simpson was not Edward's first mistress, and his earlier affairs had excited no comment. Neither, to begin with, did his relationship with Mrs Simpson, but as it progressed it became impossible for even the most tolerant to avoid becoming aware that what had started as a harmless and carefree liaison was developing into an obsession. The public mood then began to change. There were certain well-understood though invisible parameters to royal behaviour which justified the special status and privileges enjoyed by royalty, and the feeling grew that these unwritten laws were being breached and our famous unwritten constitution suddenly being made to look frail. It was unthinkable that a divorced woman should even become our English queen, or even our king's consort, and Edward's clearly growing fixation set off the first splash of anxiety that soon began to ripple outwards.

No doubt like any other man in the grip of an obsession, Edward was convinced that the public would eventually come to see his beloved in the same golden light as he pictured her himself. It never happened. Instead they saw Mrs Simpson as a divorced adventuress who had exposed a weakness in the king they loved and by so doing had lessened the majesty of the crown. The impression grew that Edward was not only devastated by the nation's rejection of the woman who filled his life, but also incredulous that it should so do. He continued to underestimate the strength of ublic feeling, while Mrs Simpson continued to dominate his life. Finally, with much sadness and regret, his subjects decided that he lacked the dedication essential for the role of head of the British Empire and rejected him as well.

I have to confess that I listened to Edward's abdication speech with far more emotion than I was able to muster when it came to Neville Chamberlain's announcement of a state of war. While I could understand the conflict that had been tearing Edward apart, I also felt let down, along with most people in Britain. The respect had gone; it had been shown to be misplaced. The king to whom I gave my oath of allegiance had feet of clay cruelly exposed. On a personal level I could only hope that he would come to terms with his decision in the long years that were to follow. Sadly I felt he never did, if the expression on his tragic face was anything to go by as we saw it from time to time in press photographs. For the rest of his life I thought of him as a charming, well-meaning man, haunted forever by knowledge of a destiny forsworn, and that he had not been man enough for the job he was born to. The truth was that the abdication, when it came, came as a relief.

Edward's younger brother, 'Bertie', Duke of York, who was crowned King George VII in the early summer of 1937, my second year at Cranwell, was the opposite of his brother in almost every respect. On the several occasions when I had the honour to meet him I always felt I could sense the core of steel behind the shy, introverted façade of a gentle man who had a strong dislike of publicity but an even stronger sense of duty. The last thing he had wanted was to be king, but, supported by his intensely loyal and supportive consort, Queen Elizabeth, herself a woman of unflinching courage, they were to be the perfect focus for the emotions of a war-torn people and to capture the hearts of the nation.

With the announcement of the coronation of George VI there came the news that Cranwell cadets were to form a section of the troops lining the route. For the great occasion there were to be personnel from all the fighting forces from every corner of the British Empire, and Cranwell was greatly privileged to be allotted the palace end of the Mall, almost directly opposite Buckingham Palace itself. The downside to the excitement was that parades at Cranwell immediately turned into the most crashing bore. Several times a week we were rallied on parade, brought to attention, then simply left standing, sometimes for hours at a stretch. The theory was that this endurance experience would toughen our stamina and prepare us for long hours of lining the coronation route. In reality it was an excellent wheeze to allow our instructors an excuse to take a few hours off. I can only say that the experience left me with unabated sympathy and admiration for those guardsmen and policemen who are called on to do sentry duty or to decorate the front doors of Downing Street and other official buildings.

The problem is mental rather than physical. You need to try and empty your mind, which is never as easy an exercise as it sounds. Happily for me I had already, as a schoolboy in class, developed my special skill for putting an intense expression of interest on my face while my mind roamed independently wherever it might care to wander. This tactic now came into its own as I was able to turn it to practical advantage. From the moment we were on parade all I needed to do was shut off my mind from the immediate surroundings and sink into a semi-trance.

We moved to London the day before the coronation and camped under canvas in Hyde Park. On the first night it poured with rain, and, confined in those rain-soaked tents, the duckboards awash with puddles, we had to clean all our own buttons, boots, webbing and rifles to such a standard as they had never before experienced. At crack of dawn on the great day we were marched to our stations in the Mall, forewarned to expect to remain standing all day with no relief. We had also been advised to drink nothing if possible, but told that if we must drink something, then stick to whisky, since that would dehydrate us. In the event, the exercise proved far less demanding than its somewhat inhuman scenario had led us to expect. Rather than being stood at attention for eight hours without moving a muscle, we were most of the time stood easy, with alternate numbers being fallen out every two hours for ten-minute breaks. The general activity going on all about us in the public throng was, in any case, interesting enough to make the time pass quickly.

The coronation itself was incomparable. Nowhere else in the world were such pomp, pageantry, richness of costume, colour, equipment, such impeccable timing and faultless manners to be seen. We swelled with pride at our unique possession, this irreplaceable tapestry of tradition and ceremony, of discipline and creativity: an emotional focus centred on the monarchy to stir anew dormant feelings of patriotism and appreciation in country and heritage. The British talent for national celebration was, and continues to be, the envy of the world.

Some time towards evening we were marched back to the tents in Hyde Park, and stood down under reveille next morning. We climbed out of our uniforms and into our damp civilian clothes before, full of youth and whisky, setting off to roam London. I am sure we had a glorious time of it. Mercifully no memories survive for me to be able to regale the reader with them here.

* * *

Towards the end of a cadet's final term at Cranwell he was allowed to state what preference, if any, he had for his posting. The choice lay between Bomber, Fighter and Coastal Commands, a command structure born out of the 1935 plan for the expansion of the RAF to face the threat already being posed by Nazi Germany. There were also the lesser-known Army Co-operation squadrons, but these came under the banner of one of the three main commands. Vacancies in all options were strictly limited, especially in Fighter Command. There were therefore no guarantees of getting what you asked for.

Bombers certainly never held any appeal for me. They seemed too vulnerable – sitting ducks with an obvious death wish. When the war did come, their crews proved themselves second to none in bravery as they flew night after night into odds heavily stacked against survival; and although we were not at the time to know the pattern the war would take for them, the idea of droning off into a hostile night, a target not only for enemy fighter planes but also for any half-trained German conscript blindly peppering the sky above him with shrapnel from an anti-aircraft gun, seemed singularly lacking in attraction.

As for Army Co-operation, the word had gone about that a good deal of it took place in the mess. This obviously had its attractions, but the aircraft used by these squadrons were mostly slow, unarmed light machines capable of landing in a confined area. The Lysander, for instance, which could 'land on a postage stamp', was originally designed for Army Co-operation. Later it achieved fame as the aircraft used by the Special Operations Executive (SOE) for landing Allied agents in seemingly impossible clearings in occupied Europe. Such aircraft, however, looked like deeply unexciting prospects as weapons of war. Flying those clockwork mice hardly seemed a justification for two and a half years of training at Cranwell. In any case, the flying, mainly over enemy lines, spotting for artillery and feeding back information on troop movements, would clearly not be lacking in its anxious moments. As with the bombers, you would be frighteningly vulnerable to fire from the ground, and — here came the nub of the matter — would stand very little chance of hitting back.

The Coastal Command of the 1930s quite definitely held at tractions for anyone of hedonistic inclination. Equipped with Sunderlands, those giant four-engined long-range flying boats, each with a crew of nine and furnished with mess, cooking galley and bunks, they were self-contained airborne hotels. With their enormous range, they roamed the vast island and coastal possessions of the British Empire, landing in crystal-clear lagoons that flanked untouched, story-book tropical islands, where the white man was still a curiosity. There their happy crews could swim, fish, laze a few days before moving on to the next island in the sun.

Naturally such a lotus lifestyle was doomed to change dramatically with the coming of war. The crews of the Sunderlands, like those of the bombers, also did a heroic job that went largely unsung and unrecognised. They were the ones who flew endless long patrols in foul weather over a grey gale-lashed Atlantic or a savagely hostile North Sea, protecting our convoys, locating and attacking enemy U-boats and shipping, calling up rescue operations for the crews of our stricken merchant and naval ships, drop ping life-rafts and supplies to those already in the water. They carried a reasonable armament in three or four gun turrets, but even so had a massive vulnerability, like that of a whale to a harpoon. Their majestic but ponderous response to danger inevitably made them easy prey to German long-range fighters, as well as to the guns of any enemy ships they located and shadowed. And once they were down they were on their own.

In the sybaritic 1930s sombre thoughts of this nature rarely or never intruded into our minds. We accepted that war must one day be inevitable, but were untroubled by speculations about its harsh realities and more concerned with today than tomorrow. The siren calls of the peacetime Coastal Command were strong, but I was already clear in my mind which command I was going to aim for. I had not joined the RAF to make myself into a sitting target. If shooting there was to be, then I was determined that I would be among the shooters, not one of the shot at. Still under the influence, I suspect, of the old First World War flying films, I harboured the romantic notion that the single-seater aircraft represented the last faint echo of the medieval field of honour. if the conduct of warfare had come to be defined by weapons technology, then at least our aerial duels might be seen as taking the place of the knightly jousting lists of more honourable times, the rules of chivalry once again made sacrosanct and enshrined.

Yet, aside from such callow romanticism, there was also a sound if mundane reason for seeking a posting to a fighter squadron. The very nature of Fighter Command's task, the air defence of the United Kingdom, made it essential for its front-line squadrons to be grouped close to all the most important concentrations of people, government and industry in the country. London, being the most concentrated centre of all, thus had the largest number of fighter squadrons grouped protectively around its perimeter. Hence a posting to Fighter Command carried the best chance of a posting to the London area, a prospect greatly pleasing to my social instincts.

I therefore put Fighter Command down as first choice, with Coastal Command listed second. Since there were only five vacancies in Fighter Command that year, several days of nail biting followed as I waited for the lists to be posted up. When the list was revealed I found to my deep content what my new home was going to be: No.65 Fighter Squadron at Hornchurch, a front-line fighter station on London's eastern rim. Again, it seemed like a dream come true.

1 Brian, Aunt Madge and sister Pat.

2 Brian aged six years and ten months.

3 *Above:* Brian aged eleven, with one of his tame jackdaws.

4 *Left:* BK (right) and sister 'Bubbles'.

5 The Kingcome and Smith family on holiday at Port Gavern in 1928. Brian is sitting second left in the foreground; his mother, Ruby, is behind him (first left) and his father, Charles, is on the right in the foreground.

6 *Above left:* BK (with Dungie the spaniel) and Alec Smith.

7 *Above right:* Paxton Park.

8 Above: Cricket at Bedford (BK middle).

9 Right: 'Anyone for tennis?' BK at Bedford.

10 Below: Rugby at Bedford (BK second from right, back row).

11 Above: Alec Smith, BK and Lady Smith on *Leonid*, the Smith's yacht, at Falmouth.

12 Left: Sister Pat, in her Riley, and BK.

13 BK on the Vickers
gun on the ranges.

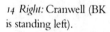

14 Right: Cranwell (BK
is standing left).

15 Below: 92 Squadron
pilots including BK
(fifth from left), Allan
Wright (third from
right) and Bob Holland
(fourth from right).

16 Tony Bartley,
Allan Wright and
BK. December 1940.

17 Above: 92 Squadron spitfires at Manston,
February 1941.

18 Left: Bob Stanford Tuck as a flight
commander with 92 Squadron.

19 92 Squadron
pilots: Sgts Lloyd,
Ellis, Morris and
Allison (standing
on wing). Left to
right: Tommy Lund,
Bastion Thomsen,
Bob Holland,
'Wimpy' Wade,
Bill Watling, Jock
Sherrington, 'Tich'
Havercroft and
'Monty'.

20 92 Squadron dispersal point.

21 92 Squadron Mess at Pembrey.

22 Right: Brian at Bibury, Gloucestershire.

23 'Boy' Wellum, Don Kingaby, Ronnie Pokes, Bastion Thomsen and Tom Wiese.

24 Johnny Kent and Tom Wiese.

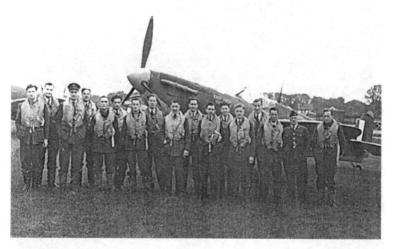

25 92 Squadron pilots (BK wearing cap).

26 Brian's Spitfire 'F' at Biggin Hill.

27 Left to right: (?), Neville Duke, 'Wimpy' Wade, Bob Holland, Jamie Rankin, (?) and Brian Kincome attending Don Kingaby's wedding.

28 Jamie Rankin, Tom Wiese and Brian Kingcome.

FOUR

THE TRAINING GROUND

I arrived at Hornchurch to join 65 Squadron on a lovely summer's day in August 1938, a brand-new pilot officer in His Majesty's Royal Air Force. On passing out of Cranwell we were given a month's leave (annual leave entitlement being sixty-three days, taken at the discretion of your unit), which meant that reporting in at Hornchurch would be a mere formality before I made a carefree departure to enjoy the summer. It so happened that the station commander was also on leave at the time. I therefore paid the station adjutant a courtesy call before setting off for St Mawes, where my family was already established in the usual rented holiday house with the Rowland Smiths.

For my drive down to the West Country I had commandeered sister Pat's car. Poor sister Pat, she hardly ever had a car she could call her own; after the loss of my Clyno I seemed to have hers on permanent loan. The car she currently ran was a Ford 10, a gutsy little motor with a recommended top speed of 70mph, though I found it quite easy to wind it up well into the eighties – treatment to which it never seemed to raise an objection. London to St Mawes, spinning along the old A30 most of the way and traversing the panoramic wilderness of Bodmin Moor (a wilderness then little touched by modern road development), was something of a long haul. It usually took about nine hours going flat out, but I loved driving and it raised my spirits especially whenever I was making that westward journey.

Those were still the days before compulsory driving tests, or provisional or learners' driving licences. To be thought fit to drive, all you needed to do was to reach the age of eighteen and pay

your five shillings (25p) for your annual licence. This legally enti-
tled you to step into a bought or borrowed car and drive it off,
even if you had never sat behind the wheel in your life before.
You then proceeded to learn the ways of the road by trial and
error. Like almost everyone else, that was how I began driving.
The greatest challenge facing most novice drivers was mastering
the crash gearbox, a standard fitting on most cars until the latter
part of the 1930s, when synchromesh gears began to be fitted to
all new models. Personally I felt that the old crash boxes added
a good deal to the joy of driving. There had been an occasion
when one of them served me well.

I bought my licence and began driving legitimately on my
eighteenth birthday in May 1935, which also happened to be the
first year in which driving tests were introduced, though they
remained voluntary for the time being. Out of curiosity I nevertheless decided to take one, just to see what these newfangled
tests involved. At that stage sister Pat owned a Riley 9, an open
tourer with a light fabric body, which was capable of quite a
sporty performance given the right encouragement. Early on in
the test it emerged that I was my examiner's very first candidate
and he was more nervous than I was. After all, I had nothing to be
nervous about and nothing to lose. No one could stop me driving
on the same licence, pass or fail. But the most important factor of
all in this saga turned out to be that the examiner was himself an
ardent Riley fan. He was far more interested in seeing what the
car could do than he was in my standard of driving.

The trump card was my gear change on the crash gearbox,
for which I had perfected a racing change from top gear down
through the box, a technique of which I was inordinately proud.
I could execute it perfectly silently when driving flat out, and so
smoothly that the increased engine revs were the only indication
of a change having occurred. Plymouth was the official venue
for the test, but under the influence of the examiner's enthusiasm
for the car we soon left the town for the moors behind the city.
Up there, on those hilly undulating roads, I was able to show off

my gear change incessantly. Finally and reluctantly the examiner told me to head for home, but as we went he turned his head to inquire, 'By the way, have you read *The Highway Code?*'

'Don't think so,' I said. 'Sounds rather period, highwayman and so on. Who wrote it?'

'No, no,' said the examiner in a dispirited tone. 'It's not that sort of book. It's a kind of manual. It tells you how to drive safely, when not to overtake, that sort of thing.'

'Good grief,' I replied, 'surely you don't need a manual to tell you all that. Isn't it just common sense?'

The examiner sucked his teeth rather gloomily for a few moments, then, 'I suppose you're right,' he concluded, and passed me competent to drive. My original red hard-backed driving licence, with a Devon County Council stamp on the inside back page, duly certified how, in July 1935, I had passed my driving test and become fit to drive 'all groups', this including, it gives me some satisfaction to record, steamrollers.

Driving was a very different experience then from how it is today. Roads were narrow and winding, improved versions of the original horse-drawn vehicle tracks, which had taken the lines of easiest resistance around hills and woods and along or across valleys. There were no dual carriageways, except for a few through the hideous ribbon developments of housing that were already reaching out all around London – the early stages of the Home Counties' relentless urban sprawl. With relatively few other cars on the road, the expressions 'traffic jam' and 'parking problem' were almost unknown. The main hazard was the surviving horse-drawn traffic, especially in rural areas. Tractors were only just beginning to be accepted and farmers still used horses as their most common means to transport produce or to power farm machinery. When flying round blind corners in narrow country roads you had to be ever alert to the risk of finding a slow-plodding horse and hay wagon suddenly materialising in front of you at the same moment as the only other automobile on that stretch of road for a week was coming in the opposite direction.

I encountered no such incidents during my drive to St Mawes in Pat's Ford 10, and began to unpack, heartily thankful to be able to relax in our haven of peace on Falmouth river. Hardly had I undone my cases, however, before a message arrived from the Hornchurch station adjutant. The station commander had re turned from leave and wished to see me immediately. Back I climbed into sister Pat's car, hammered out the many miles along the return route to Hornchurch, marched smartly into the station commander's office and saluted. He had recalled me, he said, because he thought it only right and proper that he should meet me personally before I began my leave. With my Cranwell training, he added, he felt sure I would be able to help him with some of his paperwork (an anticipation happily never fulfilled). With that he dismissed me to complete my leave. As I was to discover, the commandant was not exactly an electric personality; merely someone who meant well but who was overawed by his rank and felt the need to exercise it. I had been put through eighteen hours of hard driving for a ten-minute interview to bolster an ego. Of its kind, it was another lesson.

★ ★ ★

Life at Hornchurch in its pre-war days as a front-line fighter station was a further source of joy. I could think of no more satisfying existence for a fit young man.

A fighter squadron at full strength consisted of sixteen aircraft and a dozen or so pilots. In the air it fielded twelve aircraft, split into two flights, 'A' and 'B'. The CO would be a squadron leader, and under him came two flight lieutenants, each commanding one of the two flights. The balance of pilots was made up of flying officers and pilot officers (the latter being the lowest form of commissioned life in the RAF). As a rule, there were also three or four non-commissioned pilots − a warrant officer, a flight sergeant and a couple of sergeant pilots. A pilot officer was normally promoted to flying officer after eighteen months of service, but further advancement depended on passing promotion exams, a practice fortunately suspended with the outbreak of war.

Between the wars it was assumed that Fighter Command's operational role would be purely defensive, limited to the protection of the country against air attack. The aggressive role of the fighter as it emerged later was a response to new realities of war that were not as yet foreseen. To fulfil its defensive role, Fighter Command had to make a series of assumptions, the first being that enemy raids would be undertaken only by long-range heavy bombers. Secondly came the assumption that they would take place in daylight, since the technology for night bombing was still very primitive; thirdly, it was anticipated that these bombers would arrive unescorted over the country, for no fighter then had the range to reach England from Germany (and the fall of France never occurred to anyone even as a possibility); from all this it followed, fourthly, that they would invariably fly in massed formations, relying for defence on a lethal hail of cross-fire from their waist and rear-gun turrets.

To combat this perceived threat, Fighter Command devised a number of basic textbook attacks for its pre-war squadron of twelve aircraft. The Fighter Command attack plans were therefore confirmed to the varieties of formation possible for a force of that size.

(Fighter wings consisting of three or four squadrons only began to be developed a year or more after the outbreak of war.) There were six or so plans in all, though I recall only four of them: line abreast, line astern, and echelons port and starboard, all designed to be delivered from the beam, the aft quarter, or directly behind. The idea was that the leader of the defence aircraft would, having located the hostile invaders, decide which attack plan was most likely to be effective against the particular formation adopted by the enemy. Then the order would be issued: 'Stand by for Fighter Command attack number so and so.' As the squadron took up the relevant formation, the leader would manoeuvre it into the best position for launching the attack before calling out, 'Number so and so attack, go, go!' With that the squadron would close to firing range, pick its targets and hopefully create hell. These tactics were not very cerebral, perhaps, and they were certainly limited in scope, but then so were the available options. And when it came to the real thing, they were all totally irrelevant anyway.

Most of our days were spent in the air, our flying practice falling into five broad categories: aerobatics, air gunnery, formation, fighter tactics and cross-country. Aerobatics were not merely for display, but an important part of a fighter pilot's repertoire. To be in aerial combat means you have to be prepared to fly your aircraft in and out of all conceivable and inconceivable attitudes, angles and speeds, right way up and inverted, tightly in control and deliberately out of control. A fighter pilot therefore has to know his aircraft's limits precisely – what it can and cannot do, its strengths and weaknesses, its virtues and mean streaks. The only way he can achieve this level of awareness is by constant experiment in the air, pushing a plane to its limits and checking its reactions to unnatural forces. Aerobatic displays are nothing more than the aesthetic demonstration of some of the more controlled capabilities, put on for fans at air shows. The less controlled manoeuvres would take up too much air space for convenient public viewing.

Another purpose of aerobatics is to allow pilots to become accustomed to 'G' forces, or varying gravitational pulls, and also to 'blacking out', the result of too much 'G' and, contrary to public perception, the fighter pilot's friend. When the stick is pulled hard back, as it constantly is in aerobatics and aerial combat, centrifugal force, the same force that would send a conker twirled on the end of a piece of string flying into outer space if it were not for the retaining knot and the restraints of gravity, presses down hard, squashing you into the bottom of your seat. The harder you pull, the more you tighten your vertical or horizontal turn and the heavier the force you invoke until you become unable to move, your hands and feet growing too heavy to lift. Most dramatically, the blood is also forced down from behind the optic nerves, causing you to 'black out', which means a loss not of consciousness but of vision.

Individual tolerances to 'G' vary considerably, but most pilots begin 'greying out' at around four 'G', or four times the pull of the earth's gravity. This may sound like a frustrating handicap in a fighting situation, but it can also be a useful defensive ploy. The explanation for this apparent paradox becomes clear in considering circumstances where you have an enemy on your tail who is difficult to dislodge. If you pull the stick hard enough to black yourself out, then whoever you have on your tail is going to need to pull his back even harder. To allow for deflection, he can only turn within your trajectory, and thus will attract more 'G' than you do. If you are blacked out the chances are that your opponent, unless he is Superman, will be blacked out as well, which will prevent him being in the position to get a clear shot at you. Blacking out is a controllable condition which does not affect thinking. This means you can ease it off briefly now and then to snatch a quick look round, or else you can hold it for as long as you need to think up a new ploy.

Single-seater fighter pilots have to do everything for themselves. They fly the aeroplane, work the radio and navigate and also fire the guns. Location of controls is designed with this operational need in mind. The gun trigger of a single-seater fighter, the thumb-operated push button, was situated on top of the control column, known as the 'stick' (never the 'joystick'!). It meant a pilot could fly his plane and fire his guns simultaneously. The guns themselves were rigidly fixed within the wings or fuselage to fire directly along the line of flight of the aircraft. They were usually calibrated to converge at between one and two hundred yards, either at a single point or with an agreed spread pattern, depending on individual preference. Any closer and there was a danger of flying through the wreckage of your target aircraft. It was therefore not his guns that the pilot of a single-seater aimed at a target; he aimed his aircraft.

That was the easy bit; hitting the target another matter. Air gunnery practice was carried out with live ammunition against target drogues – airborne wind socks towed behind tug aircraft – but firing at a peace-loving drogue being dragged through the air at a constant speed on a steady course presented few problems. It was quite another matter to score a hit on an enemy aircraft travelling at several hundred miles an hour as it changed direction, speed and altitude every second or so, climbed, dived, turned and skidded. What was more, your gun platform (this being the aircraft itself) was not so nice and steady as gun platforms are intended to be, but followed the same wild antics of the target. This meant that the trajectories of your bullets could be another flexible factor to complicate the equation; and finally there came the time factor. Because your bullets took several seconds to reach their target, varying with range, you needed to aim not where the enemy was when you pressed the 'tit', but where you calculated he would be when your bullets arrived. In other words, you had to map a converging course mentally, the difference between your aiming point and the target itself being known as 'deflection'.

Technology had as yet done little to provide us with any aids to assist us in all of this. We did have a reflector sight, so called because it was a red dot reflected on the underside of the angled windscreen from a light located below. It was flanked by a pair of adjustable range bars which could be set manually to indicate the size of the aircraft you expected to encounter (bombers or fighters) at whatever range you preferred. It was quite helpful in assessing distances, and the red dot simply indicated the line of flight of your bullets. In other words, if you lined it up on a static target and were also stationery, you scored a hit. What it regrettably did not tell you was where to aim at a moving target, or how much deflection to allow to take effective care of all the jokers in the pack. Such judgements only came from experience combined with instinct.

Later in the war a gyroscopic gun sight was introduced which was reputed to be most helpful, though I personally never used one. It was still a reflector sight, but the red dot moved according to 'G' forces and turning circles, and indicated how much to lay off for deflection. By the time it was introduced I was commanding a Spitfire wing in Desert Air Force in support of Montgomery's Eighth Army in its thrust up through Sicily and Italy. The new sights never filtered through to our theatre, but went to the wings supporting the invasion and campaign in Northern Europe. It was fair enough. Enemy air activity was virtually non-existent by that mopping-up stage of the war in Italy.

Formation flying came high on the training priority list, and was an activity I always found deeply satisfying, an apotheosis of the pride felt in being part of a first-class drill squad. It was an essential skill, enabling squadrons and even wings to be flown intact as one unit, through cloud and bad weather, to arrive at their destination as a unified fighting force rather than a leaderless gaggle. Even when you were flying blind in the thickest cloud, there was always enough visibility to see the aircraft immediately next to you, if little else. Each aircraft had its place in the formation and each pilot had to concentrate one hundred per cent on his immediate neighbour. You also needed to have implicit faith in your leader. As the only one among you who was flying on instruments, he held the fate of the formation in his hands. While everyone else formatted on his immediate neighbour in a chain that led back to the leader, they fought back all their primeval instincts, all their doubts about speed and attitudes, to concentrate utterly on staying tucked close in behind their neighbour's wing and letting the rest of their minds go blank.

And the amazing thing was that it worked. Many a time in later years I took wings of three or four squadrons up through 20,000ft or more of grey forbidding cloud and broke through into blinding sunlight with everyone as immaculately in formation as when we entered. Sometimes I did wonder what the consequence would be if a leader suffered engine failure on the way up. So far as I remember, the only provision we made for this was to keep our fingers crossed and hope such a thing would never happen. If it had occurred, the result would have been a bit untidy, to say the least. The leader's numbers two and three would have lacked the experience to take his place, and so would have had to follow him down to let the leader of the section immediately behind take over. In my experience the contingency never arose.

* * *

Pre-war pay in the armed forces was recognised as miserly. This was a hangover from the days when commissioned officers were expected to be of independent means. Officers had only a few years earlier been required to purchase their commissions while receiving no pay whatsoever. It had been rather like joining an extended club, with the services acting as a socially acceptable refuge for the younger sons of the landed or moneyed classes. The eldest son inherited, the second went into the army, the third into the church, the latter two remaining stand-ins in the wings in case the lead player came to grief. Additional sons, if any, sometimes followed their elder brothers into the forces or else ended up as remittance men, scattered about the globe and living on the regular stipends sent by their families, on the understanding that they stayed away.

This generalised mould was largely broken by the air force. It was too young and newfangled to have achieved respectability, or to be accepted as a desirable refuge for spare sons. Instead it tended to attract lively young men from every background and social class, who were excited by the new horizons then materialising and attracted towards careers in a technology that offered ever-expanding opportunities rather than staging-posts in a waiting game. For myself, as a young pilot officer, the future played little part in my thinking. The present was all-absorbing. I was in a constant euphoria at my good luck to find myself actually being paid to lead an existence that I felt sure must be the envy of all my young male contemporaries. For one thing, I was flying the best aircraft in the world; for another, I was enjoying a highly civilised standard of off-duty life, with comfortable quarters among colleagues who all more or less clicked on the same wave-length.

Comparisons between standards of living then and now have become largely irrelevant, since the value of money and the costs of living have changed profoundly in the meantime. The pay of a pilot officer (a fully qualified pilot holding a commission in His Majesty's Royal Air Force) was fourteen shillings (75p) a day, £5 5s (£5.25) a week, in peace and in war. Living in mess cost six shillings (30p) a day, excluding drink but including all else − food, laundry, heating and lighting, plus − the biggest plus of all − one's own personal batman.

No words can describe the contribution to the quality of forces life made by batmen, the biggest boon to living and the most underrated of all forces personnel. They cleaned your boots, your shoes and your equipment, pressed your clothes, made your bed, packed your bags when you went on leave, stayed up late and unpacked them when you returned. They woke you on time in the morning with a cup of tea (which could be at 3.30 a.m. if you were at dawn readiness, or midday if you had a morning off), sobered you up when necessary, walked 'on egg-shells' when you had a hangover, made sure you were never late for an appointment or missed a parade, briefed you in your early days on the mysteries and niceties of service etiquette, kept you up to date with the local service and other gossip and generally spoiled you ruinously. A batman was confidant, friend and adviser, and there is no doubt that without him many a promising career would have come to a premature end.

Standards of comfort were general for all ranks, commissioned officers and non-commissioned personnel having their separate messes. Pre-war meals in the officers' mess always consisted of four or five courses, served by mess stewards in white jackets and gloves. It was usual to start with soup, which invariably seemed to be either brown Windsor or mock turtle (perhaps pre-war chefs were taught only these two), followed by fish. Then came the main course, usually a roast. After that came a pudding and finally a savoury. Cheese was served at the end of lunch, but never after dinner, when the savoury replaced it.

Following the savoury (whose post-war demise I miss), fruit was put on the table, the port was circulated, and the ritual of the Loyal Toast gone through, proposed by the president of the mess committee (PMC), responded to by the vice-president, and drunk standing. I only mention 'standing' because the Royal Navy, alone of all the services, had been granted a dispensation by Queen Victoria some time early on in her reign to drink the toast sitting down. This was a concession to the very limited headroom between decks in the old ships of the line. There simply was not the clearance for officers to stand up straight when drinking the toast at sea. Perhaps Her Majesty feared lest a constant cracking of heads against wooden bulkheads might lead to a thickening of their skulls.

There were no bars in RAF officers' messes in those days. These only came into being in about the second year of the war, initially contrary to King's Regulations. The first was at Biggin Hill when I was there with No.92 Squadron. Previously drinks were served in the ante-room, and if you wanted one you rang for it and ordered it from a white-jacketed bar steward. Cash never changed hands in the mess. You signed for your drinks and they were put on your mess bill. In this way Big Brother could keep an eye on his pilots' drinking habits, or so he thought. Heavy drinkers tend to be heavy drinkers wherever there is access to booze, and no check could be kept on outside activities.

Thursday nights were guest nights, when the black ties and blue waistcoats of our No.2 mess kits were changed for the white of our No.1s. Hornchurch guest nights always followed the same ritual. The station band would be on duty to play non-stop throughout the meal. They belted out the National Anthem when it came to the Loyal Toast and wound up with the 'Post Horn Gallop' played with deafening gusto. Then everyone retired to the ante-room for a few post-prandial drinks, after which the furniture was pushed back against the walls and the traditional games began: rough and ready schoolboy games like 'high cockalorum', rugger scrums, or anything competitive requiring team rather than individual effort and involving plenty of body contact and head-on charging. Eventually senior officers and guests retired, the games petered out, a few more drinks were consumed, and one by one we drifted off to bed.

Virtually all squadron pilots pre-war, with the exception of COs and the odd flight commander, lived in the mess. This was because marriage below the rank of squadron leader or under the age of thirty was, while not specifically forbidden, actively discouraged. An 'unqualified' married officer received no recognition, no allowances, no contribution towards living expenses or children's education, no married quarters, nothing. His rate of promotion, moreover, was likely to be sluggish. Harsh though this may sound to today's enthusiasts for individual rights, it made a good deal of sense and rendered the air force into a more efficient fighting machine than it would have been otherwise. What the RAF needed was operational crews who were free from family responsibilities and ready to be posted to any part of the world at a moment's notice without having to worry their heads over dependants left behind.

The policy certainly worked, and it had one very important spin-off. It fostered and intensified the squadron spirit. Aircrew, unlike office or other sedentary workers, who are not necessarily affected by their colleagues' levels of responsiveness, are in a job where their lives are at risk even during routine practice. Here the reactions of colleagues can be a decisive factor. If they therefore not only work together but virtually live together, they come to know each other that much better, along with individual strengths and weaknesses. Their sense of responsibility towards one another is reinforced and they meld into a single, dedicated team with instinctive responses. In effect, their squadron becomes their family and the most important relationship in their lives. A side-effect of the system was that a mess after dinner tended to be full of junior officers with two or three hours to kill before bedtime and an impressive charge of energy to dissipate. The usual simple solution to this was a local pub crawl.

To initiate an evening's pub crawl three or four of us would club together and each put half a crown (25p) into the kitty. We would then climb into the handiest car, which to buy probably cost any thing between £10 and £25 (more than a month's pay: £23.25 if it was a month of thirty-one days or £22.50 for a month of thirty days). To fill the tank with petrol cost us a shilling (5p) a gallon for the best grade, which we called 100 octane (or 'four-star' in to day's language), or tenpence (a little over 4p) for standard grade (or 'two-star'). Once we had downed several drinks costing eight-pence (4p) for a pint of beer or a measure of whisky, we would still have some change over to share out at the end of the evening.

At weekends, if you felt like going into London, then ten shillings (50p) would get you there and back by train and allow you to enjoy an evening at Shepherd's, a pub in Shepherd's Market run by a Swiss called Oscar, a charmer who bent the licensing rules for fighter pilots and whose pub became Fighter Command's drinking headquarters in London. If you upped your ante and set out from Hornchurch with a pound in your pocket, you could also treat yourself to a night club after the pubs had closed.

Oscar endeared himself to me in perpetuity during the war. I had a theory, never yet disproved, that if I drank whisky and milk together, then the milk would not only line my stomach and allow me to drink more without getting drunk, but it would also, being a food in itself, save me time otherwise wasted sitting down to a meal. Since both whisky and milk were rationed during the war, Oscar always kept a bottle of whisky and a pint of cow juice hidden behind the bar for me, for what he christened my 'moose's milk', and stubbornly refused it to anyone else.

I never did hear what happened to Oscar in the end. When I returned from my three years away in Desert Air Force, he was gone from the pub and there was no more moose's milk.

★ ★ ★

One of the most marvellous aspects of pre-war and early post-war flying was the freedom. All you needed to do, if you wanted to go anywhere – for lunch or to call on friends, on air force or purely social business – was to climb into an aeroplane and go. You did not even have to obtain permission, other than from your flight commander, nor did you have to file flight plans or obtain instructions on which altitude to fly at or route to take. You simply took off, map-read your way there, and landed. While you were on the ground enjoying lunch, the aircraft would be refuelled and checked over, and then be ready and waiting for you to climb back in at your convenience.

Ad hoc flying was constantly encouraged, the view being that every flying hour added to the sum total of a pilot's experience could only be of benefit to the force. New situations and unfamiliar weather conditions would constantly be encountered, and by dealing with them continually pilots would add to their store of knowledge and self-confidence. The main hazard we faced in pre war days probably was the weather. The flying itself was never the problem, but getting back down on the ground could be. Sophisticated radar systems did not as yet exist, and weather reports were less reliable than they became later. Single-seater pilots needed to rely largely on map-reading, which meant maintaining visual contact with the ground. You might work out your course before take-off, but once you were in the air a change of wind speed could reduce your best calculations to nonsense. If you had to fly in or above cloud, it became impossible to check your course against the map, and you could drift miles away from where you thought you were.

It was always possible for ground control to give you a vector back to base and an approximate distance, but neither of these readings would be over-accurate either. Your altimeter gave you only your height above the airfield from where you took off, so if the weather clamped down and there were hills between you and your destination, then you needed to hold your breath as you began to let down, and pray you had not picked a spot where the clouds were shrouding the hills − 'clouds with hard centres', as they were known with ominous wit. And once you were safely down through the cloud, you were likely to find yourself in unfamiliar territory amid-poor visibility. The usual trick then was to try to spot a railway line and grope your way along it until you came to a station, when you could read its name. Among all the pieces of navigational advice passed on to us at Cranwell, this was one of the first, and it was certainly the most practical.

Not long after my arrival at Hornchurch, I was dispatched to sit a navigational course at Manston, an RAF aerodrome on the north-eastern tip of Kent, close by the North Foreland. It also lay pleasingly within striking distance of such watering holes as Canterbury, Margate and Ramsgate. Manston's courses for student navigators were of the grown-up sort, where you sat at a chart table and plotted courses using all the paraphernalia of a proper navigator − parallel rules, slide rules, dividers, sextants and the rest. Why they should have sent me, a fighter pilot, on so cerebral a course I never could figure out.

We were given a few lectures on the ground, these taking in the then rather limited but fascinating new science of meteorology. Most of our time, however, was spent in the air on Ansons, laborious but useful twin-engined aircraft which carried a total of five or so passengers, including crew. The undercarriage of an Anson needed to be physically wound up and down by hand and elbow grease. It took some 120 turns of the wheel each way, heavy on the way up though easy on the way down. Naturally this labour fell to the junior crew member on the navigation course, who needless to say was the student navigator. I took the task on in good cheer once it occurred to me that no one could possibly have a worse job than the wretched pilot, doomed to drone endlessly over the North Sea, following erratic courses set by a student navigator.

The exercises themselves were quite demanding. We would fly three- or four-leg courses to three or four specific points, one leg being the interception of one of the ferries plying between the east coast ports and Scandinavia. Armed with a boat's time of sailing and estimated speed, we had to rendezvous with it at a given time and position, beyond sight of land and somewhere above the wastes of the North Sea. Having succeeded in this, we made a couple of landfalls and headed for home. How I ever passed the course I shall never know, but I did, and I was given a certificate to prove it. Yet it was not the flying, nor even the miracle of winning the certificate, that fixed this stay at Manston in my memory. Rather was it a childish off-duty escapade that for ever after acted as a salutary corrective whenever I found myself becoming irritated by the antics of the young of later generations making asses of themselves.

I had an afternoon off in Margate with a couple of chaps from the course, and we took a few drinks in various pubs before I somehow lost contact with the others. Somehow, sometime during the evening, I found myself in a theatre watching a music-hall act from the front row of the stalls. Somehow it then became necessary for me to begin lecturing the artistes about their act on stage, pointing out flaws in their performance and giving tips on how the show might be improved. Impervious to the angry hisses of the audience and the shouts of, 'Shut up or get out!' I was into that euphoric state where I *knew* I was being devastatingly amusing; that anyone who thought otherwise was clearly short of a couple of marbles. In other words, I was being the archetypal youthful drunk at his most boorish. On three occasions I was approached by the ushers, but each time I waved them away imperiously, confident that audience and actors were revelling in my witty repartee as much I was myself. The fourth time they approached me they were accompanied by two policemen. In a sudden thinning of the alcoholic mists it occurred to me that perhaps I was not cutting as popular a figure as I had thought. On the other hand, I was blowed if I was going to submit tamely to being apprehended.

Leaping from my seat, I darted out through the nearest exit. Emerging into a main thoroughfare, I sprinted down a side-road.

Then, with devilish ingenuity, I doubled to and fro, up and down a maze of back streets, till I cunningly doubled straight into a cordon of wall-to-wall policemen, their arms outstretched as they gripped one anothers' wrists to form a phalanx that blocked the road entirely. Like a cartoon character I screeched to a halt, but by now I was as intoxicated with the thrill of the chase as I was with my diminishing alcohol blood level. I shot off down another alley, and almost into the arms of another police cordon. Nothing daunted, I spun about and started back: more police. It seemed the entire Kentish constabulary had been called out to capture me, and while such attention was very flattering, the elation was short-lived. Finally I was cornered, and Kingcome's brief career as a fugitive from justice came to a finish in the local lock-up. It did not take long to establish my identity, whereupon Manston was informed. The police released me into the custody of the station adjutant, who collected me and took me back to camp.

The next morning, wheeled into the station commander's office, I was deservedly torn off the most almighty strip. The entire course was then assembled to be addressed by the station commander, who went into every detail of my conduct with relish and held me up as a prime example of how officers and gentlemen do not behave. And that, to my surprise, was that.

It came as a considerable relief. I had expected to be fired from the course and returned to Hornchurch in disgrace. Perhaps, I thought on reflection, the station commander's leniency had been inspired by a similar incident in his own past, and he had tried, as I would many years later, to see beyond the nauseating arrogance which is the hallmark of the youthful drunk to the often pleasant young person behind the foolishness. I returned to Hornchurch, career prospects seemingly unscathed. Manston was to feature twice more in my life, but both these later occasions would be after the outbreak of war.

★ ★ ★

There was one particularly tragic incident at Hornchurch. On a summer evening three or four of us were coming back from a pub crawl and went into the mess ante-room for a night-cap. It was a Friday night. There was a mess ball scheduled for the following evening, and among those already there and holding the floor was an Australian known as Mac, a pilot from one of the other squadrons. As the whole room was soon aware, Mac had lined up two girls for the ball and could not make his mind up which to settle for. That was fairly vintage Mac for you. He was attractive and athletic. He swam for the RAF, was highly popular with the opposite sex and seemingly permanently entangled in mild girlfriend problems. Little notice was taken of his agonising, and Mac himself seemed every bit as interested in choosing records for the gramophone as in sorting out his dance dates. Then, all at once, he stood up, said, 'Goodbye, everybody,' in rather a sombre tone, and left the room.

We dismissed Mac's sudden change of mood from our minds as a routine case of a drink too many. Ten minutes or so later there came the sound of a shot from somewhere outside in the gardens. Again, no one paid more than the barest attention. Mac had a well-earned reputation for eccentricity. Somebody made a casual remark about him probably playing silly buggers with his service revolver before, one by one, we drifted off to bed.

Still no alarm bells rang when he failed to show up for duty next morning. It would not have been the first time when he had decided on the spur of the moment, last thing at night, to nip up to London to call on one of his girls. What other conceivable reason could there be? Not until the day after that did an alternative explanation finally emerge. One of the mess gardeners, working in the beautifully maintained rose garden, came upon Mac lying face down on a grass path between two rose beds. He had stretched himself out on his stomach with his arms in front, reversed his service revolver, rested the butt on the ground and the barrel against his forehead, put his thumb through the trigger guard and pushed the trigger. The deed was methodically, carefully and expertly done.

The part of the story that shattered us utterly was the apparent lack of any connection between the Mac who had so light-heartedly chattered on about his plans for the forthcoming mess ball, changing records on the gramophone, jiving to the music and generally carefree and cheerful, and the Mac who moments later did himself to death in as tidy and efficient a way as might be imagined. My true belief, then and afterwards, was that he had gone so far as to choose the garden to minimise the clearing-up work for his batman.

The post-mortem showed no physical problems and mentally there seemed nothing to distinguish Mac from any of the rest of us. It was an incident that made me begin to realise that the standard phrase once used by coroners, 'While the balance of the mind was disturbed,' had more significance to it than simply being a ploy utilised by kindly people to circumvent the banning of suicides from burial in holy ground.

I never saw Mac's body, but another unhappy incident at Hornchurch did bring me face to face with the physical aspect of death for the first time, after one of our pilots had crashed near Andover. His body was taken to the town morgue and the job of formal identification filtered down to me as the junior member of the squadron. I borrowed a Lysander from the communications flight and flew to the RAF airfield just outside Andover. There I was met by a friendly policeman, who drove me to the morgue. He was a considerate man, obviously experienced in death but sensitive to the fact that confrontation with it at its most violent and ugly could be deeply disturbing to those who lacked such experience, especially the young and healthy who had not yet come to terms with it.

The body had been quite badly battered, he warned me, and I braced myself for the worst. Gently he drew back the sheet. He had gone to the trouble of covering the worst of the damage to the shattered face with dressing, so that little more than half was left visible. 'Is that enough?' he asked. 'Can you see enough to be sure it's him?'

I looked at the broken body and felt curiously unmoved. I have no idea what I had expected, but it was certainly a more positive reaction within myself. The waxen features, more like those of a Madame Tussaud look-alike than human flesh and blood, were undoubtedly those of my colleague, last seen only a few hours before as an active young man. Yet somehow the living man and this lifeless effigy were so remote from one another that it was impossible to make the connection. 'Yes,' I replied. 'Thank you. Certainly it's him.'

The policeman replaced the sheet and we left.

On my way back to Hornchurch I briefly wondered whether there was not a lesson here: whether I ought to be more careful, stick more closely to the rule books, heed the sound advice of my flying instructors. But as with all such good intentions − like those we have on the road when passing the consequences of a serious traffic accident − the mood was short-lived.

★ ★ ★

I remained at Hornchurch from the late summer of 1938 until the Dunkirk rescue operation in the early summer of 1940. When I first arrived 65 Squadron was equipped with Gloster Gladiators, the most up-to-date aircraft then in service. These were single-seater biplanes with radial air-cooled engines, sliding cockpit canopies (a rare luxury: the only fighter aircraft without cockpits open to the skies) and cantilever undercarriages (another unique feature). They carried four .303 calibre machine guns, two of which were mounted on the engine cowling in the front of the cockpit and fired through the revolving airscrew. These were controlled by an arrester gear designed to ensure the bullets missed the whirling propeller blades, which, to my perpetual astonishment, they did. The other two were mounted in the wings, just outside the airscrew.

Gladiators were lovely aircraft to fly, docile and vice-free, but they marked the end of an era. The biplane, alas, was about to slide into history. The Gladiator, the best of its kind in its short day, would have been no match for the monoplane fighters then coming off the drawing boards – the British Spitfire and Hurricane and the German Messerschmitt 109 and, later, the Focke-Wulf 190. Although Gladiators were withdrawn from service in the United Kingdom well before the start of the war, three of these machines, nicknamed 'Faith', 'Hope' and 'Charity', did achieve considerable battle fame in the air defence of Malta in 1941–42, when the island resisted the might of a combined assault by German and Italian forces with a gallantry that uniquely earned it the award of the George Cross.

The most significant event at pre-war Hornchurch came about when we re-equipped from Gladiators to Spitfires, somewhere between six and nine months before the war began. As one of the first squadrons to be re-equipped, we gained the huge advantage that we were already experienced Spitfire pilots by the time we came to the outbreak of war, and most importantly by the time of the Dunkirk evacuation. Dunkirk was, indeed, the first occasion on which the home-based fighters saw any sustained action. The Spitfire and Hurricane together represented a huge breakthrough in fighter-aircraft technology. They were the first of our monoplane fighters, the first to reach 400mph in straight and level flight, and the first to carry eight machine guns – an unheard-of weight of firepower at the time.

At the outset there was endless friendly banter between Hurricane and Spitfire pilots as to which was the better aircraft, but in the real world there could only be one answer. Even if I had been a Hurricane pilot, I would still have had to award the supreme accolade to the Spitfire in any final judgement. The Hurricane was a solid, reliable, uncomplaining workhorse, but the Spitfire personified symmetry and grace. She was a thing apart, defying comparison. She was as relaxed, as elegant, as obviously and effortless at home in her natural environment as a swallow; and equally poetic in motion. To compare the two models would be as invidious as comparing a champion ice skater with the most skilled of Morris dancers: each is brilliant in his or her own way, but each displays a widely different talent and technique. There is an old truism that, if a car or an aeroplane looks good, then it almost invariably is good. And nothing looked better than the Spitfire.

Not that the Hurricane failed to possess one or two advantages over the Spitfire. It was more robust and could take more punishment; it had a more concentrated fire pattern, its guns being grouped more closely together. It was also marginally more manoeuvrable, and was far more stable on the ground − the result of its undercarriage being wider and positioned farther forward, a characteristic which often proved useful on the rough terrain of temporary landing strips. The Spitfire, on the other hand, was faster and could out-dive and out-climb the Hurricane; and since it could also out-turn the German front-line fighter, the Me 109, it had all the manoeuvrability it needed. Yet in the end these are only details of performance, and it was in the respective operational life of the two aircraft that the truly huge difference between them became crystal clear.

The Hurricane was already more or less at the peak of its operational and design potential when it first came into service. As time passed, it was given bigger and better engines, heavier and more powerful armament, and was tried out in various ground-attack roles. Nevertheless its future was strictly limited by its rugged, uncouth airframe. In other words, it had virtually no development potential. The Spitfire, by contrast, possessed a unique capacity for development. On one occasion Jeffrey Quill, the legendary test pilot who nursed the Spitfire from cradle to grave, gave me his definition of the range of its development throughout its life as a fighting machine. The difference in capability between the first Spitfire off the drawing board and the last to be built was to be measured, he said, by the fact that the latter could carry an extra load equivalent to an additional thirty-six airline passengers, each with his or her regulation forty kilos of luggage.

Only by evoking such a graphic example as this is it possible to convey a glimmer of understanding of the supreme concept which enabled an aircraft conceived in the early 1930s to sustain revolutionary improvements in performance without any significant modification to its basic design. This extraordinary capacity for development maintained the Spitfire as Britain's front-line fighter in the late 1930s through to the early 1950s, when it was finally ousted. It bowed out gracefully at the close of a remarkable chapter in aviation history, of which, with vastly different capabilities, it had marked both beginning and end. Its demise was brought about not by yet another piston-engined aircraft, but by the next major breakthrough in aviation technology – Frank Whittle's jet engine.

But to return to the beginning, and the impact the Spitfires had on pre-war Hornchurch, the initial point to be made is that a first flight in a single-seater fighter is always a voyage of discovery. Lacking dual instruction, you have to find your way around it on your own. Where the Spitfire was concerned, a first solo presented no problems and the classic aircraft responded in the air in a classic way to any demands you cared to make on it. Its main weaknesses became manifest when it had contact with the ground. The very long nose allowed the pilot no forward vision in the tail-down position when taxiing, which created a need for him to weave from side to side so he could see where he was going; and the centre of gravity lay uncomfortably far forward on the ground, so that any but the most delicate handling of the brakes could well tip the whole machine unceremoniously on to its nose.

In the air it was another matter altogether. I was once quoted in a publication as remarking that you didn't fly a Spitfire; you wore it like an old jacket. I never did recollect saying such a thing, but while as a comment this may sound a trifle contrived, it contains an element of truth. The Spitfire was so natural, and responded in such a natural, uncomplicated way to the controls, that any pilot felt instantly at home in it. The only initial anxiety to haunt me was what in the world it could be that kept the wings from breaking away in full flight.

Those of us who were brought up on biplanes were accus-tomed to be able to see the flying wires that kept the wings on in the air and the rigging lines that held them up on the ground. Such visual evidence of straightforward engineering could be deeply reassuring, but in a monoplane you had to place your trust in a new concept called 'cantilever construction', and convince yourself that, even if you could not see it, it worked. Most of my first few flights in a Spitfire were spent casting anxious sideways glances at the wings, expecting them to break off and disappear at any moment. Once I was persuaded that the cantilever principle was sound, then the Spitfire cockpit became a second home. Considering the events of the next few years, I could hardly have asked for a better one.

FIVE

THE PHONEY WAR AND THE REAL THING

After the declaration of war in September 1939, life for the fighter squadrons committed to the air defence of Britain wound slowly down from the initial period of intense anticipation into one long yawn. The 'phoney war', as this early period of inaction came to be known, lasted up to the summer of 1940 and the fall of France. Its chief characteristic was a feeling of unreality, and the event that summed up its phoniness for us was an inglorious mix of farce and tragedy dubbed 'The Battle of Barking Creek'. This happened on the first or second Sunday of the war after all pilots had been moved out of the comfort of the mess and into tents pitched around the perimeter of the airfield, the idea being that this would make us less vulnerable to air attack.

Naturally we were on edge. We had been expecting to hear the drone of approaching bombers at any moment from the time when Chamberlain finished broadcasting his warning to the nation. Yet nothing had happened. A season of perfect weather, with blue unclouded skies and almost no wind, connived with the feeling of anticlimax. Meanwhile we itched to get airborne but no flying was allowed. A deep boredom set in, at which point a Hurricane squadron from a base in East Anglia asked for and was granted permission to air-test one of its aircraft. The aeroplane took off and was immediately plotted as a 'bogey' – jargon for an unidentified aircraft ('bandit' being the term for a confirmed enemy). Three aircraft were scrambled to investigate, and these in turn were plotted as bogies. More aircraft were sent to investigate, which led to more bogies and further investigations. Finally almost the whole of Fighter Command was airborne, flying in ever-decreasing circles as it investigated itself.

I was with my own squadron, cruising along the Thames at 5,000ft, when we were instructed to orbit while operations control got down to deciding what it should do next. There were various ack-ack batteries based on the isle of Sheppey, and each time we passed above them they opened up at us; they ceased firing as we circled away over the river then let fly again as we came back round over the guns. It would have made no operational difference to us if we had simply edged out of their range, but instead we continued blindly orbiting in and out of their line of fire. Orders were regarded as sacrosanct, never to be subjected to interpretation, and common sense was yet to prevail. The man on the ground was deemed to know better than the man in the air. Happily all of that was soon to change.

It was no thanks to the man on the ground that we all landed back at Hornchurch unscathed. At once our CO got on the phone and tracked down the battery commander at Sheppey, intending to let him have an earful. He was disarmed from the start. The battery commander said he was frightfully sorry, and he could see how upsetting it must have been, but he was sure we would understand his position. His chaps had all been on alert since hostilities were declared but with nothing to fire at they were getting rusty. Our appearance in the skies had presented a god-sent opportunity to get in some real target practice, which could only be for the good of the war effort in the long term. He was sure we would see the incident in that light. After all, the fact that they had hit nobody showed how important it was for them to have some target practice, didn't it? Our CO was rendered speechless.

That was the farce for you. The tragic side came when a Spitfire squadron bounced a squadron of Hurricanes and briefly opened fire before it realised its error. Two of the Hurricanes were shot down and one of the pilots was killed, though the other pilot bailed out safely. The Spitfire section leader who fired the fatal burst was an old friend, Paddy Byrne, who had impressed himself on all at peacetime Hornchurch as an unforgettable, unbelievable, impetuous Irishman. Among Paddy's many eccentricities was his incurable habit of being a jackdaw. He would fly off to another RAF base to have lunch with friends and return with an assortment of hats, greatcoats and gloves that he had somehow contrived to sneak out of his hosts' mess and into his aircraft. He would get up to the same tricks in oar own mess at Hornchurch. 'What's wrong, me old cock?' Paddy would ask you. 'Lost something?'

'Yes, as a matter of fact I have. Can't seem to find my gloves.'

'Ah,' Paddy would say. 'I may be able to help. I think I've a spare pair about your size. Come along up to my room and take a look.'

Off you would trot to Paddy's room, to find it fitted out like a haberdashers with rows of hats, gloves and coats neatly laid out and graded. There, among them, would be your pair of gloves, His Majesty's issue, which Paddy, exuding innocence, would try to sell back to you.

'Barking Creek' was an episode that the authorities hoped would remain tucked under the carpet in decent obscurity. Meanwhile the only things to remind us of the fact that we were technically at war were all negative – blackout and shortages. The food shortages affected us little inside the mess, but in the world outside, in restaurants, hotels and pubs, it was a different story. The most a restaurant or pub was allowed to charge for a meal was five shillings (25p), plus a cover charge of one and sixpence (9p). Nevertheless it was always surprising how excellent a three-course meal could be supplied within these limits. One of the advantages for a junior officer on his meagre wage of fourteen shillings a day was that the catering regulations did away with price barriers and made regular haunts out of smart places which he could otherwise have afforded to patronise only rarely.

At this stage every fighter station kept at least one of its squadrons at permanent readiness, with the others on varying degrees of availability. This meant that we were, to begin with, permanently confined to camp. At the outset of war, and for the year or so afterwards, the business hours for fighter squadrons were extended round the clock, with the same squadrons operating night and day. This phase of things slowly came to an end as the new Radio Direction Finding system (RDF), began to live up to its huge potential. RDF was a British invention, the development of which was, true to form, slowed down by lack of funds until the Americans took it up enthusiastically and renamed it 'radar' (radio aid to direction and range). Soon it became apparent that radar could, among its many other qualities, 'see' far more efficiently at night than the naked human eye. It also enabled us to pick up approaching enemy aircraft before they crossed the coast, giving invaluable extra time to intercept. Before that we had relied on the ground wholly on the Observer Corps, an admirable band of amateurs equipped with binoculars and field telephones − a gallant but decidedly low-tech force.

As the development of radar progressed, so the limitations of single-seater fighters in a night-fighter role also became more and more obvious. As a result the single seater was gradually replaced by specialised night-fighter squadrons flying twin-engined aircraft with specially trained two-man crews − pilot and radar operator. The single-seater fighter meanwhile slowly reverted to a daylight only role, and the emergence of a specialised night-fighter role produced a new breed of pilots, among whom probably the best-known, and certainly one of the most successful, was the great John Cunningham, dubbed 'Cat's-eyes Carrots' Cunningham by the press. The story put about was that his phenomenal success could be attributed to an addiction to carrots, which gave him exceptionally keen night vision. This likely tale was instigated, so he told me, by the Ministry of Food as part of its propaganda drive to encourage people to grow more of their own vegetables and make the country less reliant on imports. It was perfectly true that Johnny's off-duty passion was gardening, but his success was the result not of overdosing on Vitamin A from home-grown carrots but of first-class teamwork between an inspired pilot and a brilliant radar operator.

Cunningham was one of the rare few who carved out an exceptionally distinguished career at the sharp end of aviation in both peace and war. Before the war he was one of de Havilland's test pilots; during it he grew to be one of the greatest night-fighter pilots; and after it he returned to de Havilland to become their number one and a leading test pilot of the post-war era. Like all the great test pilots, he combined a cold courage with an extensive knowledge and an instinct for the air. There were no computer simulations to check design, detect and correct problems and minimise practical risks at the time when he was testing. His aircraft were tested, in the air, to their very limits, all the way to the point of break-up. The only method of discovering what those limits were was to fly the beast, and many a test pilot sacrificed his life on such hazardous, pioneering flights of discovery.

It was Johnny who, in the early post-war years, developed the Comet, the first commercial jet airliner, from drawing-board to maiden flight. This breakthrough for British industry took the international aviation world by storm, but regrettably the Comet came to a tragic end after two crashed mysteriously and killed all on board. For a while the cause of these disasters eluded detection, until a whole aircraft was put into a specially designed tank at Farnborough, which flexed the metal components cease-lessly round the clock until the main wing-spars developed metal fatigue and snapped. This was a weakness no amount of test flying could have revealed, and the discovery played a vital part in the development of high-speed, high-altitude military and commercial jet planes. It was a sad conclusion to the story of the Comet, but she represented a vision of an aircraft that had simply gone one step in front of the technology of her time.

Cunningham deserved a recognition he never received for his outstanding contribution to the aviation industry. The irony of our honours system is that it seldom recognises the Cunninghams of this world, whose daring and innovative efforts positively enhance the nation's status – in the case of Cunningham at a constant risk to his own life. In the meantime it routinely rewards senior civil servants with knighthoods and other lofty honours purely for the negative achievement of hanging on within protocol and never rocking the boat. This, at any rate, is the conclusion to which my own observations have led me, though in 1940 my main concern was with the fact that there were people like Cunningham who were apparently daft enough to sacrifice their social lives on the altar of night flying.

No one could have been more delighted than I was when night operations were phased out for single-seaters. Of itself, night flying held a certain fascination, but as a *modus vivendi* the timing seemed thoroughly unfortunate, for what could be more vexing than to go on duty during the evening, just as the pubs are opening, and seeing the crews you are relieving drive away for a night's jollification? The off-duty hours on the ground were for me almost as demanding and interesting as the operational ones in the air, and with the change to a day fighting role our hours of business became generally more civilised. The level of advantage to our social lives, however, hinged a good deal on the seasons, since our official duty began thirty minutes before dawn and lasted till thirty minutes after sunset. We therefore got the best of the bargain at midwinter. At midsummer, with double summer time in force, our day could begin at around 3.30 a.m. and not finish till after eleven at night.

Opportunities for social activity were limited at the best of times, and we felt a terrific pressure to live any we could grab to the full. The licensing laws were strictly enforced, which meant that every hostelry was shut after closing time. London's night-clubs were always an after-hours option, but the travelling time to get to them left us little margin for drinking once we were there. As the phoney war dragged on, we slipped into a new routine and almost forgot there was a real war on as well. We grew blasé about the blackout and accustomed to the shortages. We took in our stride the stock response of shopkeepers to requests for some routine commodity which was suddenly unobtainable, 'Don't you know there's a war on?'; and the equally routine admonishment of traffic policemen hauling us up for speeding, 'Must remember we're not flying our Spitfire now, sir, mustn't we,' before benevolently waving us back on our way. (It was never 'our Hurricane', I noticed.)

Slowly we reverted almost to a peacetime routine. Time of year and hour of sunset permitting, we usually ended our day with a beer or so in the mess before setting out on a pub crawl, pooling our petrol coupons or occasionally filching the odd gallon of 100-octane aviation fuel from the bowsers at dispersal. On rare occasions, if sunset came early enough, we might take a train to London, start off our evening at Shepherd's, where as like as not we would meet an old mate or two, then move on to a night-club. But if it was still early in the month, a trip to London might necessitate first calling in at the mess office to cash a cheque for ten bob or even a pound. It was a harmless and relaxing way of emptying our pockets, and why not? There was no tomorrow. So far as we could see we might well die of boredom waiting for action that never came.

The knotty problems of inaction and limits on our social life found no solution until the Battle of Britain, when the risk of airfields becoming prime targets for enemy bombers grew very real indeed with the Luftwaffe's determination to flatten the RAF once and for all. We were not to know it at the time, but one of the reasons why Germany lost that battle in the air was its curious failure to follow up the few highly damaging attacks it made on our bases. It is clear that for a squadron to have all its pilots wiped out by a single high-explosive bomb as they slept unproductively in their mess would have been the opposite of cost-effectiveness in today's jargon. To lessen the chances of such a disaster air crew were quickly dispersed and billeted in houses several miles from the airfield – usually empty ones the owners had vacated for the duration. With no one else to annoy, we were soon improvising our own in-house night-clubs and the quality of off-duty life improved dramatically as a direct result of the Nazi war machine having finally awoken, yawned, growled and rolled into action.

In Europe one of the main linchpins of the French defensive system was the Maginot Line, a massively armed and armoured string of fortifications linked by rail through an underground net work of tunnels. The line ran north and south along the Franco German border and was said to be impregnable to frontal assault. As the pride of the French High Command and the keystone of France's defensive system, it may have been impregnable to direct attack, but it had one fatal flaw: it was not endless. On its north-ern flank it stopped short of the border between Luxembourg and Belgium, in the spectacularly beautiful Ardennes countryside, where, it was thought, the rugged hills and dense forests would be sufficient to deter any advancing army. They were not, and neither were the neutral borders of Holland and Belgium. To the anguished disbelief and dismay of the French military leaders, the highly mobile Panzer (tank) divisions crossed the Ardennes on the northern flank of the Maginot Line and swept through Holland and Belgium, driving a forty-mile wedge between France's two main armies in the north and south. Their mobility and speed confounded the Allies. The British Expeditionary Force (BEF) in the north, along with a corps of the French First Army, found itself trapped between the English Channel and a tidal wave of German steel.

In retrospect, the Maginot Line was always doomed to be an expensive fiasco. The concept behind it had long since ceased to be valid. As the French should have realised, the theoretical rules of war drawn up by victorious nations in times of peace are likely to be flouted when war becomes a fact, especially any that are based on 'schoolboy' honour, such as the inviolability of neutral borders. More importantly, they should have realised that the tactics and strategies of war are dependent on the weaponry available and need to be constantly updated. Up to the First World War it was the vulnerable cavalry units that provided armies with their mobility. These were gradually phased out in the face of heavy artillery and the early developments in war planes and tanks, leaving the armies with no option but to dig in and slug it out. A Maginot Line built at that time might well have had a decisive influence, but twenty years later the advances in aircraft, tanks, armoured vehicles and communications had revolutionised the conduct of war.

For their part the Germans had realised the significance of these changes and exploited them brilliantly with their blitz-krieg ('lighting war') technique, which used dive-bombers and airborne troops as the inheritors of the mantle of the old cavalry unity. These proceeded to harry the enemy from behind, cutting lines of communication and supply, immobilising airfields and clearing the way for the Panzer divisions, which were followed in turn by the infantry and administrative forces of occupation. Once they were on the move, the Germans became unstoppable both in the air and on the ground, and the Allies had no answer to give back to them.

In the air the RAF meanwhile began to pay the price of Whitehall's peacetime obsession with defence budget cuts. It was the same price the fighting services have so often had to pay in the past, through being such obvious targets in any peacetime economy drives. It takes a war to reveal any dangerous weaknesses which may have been exposed, but the price of the pennies saved by ambitious civil service mandarins is always the blood of the men who trusted them. In the case of the RAF, the budget cuts of the 1920s and 1930s became manifest mainly in the form of second-rate equipment and a ragbag of machine types.

As the German advance got under way, a bomber squadron equipped with Fairey Battles was dispatched to destroy the bridge at Maastricht in an attempt to delay the enemy impetus through Holland. The Fairey Battle was arguably the most useless aircraft ever to achieve lift-off from the drawing-board. Not one of those battle planes returned. Every single one of them was blown out of the sky and every member of their aircrews was killed, something that none of those dead men would have been in the least surprised to know. Each must have realised as their squadron lumbered ponderously into the sky that any chance of returning from this mission was going to be remote in the extreme. It represented something more than a tragic, unnecessary sacrifice of young life. Members of aircrew who manned the front-line squadrons at the outset of the war were the most highly trained and experienced in the RAF. Nevertheless their lives were thrown away, bartered for a few knighthoods as a reward for saving money.

The Fairey Battle may have been an unmitigated disaster among aircraft, but it was not uniquely so. It was just one amid a medley of outdated sub-standard machines – Hampdens, Blenheims, Defiants, Swordfish and many others. With these a whole phalanx of doomed young men was expected to fight a war, and to go to their wasted if heroic deaths, victims of misplaced economy drives. If it had not been for the persuasiveness of Hawkers and Supermarine, who developed the Hurricane and Spitfire respectively, coupled with a campaign of exceptional pressure from worried RAF chiefs, then we would not even have had the few squadrons of modern fighters that we did possess in 1939. Even so, some of our front-line squadrons continued to fly and die in outmoded biplane fighters long after war was declared. Had the Germans moved a few months earlier than they did, then the overwhelming invasion of the British Isles by Germany would today be a long-ago fact of twentieth-century history.

The handful of fighter squadrons with the BEF in France in 1940 were at least equipped with Hurricanes, even if the planes they had were still the earliest marks. Unbelievably, some of them still had the fixed-pitch two-bladed airscrews of the prototypes. Heavily outclassed by the Messerschmitt 109s, they did their gallant best and took heavy casualties, and were soon brushed aside by the German war machine, which swept the Allies towards the English Channel in relentless retreat. Churchill had ached to send out our few squadrons of Spitfires from the slender home air defences, and he would have done so if Dowding's warnings had not dissuaded him. They could never have provided more than short-term help; the problem was too fundamental. The BEF and the French were outnumbered, out-trained, out-equipped and outclassed, and the conclusion was inevitable.

At Hornchurch the taste of war at last began to tingle our palates as we anxiously followed the desperate retreat of the Allied troops as they were slowly driven into a coastal trap around Dunkirk. Soon the Channel would block their escape route and some form of rescue operation would have to be mounted. To the surprise of many, it emerged that plans for just such an operation were already prepared. The sheer speed of the Allied retreat had caught everyone on the wrong foot, but contingencies had indeed been set in train by Admiral Ramsay, the far-sighted Flag Officer Dover. Since 20 May, with the writing clearly on the wall, he and Captain Tennant, the Senior Officer Ashore, had begun to gather together a motley fleet of ferries, coasters, barges and Dutch lighters. The original plan was to rescue the men from the town and harbour of Dunkirk itself, the third largest port of France, but heavy bombing and shelling had reduced its installations and loading quays to a shambles. By Tennant's calculation, limited use could still be made of no more than the harbour's east mole, and evacuation from the beaches, previously dismissed out of hand as entirely impracticable, became a serious option.

Less than a week earlier, on 14 May, the Admiralty had sent out an edict requiring all private owners of self-propelled pleasure craft of between 30 and 100ft (10 and 33 metres) to register them. They were to be placed at the disposal of the Admiralty, but would be skippered by Royal Navy personnel as an emergency back-up to the main evacuation plan, which was given the code name 'Dynamo' and put into operation on 26 May. With the veil of secrecy lifted, the navy relaxed its rule about skippering, and in the end many private owners got to skipper their own boats. As the news of 'Operation Dynamo' became public knowledge, it had an instant snowballing effect on other boat owners. Everyone wanted to take part, and the battle of the small ships was on.

My vantage point for the unfolding epic was in the air above the beaches, where I found the activity less exacting than I had expected. As I sat in the relative safety of my Spitfire cockpit, it was the clouds that were my main problem. Our orders had sent us in at 30,000ft, too high for the best of the action, whereas the Hurricanes were patrolling at 15,000ft. Needless to say we cheated and kept slipping down to see what was happening. Even then, though we ran into a few Germans, there did not seem to be the masses I had anticipated. If the Hurricanes had been deployed at 5,000ft, and the Spitfires at 10,000, then between us we could perhaps have been rather more effective.

Fortunately for the small boats there was not a breath of air and the sea remained flat calm. But the task of providing air cover was hampered not only by the extent of the cloud cover but also by its nature. It stood in patchy layers from about 1,000ft upwards − ideal for marauding bombers but not for our purposes. The German aircraft could pop out of a cloud, carry out a quick bombing or strafing run and slip back into the cloud cover, allowing little time for interception. Nevertheless I managed to fire my guns in anger for the first time, and had the basic fact brought home which I had tried to forget: namely, that while the aircraft in your sites was an inanimate object, the human beings it contained were frail flesh and blood. In those early days the German bombers carried little or no armour, and one of the first indications that you were registering hits (especially on the Heinkel 111) came with the spectacle of the guns arching suddenly upwards as the unfortunate gunners died and slumped forward on to their weapons.

I have already included the Defiant in my list of dud operational aircraft, and at Dunkirk it moved rapidly in and out of the spotlight of fame and notoriety. It was a single-engined aircraft, similar to the Hurricane in general conformation, but carrying a crew of two: pilot and gunner. It had no forward-firing guns, its claim to fame being a rear gun turret sporting four hydraulically operated synchronised machine guns, unusual for the time and otherwise unknown in a single-engined fighter. A squadron of Defiants sent out on patrol was bounced by a squadron of Me 109s, which mistook them for a squadron of Hurricanes and, as a result, attacked from above and behind. This would have been a correct tactic if they truly had been Hurricanes, but the 109s had to go through a learning curve the hard way to discover they were not. Instead it was they who presented the perfect target and the Defiants' rear gunners shot them out of the sky.

In the first flush of euphoria at this success, the Defiants were rearmed, refuelled and sent back into the fray. But inevitably their moment of glory was transitory. This time the 109s were waiting for them, the recent lesson thoroughly absorbed. They attacked from below and behind where the Defiant was defenceless; the score was evened, the squadron virtually wiped out. Thankfully this was the last appearance in hostile skies in daylight for that abortion of an aircraft. Briefly it reverted to a night role before being consigned to the scrap heap which should have been its original destination.

The CO of the Defiant squadron had been my flying instructor at Cranwell. He was a gifted and sympathetic instructor, but after I heard he was dead the thing that stood out most clearly in my memory of him was his passion for rhododendrons. Whenever we had to find our way along some practice cross-country route, he would ensure that it took us over the area of scrub and conifer country to the south and west of Camberley where rhododendrons thrive. As we leisurely circled the area, he would practically fall out of his cockpit as he exclaimed at the flowering shrubs, which, viewed from above at the right time of year, transformed that rather dreary stretch of countryside into a vast sea of colour.

On the face of it, history should have remembered Dunkirk as nothing more than a tragic memorial to the obliteration of an army. But most packs of cards have their jokers, and the one in this particular pack was the curious genius for improvisation of the British, their sort of 'backs-to-the-wall' rubber-ball ability to bounce back in the face of disaster − even, in a way, to revel in it. Within hours of the realisation that nothing but a magic wand could save our troops, the magic wand had appeared in the shape of 'Operation Dynamo'. Out of nowhere came history's most improbable armada: a unique collection of boats of every size, shape and degree of seaworthiness; yachts, pleasure boats, fishing smacks, sailing barges, motor cruisers, dinghies — some beautiful, some tottering on their last sea legs, some owned by professionals many by amateurs. Everybody with a craft which floated and was within reasonable range of Dunkirk was determined to be in on the act, like Henry V's soldiers on Crispin's Day.

Many of the vessels in this extraordinary flotilla would no doubt have reduced a safety inspector to tears, but they set course for Dunkirk and, under the noses of the German military machine and the Luftwaffe, working against odds no bookmaker would have contemplated, set about plucking the members of the BEF from the surf and sands. Thus they helped transform a shattering defeat into one of the most gloriously successful if improbable military evacuations in history. Enjoying my grandstand view, I was staggered by the orderly, controlled way in which it all took place. The beaches were a shambles, littered with the smoking wreckage of engines and equipment, destroyed either by enemy fire or else by our own troops to stop them falling into German hands. The sands erupted into huge geysers from exploding bombs and shells, while a backdrop to the scene of carnage and destruction was provided by the pails of oily black smoke rising from the burning harbour and houses of Dunkirk and hanging high in the still air. And yet there the orderly lines of our troops stood, chaos and Armageddon at their backs, patiently waiting their turn to wade into the sea towards the boats, or holding their weapons above their heads as their turn finally came and they waded in up to their waists.

The glamour and bravado of the little boats has created a leg end that might lead some people to believe that the Royal Navy played only a small part in the operation. This would be very wrong. Undoubtedly the contribution of the small boats was astonishing, and the fillip it gave to the nation's morale was incalculable, but without the navy the operation could never have begun. Without their continuous presence, organising, controlling, encouraging, shepherding and protecting, as well as picking up over two thirds of the survivors, the operation would have petered out in fiasco. 'Operation Dynamo' should be seen for what it was, an incomparable joint effort, with the navy acting magnificently in extremis, as it always does, backed by an *ad hoc* fleet of indomitable amateurs with an unflinching determination to achieve the impossible.

The figures give some idea of the scale of the achievement. At the planning stage, even before the destruction of Dunkirk harbour, it was estimated that the maximum number of men who could be evacuated was 45,000. In the event, more than 338,000 were picked up, nearly 99,000 of them from the beaches. More might have been saved, except that on the nights of 2 and 3 June, after the final remnants of the BEF were safely aboard, the boats for the first time returned half-empty. Those left behind, mostly French, were too exhausted and dispirited to move and refused to embark, preferring captivity to further war.

During the post-mortem after Dunkirk there was bitter criticism of the RAF's role and speculation on whether it could have done more to protect the ground forces. In my view such speculation was misconceived. The persistent heavy cloud hid much of our activity from sight of the ground. Those on the receiving end of a bombing dive or strafing run are understandably most acutely aware of those aircraft that they do see – the ones which are dropping bombs or trying to shoot them up. They cannot be aware of activity that is going on out of sight, or of the many more enemy aircraft launched to attack them which were intercepted and destroyed or driven off. Fighter Command's 11 Group, the sector responsible for the defence of London and south-east England, had twenty-one squadrons at the time, and most of these were little above half-strength.

I do not remember how many sorties we flew, but it certainly seemed as if we were spending more time in the air than on the ground. Between us we clocked up almost 5,000 operational flying hours, and with an average sortie time of round about an hour and a half, this suggests approximately 3,500 sorties: quite a few to cram into such a short campaign. According to official figures, the RAF lost eighty-seven of its own aircraft and destroyed 258 enemy planes, damaging a further 119. Most of us had our experience of personal losses. As my old friend and colleague, Hugh 'Cocky' Dundas, recorded in his book *Flying Start*, it was 'bewildering and distressing' for pilots to encounter the hostile question from survivors of the Dunkirk beaches, 'Where the hell were you?' 'It is not surprising,' wrote Cocky, 'that we were ourselves inclined to bitterness when it was suggested that the RAF made no effort to support and protect the evacuation.'

It was unavoidable that our land forces caught on the open beaches should have suffered casualties. They presented as soft and vulnerable a target as might be imagined – a Stuka dive-bomber's dream. This was a fact eagerly recognised by Hermann Göring. His Luftwaffe, he had boasted to the Führer, was poised to wipe out the French and British forces to the last man and would require no help from the Wehrmacht in obliterating the Dunkirk pocket. His assumption would have been right had the Luftwaffe remained unopposed in the air. It was not, and in this case it did not fulfil the Reichsmarschall's over-confidence. From the jaws of what could well have become the graveyard of the trapped British and French troops, nearly 350,000 men were evacuated and lived to fight another day.

This statistic, I think, says everything – everything, that is, except for Churchill's final comment, which characteristically put the overall picture into perspective. 'We must be very careful,' he intoned, 'not to assign to this deliverance the attributes of a victory. Wars are not won by evacuations.'

Maybe not, though I have never ceased to think that all the civilians who took part in that magnificent rescue operation could chalk up personal victories of their own.

SIX

92 SQUADRON: EARLY DAYS

The Dunkirk campaign left behind it a mixed aftertaste of triumph and disaster. Once again the waiting game began, but this
time with a difference. The threat of invasion was at last out of the
shadows and a subtle atmosphere of menace was all-pervasive.

The end of the Dunkirk campaign was also the end of my
link with 65 Squadron. Early on in the action, Hornchurch had
been sent reinforcements, as had most of the front-line fighter
stations in southern England, and one of the squadrons joining
us had been No.92. This was a unit originally formed during
the First World War as a Canadian squadron, then disbanded and
mothballed between the wars before finally being reconstituted
as a British squadron during the first few months of the Second
World War. It began its new manifestation at Croydon, then still in
use as an RAF airfield, and was initially equipped with Blenheims,
dubbed even in those early days as 'flying coffins'. Mercifully it
had re-equipped with Spitfires before being sent into any action,
or before I was invited to join it after Dunkirk.

The commander of 92 Squadron during the Dunkirk operation was Roger Bushell, a barrister of distinction who came
into the RAF by way of the Royal Auxiliary Air Force, the
part-time airman's equivalent of the Territorial Army. He was
shot down over the beaches and captured, later achieving fame
as the mastermind for the 'Great Escape' from Stalag Luft 3,
the German prisoner-of-war camp which housed the majority
of captured RAF crew; a role for which the Germans sadly
executed him. I hardly knew Roger Bushell myself, but those
many former PoW aircrew who did invariably talked about the

example he had set, the way he had raised morale, the inspiration he had given. His death was in direct contravention to the internationally accepted rules of the Geneva Convention relating to the treatment of PoWs. It was a brutal, vindictive reaction of a local German military authority, infuriated at being made a fool of by the escape operation planned and prepared right under its nose. To put the matter at its simplest, Roger Bushell was murdered, but Nazi Germany never lacked henchmen to perpetrate its worst crimes.

Bushell's two flight commanders at 92 Squadron had been 'the Paddys', Byrne and Green. Either one of them would have been an outstanding personality in any gathering, though as physical types they were total opposites. Paddy Byrne, who precipitated the one fatality during the 'Barking Creek' fiasco, was short, dark and stocky, the archetypal version of an Irishman as the world pictures it, with lilting brogue and irrepressible humour. Paddy Green, by contrast, was a large fair-haired South African, a distinguished athlete and legendary high-living playboy. Occasionally, as the joke went, on one of his really good days he looked as if he had only been dead a fortnight. Yet behind that dissipated face, so lived in you felt it must be home not only to Paddy himself but also to most of his loose-living friends, there lurked a huge zest and appetite for life. It was predictable that women should be fascinated by his ravaged features and war-weary air, and he was never short of girlfriends.

Paddy Byrne was, like his chief, Roger Bushell, shot down over Dunkirk and packed off to a prisoner-of-war camp. Paddy Green, although he stopped a bullet with his thigh over Dunkirk, succeeded in getting safely back to base. The wound was enough to put him out of the picture for a while, though he was satisfactorily patched up and returned to operational flying in due course. Paddy Byrne was not destined to share Bushell's fate at the hands of the Nazis, but instead used his native wit to work the trick of repatriation on the grounds of insanity, though that did not come about till 1944.

Meanwhile Bob Tuck from 65 Squadron, who was a flight commander by this time, had been further promoted to squadron leader to replace Bushell as CO of 92 Squadron. It was through his invitation that I now went to fill the gap in leading 92's A Flight that had been left by Paddy Byrne. To my mind 92 Squadron always had the special ingredient which sets certain people or groups apart from the rest − a small, indefinable quality in the alchemy that gives an edge, a uniqueness. This quality can never be duplicated or planned for, but somehow it comes into being and is aptly called 'spirit'. It always begins at the top, and 92's exceptional spirit undoubtedly had its origins in the outstanding personalities of the original squadron and flight commanders. It then continued to flourish in the fertile soil of the rich mix of characters who made up this exceptional fighting unit: determined, committed young men, intent on squeezing the last drop of living from whatever life might be left to them at the same time as they refused to take themselves or their existences too seriously.

They came from all walks of life and every corner of the earth. There was, for instance, Johnny Bryson, a huge Canadian almost too big to fit into a Spitfire, who made a tempting target as he bulged out of his cockpit. Sadly he became a target all too soon and died quite early on. Then there were Neville Duke and 'Wimpy' Wade, both outstanding airmen who survived the war with distinguished and much-decorated careers and became household names as test pilots. There was also Allan Wright, an ex-Cranwell cadet, extremely bright and professorial even in those far-off days, but a determined and successful pilot, and then the youngest of all, Geoff Wellum, aged seventeen and known as 'Boy' because of his age. And there were Don Kingaby and 'Titch' Havercroft, two of the RAF's most successful NCO pilots, both of whom finished up as wing commanders, Don having a unique distinction in earning a Distinguished Service Order (the DSO being a decoration reserved for officers on account of the leadership qualities it supposedly acknowledges) and three Distinguished Flying Medals (the DFM being a decoration reserved for NCOs and the equivalent of the Distinguished Flying Cross (DFC), which under the curious British honours system was the preserve of commissioned officers for performing precisely the same deeds).

Above all, there was Bob Tuck, extrovert and flamboyant, tall and very slim. His jet-black hair was oiled and brushed close to his head, and he had a pencil-slim moustache (contrary to King's Regulations, needless to say). He also sported a scar down one cheek, though it was not a duelling scar, as he used to delight in conning strangers. It had been caused far more glamorously, to my mind, by a broken flying wire when he bailed out of a Gloster Gauntlet (the forerunner of the Gladiator) after an aerial collision when practising tied-together formation acrobatics.

Bob's striking good looks and illicit Clark Gable moustache brought him a lot of good-natured ribbing, to which he responded happily with a nonchalant smile. He could afford to be nonchalant. In the air he was a total professional, and none was more highly respected. He was a superb pilot and a first-class shot, and most importantly he had the uncanny hunter's instinct for arriving precisely where the enemy was; then, as lesser mortals turned for home believing the skies vacated, he would find a few stragglers still within firing distance.

In 92 Squadron we even had our archetypal playboy in the person of Tony Bartley. He came a close rival to Bob Tuck in cultivating languidness and nonchalance, and he was so good-looking it was almost in poor taste. He was also a brilliant, successful pilot who deserved more recognition than he received. Soon after the war he married the gorgeous and talented film actress Deborah Kerr, and went with her to Hollywood, where he stayed for several years. Eventually the marriage went the way of so many in tinsel-town, and he returned to England to marry another equally lovely lady and to remain ever after a close friend to me and my family.

In my recollections of those days a special niche is occupied by Bob Holland, our cherished squadron pianist, who could have come straight out of a Hoagy Carmichael film. He would often take over the piano stool from night-club pianists on our nights off, and sit there, a large drink standing by on the piano top, his eyes half-closed and screwed up against the smoke from the inevitable cigarette that dangled from the corner of his mouth, fingers flitting deftly over keys he hardly seemed to touch. He survived the war, but ironically was killed soon afterwards when instructing at the Fighter Leaders' School, when a student misjudged and went into a collision course, killing them both. Music is a great nudger of memory. Whenever old tunes are revived, including 92's favourite number, 'In the Mood', I am back to hearing them endlessly being teased out by Bob Holland's magic fingers in every smoky night-club that we ever visited, including our own after we had set it up. The evocation never grows less and the appeal is there for ever.

There were so very many who passed through 92 Squadron while I was with it during its spectacularly successful early days of 1940–41. For each of those who survived and went onto greater things, there were many who did not. Some lasted weeks, some days, some no more than hours. Some passed through so briefly you hardly noticed them. They would be there one day, gone the next, names and faces forgotten. Generally speaking, the main hurdle for a pilot in combat was always the first two or three engagements. Anyone who survived these increased their long-term chances of survival as they picked up the tricks of the trade. Alter that they confronted an equally dangerous though more insidious problem: over-confidence.

Two important elements were still lacking when I first joined 92 Squadron, namely a motto and a crest. With the squadron having been formed in the heat of the First World War and mothballed soon afterwards, there had never been time for any one to give the matter much thought. It was a void in our identity that needed to be addressed, but it is never as easy as it sounds to pluck out of the blue an inspiring motto and a crest that tells a story. In fact the crest turned out not to be too difficult. Two things needed to be recognised: first, the unit's Canadian origins, and secondly, a new factor that had just come into the reckoning. The cost of manufacturing each Spitfire was put at 5,000, and companies and organisations were encouraged to invest that sort of money by the prospect of having a squadron named after them. One which qualified for this was the East India Co., in recognition of which we were renamed 92 (East India) Squadron. Our solution for a pictorial representation of the two factors was therefore straightforward if not wildly original: a large maple leaf as a background to show the Canadian connection; a coiled cobra in the foreground to illustrate the East India Co. contribution to the war effort.

The motto was a more difficult nut to crack. We scratched our heads for several days without result, until I remembered a famous saying of my predecessor Paddy Byrne that was always a part of his briefing of a new pilot, invariably delivered in a rich rendering of an Irish brogue: 'Now, m'boy,' he would declaim, 'you must foight or be killed or be ruined entoirely.' I had my doubts about whether this exhortation ever did much to extend the operational life of any pilot briefed by Paddy, but it was a catchy phrase and there was general agreement that it could make something interesting and individual. Laboriously we got down to translating the proposed motto into Latin, but unfortunately, while the Royal College of Heralds accepted the crest without demur, the part of Paddy's enjoinment that concerned being 'ruined entoirely' stuck in their gullet, even in the dog Latin devised by our homespun scholars. In the end, with a sigh, the college went along with the first half of the motto, and that is how it remains to this day: a coiled cobra in front of a maple leaf, set above the truncated motto *Aut Pugna Aut Morere*, 'fight or be killed'.

As Dunkirk receded into history, my enjoyable and fruitful association with Hornchurch also came to an end when 92 Squadron was dispatched to Llanelli in South Wales, charged with the air defence of the industrial towns and harbours along the coastal strip that flanks the Bristol Channel. In that especially beautiful part of Wales our airfield lay alongside a great stretch of golden sand, out of bounds to civilians because of anti-invasion mines, and consequently utterly deserted. We were able to make good use of the mine-free parts of this facility in off-duty moments, while in the air activity was negligible. There was only one occasion when I made contact with the enemy.

Early one morning I was out on patrol leading a section of three of my aircraft from A Flight when we ran into a lone Junkers 88 on the approach to Cardiff, looking suspiciously as if it was on a photo-reconnaissance flight. It was a clear morning without cloud cover, and with three Spitfires coming in on its rear end, the unfortunate German aircraft never stood a chance. We watched the pilot as he took his plane down in its terminal dive southwards, pulling up just before he hit the water and scraping the top of the cliffs on the north Devon coast, not far from Minehead, before crashing on to the headland above. He finished up on a fairly level stretch of scrub and grass, so after we had returned to base, I climbed into a Magister, a light two-seater aircraft we used for communication, and re-crossed the Bristol Channel to land in the field next to the devastated hulk.

The Ju 88 crew were all dead, and the local fire brigade and ambulance team were at the scene, clearing up the carnage and wreckage. Very generously they offered me the victor's spoils in the shape of an extremely superior and sophisticated Zeiss camera, complete with zoom lens and various appendages that were fairly out of the ordinary for the time, which had been found beside one of the bodies. There was a half-used film still in the camera, but when I had it developed later it turned out to contain nothing but shots of German military and SS parades.

One of the crew still lay where he had died, an enormous young man in his late teens or early twenties, both blond and beautiful. So much of a type did he seem that I thought at once he must have come straight off Dr Goebbels's drawing-board, a designer-specified golden boy conditioned by the Hitler Youth movement and embodying the German dream of an all-conquering Aryan race. The recent action over Dunkirk had borne in on me uncomfortably the human side of aerial warfare that I preferred to forget, hypocrite that I was: the signs of German air gunners collapsing over their weapons as my bullets hit home. Here, on the north Devon coast, the lesson should have been rubbed in even more vividly, yet whereas over Dunkirk I had felt genuine remorse for lives I was taking and families I was bereaving, here I felt none.

We had by this stage seen many newsreels of such young men in action, and here was this perfectly formed young demigod, apparently personifying all we had gone to war to fight: the essence of the evil at the heart of the Nazi movement and its Fascist clones (as the modern term goes); the cult of the licensed bully and sadist who used their strength not to protect the weak and helpless but to terrorise and humiliate, to derive an ultimate pleasure in raping, tormenting and torturing the feeble and frightened, hunting in packs to give themselves the courage they would otherwise lack and feeding on the unreasoning lust of the lynch mob. They had the audacity to claim it was other racial and genetic groups who were degenerate, yet they themselves represented the most degenerate political aberration in modern history.

Faced with this corpse, perhaps I should have brought myself to feel more Christian, more tolerant, more compassionate. I could not manage any of these qualities. The furthest I could go in charity was to recall the proverbial claim of a well-known religious teaching order, 'Give us the boy and we'll give you the man,' and think that it might be the teacher who was more to blame than the pupil. We already had our first-hand ugly evidence of the consequences of the Nazi creed from Dunkirk, when the remnants of four regiments of the BEF that had stayed behind to help cover the rear of the retreating Allies, finally surrendered under the protection of the white flag, one of the few symbols of the rules of war to be held sacrosanct. They were rounded up by the SS and nearly two hundred of them massacred before the intervention of a senior Wehrmacht officer prevented even more suffering the same fate. The Wehrmacht, the non-political regular army, was still relatively untainted by the Nazi ideology.

Gazing at the young man lying in front of me I could not accept that he had been some kind of non-political combatant. He seemed too close to the ideal Aryan mould cherished by Hitler to be a coincidence or accident, and any charitable or pitying thoughts I might normally have harboured simply remained frozen deep within me. I found myself looking at him with loathing and hoping that my bullets had not killed him instantly; that he had been fully conscious during the whole of that long, last dive, and that all the way down he had screamed out with the same terror his kind enjoyed provoking in others as he saw death and the north Devon coastline rush up to obliterate him. It was, if you like, a lesson in the way war corrupts the deepest feelings of all participants, which meant that my hatred, too, was an incidental product of Nazism and therefore another cause for resentment.

I was about to turn away when I noticed that the Mae West the German airman still wore appeared to have escaped damage. The German life-jacket was in many ways superior to our British issue, being, among other things, inflated by a small compressed-air bottle rather than by lung power. It was also less bulky and far more comfortable. It seemed unlikely that the late demigod would find much use for it in Valhalla, so I relieved him of it and wore it continually until I was posted abroad two years later.

On reflection, I was probably lucky never to have been shot down over water during that time. With no routine inspection of the air bottle or the airtight jacket — which, unlike ours, had no built-in buoyancy — I suspect the garment might well have gradually lost its effectiveness and dragged me bubbling to the bottom. I was untroubled by such thoughts as these as I was taken, complete with my spoils, to be fêted over a very good lunch by a group of generous Devonian dignitaries. A few months later, being more broke than usual, I sold the camera for £30, or nearly a month and a half's pay. All in all, in the jargon of today's accountancy-crazed world, it had been a highly cost-effective morning's work.

★ ★ ★

By this time it was around midsummer 1940, and while aerial activity was on the increase in south-east England, in South Wales the skies remained empty and there was little to do except enjoy the marvellous swimming and bask on the sands. With all due respect to the Welsh (being a quarter Welsh allows me some leeway to criticise, I feel), the pubs in the Llanelli area in 1940 were appalling: utterly basic spit and sawdust hostelries with, around the walls, lines of chairs occupied by local ancients who ached to burst into song and seized on the slightest pretext to do so.

Time therefore hung heavily and we seemed in danger of slipping back into the hazy unreality of the phoney war. The impasse was finally broken by orders from 10 Group, the division of Fighter Command responsible for the air defence of the South West. One of 92 Squadrons flights was to be dispatched to Bibury, a small viallage in the Cotswolds. From there it would operate a temporary airfield outside the village and take responsibility for the night defence of South Wales and the south-west of England. The only other flight would remain at Llanelli and be responsible for day defence only.

I drew the short straw and took off with A Flight for Bibury with mixed feelings. The village was not far from Burford and Witney, an area I knew quite well. At Witney there was an airfield owned by de Havilland, for whom my old friend Philip Gordon-Marshall now worked. It had been set up under government contract to repair crashed Spitfires and return them to service with the utmost urgency. Philip had been in charge of this operation from the beginning, and since he was the only qualified pilot in the outfit it fell to him not only to run the airfield but also to air-test the repaired aircraft. The satisfaction this job gave him compensated to some extent for his shattering disappointment at having been rejected by the RAF on medical grounds.

Philip had by this time been at Witney for several months, and I had flown over on several occasions, either to have lunch or to stay the night. While I always arrived in a Spitfire, Philip kept a few de Havilland Moths standing about, and somehow he cajoled the company into putting one of them at my permanent disposal. The aeroplane was a Puss Moth, tiny, but with an enclosed cabin seating three, and capable of landing on the proverbial sixpence. We used it for pub crawling. From the air we would spot what looked a likely pub with a field adjacent, make a few passes to move any sheep or cattle and clear a landing space, then set down as close to the pub as possible. Once on the ground, we would tether the Puss Moth to the handiest fence.

Almost invariably we would hardly have finished tying the knot before and air-raid warden or Home Guard member appeared from nowhere and offered to stand guard over our machine for us. Accepting these offers always made me feel faintly uneasy and embarrassed. It hardly seemed a correct use of His Majesty's forces, even if they were from a volunteer sector. Had the plane been a Spitfire, and had I been on a mission to sink something more war-worthy than a few pints, the case would have been different. It seemed most unlikely that any self-respecting spy or fifth columnist was going to risk his neck hijacking a toy aeroplane that was already in widespread use throughout the Continent, including Germany. However, these impromptu guardians seemed to derive genuine satisfaction from the job and it would have seemed churlish to tell them not to worry. No doubt it relieved the boredom of staring at nothing but sheep.

Bibury itself was a small and charming village, noted for its excellent pub, the Swan. Nevertheless, A Flight tended to make Burford its unofficial headquarters, mainly because of my contacts there through Philip. In those days, long before motorways triggered the 'Yuppie' explosion of traffic and the age of wall-to-wall Range Rovers, the whole area was totally unspoiled. The road that skirted Burford from Witney was lazy and winding, and Burford still lurked down a small side-road, hidden from passing traffic by the crest of a hill. Two ancient pubs dominated the village, the Bull and the Lamb, each of them superb in its different way. The Bull was black-and-white timber framing, heavy with oak beams, sagging ceilings and bulging walls. The equally ancient Lamb was cast in a different mould: built in the classic Cotswold style from the lovely honey-coloured local stone, with deeply worn flag floors and mullioned windows. One other institution of note was a small but rather grand restaurant called the Bay Tree, almost next-door to the Lamb. I sampled it once or twice and found it outstanding, but food as such never came high on our list of priorities. Whatever precious spare time came our way we preferred to squander imbibing in pubs.

Our landing field in Bibury did little to inspire confidence. It was a small meadow commandeered from a local farmer, and it really did look like a pocket handkerchief as you made an approach from the air. There were three or four bell tents erected as a mess, sleeping quarters and pilots' dispersal, where we hung about from dusk till dawn, dozing or reading while waiting to be scrambled. Our off-duty daylight hours were perfectly pleasant. As soon as we were released at dawn, we would snatch a few hours' sleep before driving into Burford for a few drinks and a sandwich. Then we lazed away the afternoons, dozing by dispersal in deck chairs, reading again, or perhaps going to watch the brown trout from the bridge that crossed the stream which ran through Bibury, hypnotised by the fluid and elegant movements of the fish and their lazy but total control over their element.

Day flying was restricted to air-testing aircraft after repairs or servicing, but the field was so small it demanded intense concentration even when landing in daylight. After dark it became a nightmare, and the few weeks we spent there were among the most alarming I spent in all the war. Operating from that dreadful little postage stamp at least kept us on our toes. The Spitfire, as I commented earlier, was at its worst on the ground — unbalanced and unstable, the nose very long and the undercarriage narrow and set far back. A bit of clumsy braking or a slight unevenness of the ground could be enough to tip it on to its propeller, while the 'nose-up' position, the aircraft's attitude when both taxiing and landing, made direct forward vision non-existent even in daylight. The pilot therefore had to cope with a restricted view of around forty-five degrees to either side of the line he wished to take.

Taxiing was not such a problem. You simply wove from side to side, and if in doubt stopped. Landing-was more complicated since it was inevitably done at speed and stopping was impossible. I adopted the tactic of coming in on a long gentle curve to gain an oblique view down the landing-strip until the last moment. Even when using this technique, from the instant you were holding off before touch-down you were committed, and if there was something in the way, you could only know about it as you hit it. Then, as you were rolling along the ground and rushing blindly forward, you braked as firmly as you dared and hoped you would slow and stop before running headlong into the boundary hedge, which remained invisible.

These daytime problems remained relatively routine, however, in comparison with the night-flying situation, when they were compounded by the flames from the two exhaust outlets, set one on either side of the engine cowling in direct line with the pilot's already limited vision. The flames, invisible in daylight, became blinding glares in the dark. To combat their dazzle, detachable metal bolts were bolted on to the cowling at night. These were effective in shielding the pilot's eyes from the glare, but they restricted his forward view even further.

On a normal airfield with normal lighting, we would all have taken such hazards in our stride. We were conditioned to flying Spitfires by night and accustomed to their little idiosyncrasies, but at this point 10 Group became particularly nervous about the prospect of night raids and obsessed with security. As a result, all airfield lighting was reduced to well below the already timorous levels that had been set at the beginning of war.

For night flying, airfield lighting consisted of a chance light − a mobile floodlight positioned at the downwind end of the landing run — and a row of glim lamps, or marker lights, placed at intervals along one edge of the strip. Unless there was enemy air activity in the vicinity, the chance light was normally switched on the moment a homing aircraft was heard approaching the air field, and switched off as soon as its landing run was finished. Because of 10 Group's security anxiety, the chance light at Bibury could not be switched on until a pilot was virtually touching down, while the glim lights were halved in number and, I suspected, halved in strength. They were also hooded, so that they could only be seen obliquely from the air, and not at all from directly overhead. These regulations, in combination with the Spitfire's known limitations at night and our tiny and dangerously unsuitable field, made every take-off and landing a hair-raising stunt in itself.

While we were still at Bibury the amount of enemy activity in the night skies over South Wales remained fairly sparse: mostly single bombers making spot attacks on ports and harbour installations. They kept us very busy, but in a way that left us feeling we were very busy risking lives and aircraft and wasting fuel without the ghost of chance of ever making contact with the enemy. When it came to the bottom line, we lacked the equipment to operate effectively, and so did ground control. For the most part we were in a moonless period, with nights very dark and slightly hazy and no visible horizon. It was like flying in a barrel of Guinness. We were completely reliant on our instruments and could only blindly follow instructions from the ground.

The experience brought back to me the first time I had flown at night in a blackout, on an exercise flight before the war. I had taken off from Hornchurch in one of our newly acquired Spitfires and was at about 10,000ft over Southend-on-Sea on a beautiful starlit but moonless night. Before me lay London, its suburbs and satellites, spread out in a glittering display of lights — a lovely, comforting sight. Suddenly Southend vanished from beneath me, and one by one all the other huge areas of light disappeared in quick succession until I found myself alone in a lightless world. In reality, it was a fairly unremarkable effect, but it had a most curious impact. For several seconds I felt divorced from all living things, entirely isolated, trapped in a small black suffocating hole in the air without a hope of escape. The sensation lasted only a few moments, yet ever afterwards, whenever downcast and low in spirits, I found the same feeling returning and experienced the same sensation of entrapment in a black, all-enveloping void, which it took a positive effort to will away.

Hunting down enemy bombers in the dark over South Wales seemed a far distance and a lifetime away from peacetime Southend, but there were certain eerie qualities that somehow linked the experiences. We would be vectored by ground patrol towards their plot of a raider, and as we groped our way towards the enemy intruder in stifling blackness we began to pick up the voices of a bomber crew chattering away in German. The sounds would at first be so faint as to be almost inaudible, and then they slowly grew louder and louder until they reached crescendo and collision seemed inevitable. You strained your eyes and twisted your neck in frantic efforts to penetrate the horizonless dark, yet however hard you tried you never saw the enemy. And then, as you braced yourself for collision, the sweat emerging from every pore in your body, the voices started slowly to fade and the crisis passed you by. Feeling as limp as a wrung-out rag, you had no idea whether you ought to be relieved to be still alive or disappointed that you had not been able to see the enemy and shoot him to blazes.

Anyway, you had survived your hour or so on patrol. All you needed to do now was find the airfield again. Ground control could vector you to the area, but after that you were on your own since they could never give you an exact position. Somewhere below you was the airfield controller, unable to switch on the chance light until he was sure you were well into your final approach, and the four or six glim lamps, hooded to make them invisible from directly above. It constantly staggered me that we managed to avoid writing off most of A Flight during this period of operation. Several pilots did opt to land at better-lit airfields they had stumbled on by accident, and one pilot bailed out, having failed to find anywhere at all to land before his fuel ran out. That, amazingly, was the full catalogue of our mishaps.

From almost our first day at Bibury I had been on the telephone to 10 Group, attempting to convince them that what they were expecting us to do was dangerously counter-productive, that our chances of shooting down a German were virtually zero, that the risk to our pilots and aircraft was considerable. All to no avail. I continued to telephone those deaf ears, making the point that we had survived so far thanks to an extraordinary run of luck which could not possibly last for ever. At last I reached a point where I had finally persuaded them. Then the worst happened.

Allan Wright, out on patrol over Cardiff, was vectored on to a German bomber and went through the usual experience of hearing the crews' natter grow louder and louder. But this time, as he searched desperately around for the source of the voices, he saw, not many feet in front and slightly above him, a pair of glowing exhausts. Two engines could only mean an enemy bomber. He pulled up his nose, opened fire at the black space between the exhausts, and sent what turned out to be a Heinkel 111 down in flames.

The consequence, of course, was that all my groundwork in trying to persuade 10 Group that their ideas were idiocy had gone down in flames as well, aborted by one impossibly lucky stroke. They would now smugly consider they had been right all along and that Kingcome was nothing more than a hysterical fool. Poor Allan returned expecting, if not a standing ovation, at least a pat on the back and a word of congratulation. Instead he found himself facing a blast of quite the opposite. How, we all demanded to know, could he have been such a twit, to do something so daft just as 10 Group was beginning to see reason? It was certain he had set our cause back indefinitely, and now here we were, stuck on this god-forsaken strip of rough field for ever. A thoroughly chastened Allan Wright crept off to bed, having in fact performed a first-class piece of airmanship that fully deserved a hero's ovation. Reader, have no fear, we made it up to him later.

It turned out that we need not have worried. A day or two after this incident news came through that the squadron was being posted from Llanelli to Biggin Hill, not far south of London in the county of Kent. Life was on the up-swing, though Bob Tuck left us just before we were posted, to take command of a Hurricane squadron in East Anglia. He, too, came to Biggin Hill a year later, as Wing Commander Flying, and built himself a deservedly great name before he was shot down on a low-flying sortie over France. He wound up in Stalag III, but escaped through the advancing Russians and made it safely back to England just before the armistice. His hunting instincts never deserted him. After the war he became friends with Germany's most famous airman and senior commander, Adolf Galland. They met up frequently to go off on hunting expeditions, tracking everything from wild boar in the Black Forest to brown bears in Alaska.

SEVEN

COMING DOWN TO EARTH

We arrived at Biggin Hill at the end of August 1940 to find the skies over south-east England becoming busier all the time, as they had been ever since Dunkirk, except for a brief lull after the evacuation of the BEF. This had no doubt been to allow the Luftwaffe a short breathing-space in which to regroup and prepare for their next phase of cutting through Europe with contemptuous ease. If there was one thing Hitler had learned, it was that command of the skies was essential to gain command on the ground. He now charged the Luftwaffe with the destruction of the RAF as a preliminary to landing an invasion fleet. Few in the world thought this would take him long; only the British were unprepared to concede the point.

I am sorry to say that the RAF was still in a time warp in which the COs of front-line squadrons were selected on a basis of age and length of service rather than operational experience and ability. It was another policy for which we continued to pay the price until 1941, when sanity prevailed and it was changed. But, leaving that contention aside, our new CO, Squadron Leader 'Judy' Sanders, was an excellent pilot and the nicest of men. His stay with us was brief, however, and the incident that terminated it would have been hilarious if it had not cost him his job and put him in hospital for several days. One morning, not long after we arrived at Biggin Hill, we were scattered in and around the dispersal hut, killing time as we waited for the 'scramble'. Along came Judy to have a chat and check the form. Just outside the hut someone had parked a petrol bowser, and Judy saw at once what a good opportunity it presented to clean some oil stains off the sleeve of his uniform. He found an old rag, soaked it in petrol from the bowser and rubbed the oil off his tunic. Then he decided to have the one cigarette he allowed himself a day… Whoosh! We put him out quickly, but not fast enough to preserve his uniform or save his arm from some painful though happily superficial burns.

In the wake of this misfortune, as senior flight commander I automatically became acting CO, pending Judy's replacement. I continued as acting CO while we had a succession of three further senior squadron leaders posted to us. The first of them, Lister, came to grief early. He, too, was a first-class pilot, who even had a DFC – a rare mark and honour in those early days of the war. His distinction had been won, however, in India, on the North-west Frontier, where local circumstances bore no resemblance whatever to Kent under attack from a modern Luftwaffe. He was sensible enough to fly as my number two, to give him time to gain a little more experience. Unfortunately he was shot off my wing on our third time up. He was wounded only slightly and survived, but it was enough to put him out of the picture.

McLochlan, our next noviciate CO, came to us from Flying Training Command, where he had been a flying instructor for two or three years, clocking up an immense number of flying hours – probably many more than the rest of us put together. He was also uncannily accurate at darts. When we asked him how this came to be, he replied that all flying instructors were good at darts. The reason was that they kept dart boards in their flight offices and, whenever the weather was too bad for flying instruction – as happened not infrequently in those days of limited aids – would kill time by aiming away with darts at a board. I suspected he would have turned out to be an equally good shot with his guns had he ever had the chance to use them. He never did. Like Lister, he flew as my number two to gain experience, and like his predecessor, he was shot off my wing on the third trip. Fortunately, also like Lister, he was only lightly wounded and survived the war, but we never met again.

It took the third incipient CO, Jamie Rankin, to break the mould. He arrived from a secondment to the Fleet Air Arm, as it then was, where he had been posted to an aircraft carrier. There he had spent the past six months, hazarding life and limb by flying some of the strange aircraft the Fleet Air Arm seemed to consider normal, but surviving unscathed. Like my predecessors, he flew as my number two for the first few sorties, but unlike them he not only stayed in the air but went on to become one of the outstanding wing leaders of the war.

Not long after he joined us I was the one who was shot down and wounded. One day he came bouncing into my hospital ward, hardly able to contain his joy. Apparently 92 Squadron had enjoyed a particularly successful engagement and Jamie had shot down his first enemy fighter. 'One-o-nines for breakfast! One-o nines for breakfast!' he kept shouting as he capered around the ward, literally beside himself with happiness.

★ ★ ★

When you are marginally older than God's dog, as I seem to have been for a depressingly long time, life's perspectives change. It is not something to lose any sleep over, but there is an undoubted heightening of curiosity about what may or may not lie around the corner. The odd thing is that however long or short a time it takes to tread the road between boyhood and creaking senility, I seem to have been alive forever. Perhaps it is the case that memory of the past fades into a hazy nothingness, with no clear-cut starting-point, while visions of the future drift into a misty hopeful blur. Life, robbed of both positive beginning and end, therefore takes on a sort of mini-eternity of its own, giving every age and stage a comforting illusion of immortality.

Eternity, understood as an infinity of time, is a difficult thing for finite minds to grasp. Maybe the normal intelligence takes such matters in its stride, but my tired brain, struggling within strictly limited parameters to grapple with the enormity of the concept, needs allegories to give it at least a vague perspective. One such allegory is the one that concerns a block of granite and a sparrow, the allegorical block being a mile high, a mile wide, and a mile deep. Even attempting to visualise this vast structure is no easy task, but now one must go on to imagine a little sparrow that once a year alights on it and sharpens its beak on a corner. After this indefatigable little bird has worn the entire block down to a heap of dust with its tiny beak, then one second of eternity will have passed.

Yet even if this allegorical vision does help a little to crisp up an understanding of eternal time, it also deepens the mystery of how such an emptiness might be satisfactorily filled. Reunion with pre and post-deceased family and friends will come high on the list of priorities, of course, but even after the most exhaustive exchange of news and gossip from both worlds, I fear the granite block would remain virtually unchanged. Funerals are not the jolliest of occasions, but there is one phrase in particular in the funeral service that is presumably intended to comfort, though it has always sent shivers down my spine. It is the one where the presiding priest implores the Lord to grant the departed 'eternal rest'. Why, for heaven's sake. Whoever wants eternal rest? The very idea of it seems profoundly depressing.

If death is oblivion – which is, after all, synonymous with eternal rest – then life itself is nothing more than a fragmentary flicker of light sandwiched between two endless oceans of drowning darkness; in other words it is meaningless, the funeral service an irrelevance. Surely the time has come for priests and prelates to get their act together. 'Life everlasting' and 'eternal rest' simply fail to match and mingle as concepts; they are mutually incompatible. Life is consciousness and memory, the very opposite of the blank moribundity of sleep. No one wants eternal nothingness. Surely what we long for is eternal action, satisfying, stimulating and fulfilling, with memory retained and ties of family and friends broken only temporarily; but still my finite mind stumbles over the 'eternal' element. No doubt the answer is there waiting to be revealed, and when it is we will fall over ourselves at its sheer simplicity. Meanwhile the shadow of the vast granite block and the ineffectiveness of the punctual little sparrow with its eternally pristine beak do little to clarify my understanding.

My thoughts were mercifully clear of any of these introspective wanderings when I was a young fighter pilot, sitting in my Spitfire cockpit at 20,000ft above the smiling countryside of Kent on a lovely morning in mid-October 1940. This was despite the fact that old man death was constantly sitting on my shoulder, scythe at the ready. Once or twice I had caught him looking at me speculatively as he honed the wicked blade, but familiarity, while it certainly did not breed contempt, fostered an easy-going, relaxed relationship. Early forebodings, based largely on what had happened during the First World War, were gradually fading.

When history, taking up the words of Winston Churchill, retrospectively dubbed this stage of the air war the 'Battle of Britain', it was given a significance of which none of us who were involved were aware at the time. Churchill, of course, had coined the phrase in one of his magically appropriate speeches, this one made after the fall of France – 'The Battle of France is over. The Battle of Britain is about to begin.' At the time he was speaking in general terms to the nation as whole. When he came to utter those famous words that encapsulated all the glamour and mystique of the aerial battle (and no doubt aided the RAF's recruiting drive).

'Never in the field of human conflict was so much owed by so many to so few', delivered in his strangely compelling voice with the emotions straining to break through the measured phrases – a tremor of anxiety ran through Fighter Command lest he was referring to our mess bills, payable by the tenth of each month and always a source of concern about how they would be met, considering the disproportionate scale of our socialising expenditure out of our salaries of fourteen shillings a day.

The so-called 'Battle of Britain' we regarded as part of a continuing routine, certainly not as an isolated historic event. Our current levels of activity were clearly linked to Germany's invasion plans, but once those had failed (never an 'if' in our minds), other plans would doubtless follow. So far as we were concerned, the 'Battle' was merely part of the normal progress of the war, which we assumed would continue unabated until final victory. In 1940, autumn had been held at bay by an exceptional summer, though it was at last beginning to give way to a touch of winter as the Battle of Britain drew to a close.

The Germans were facing up to their failure to defeat our air force and achieve the air supremacy essential for invasion. 'Operation Sea Lion', their code name for a landing on the Kent beaches to spearhead a massive armoured assault intended to add Britain's scalp to Hitler's overloaded collection of trophies, was a dying if not a shattered dream. A story tells how Reichsmarschall Göring demanded to know from Adolf Galland how it was that the Luftwaffe with its Messerschmitts was failing to subdue the RAF in the air battle. What more did he need? 'Herr Rejchsmarschall, a squadron of Spitfires,' Galland famously replied, responding to the sarcasm. As he made clear later, he never felt any loss of loyalty to the Messerschmitt as an aircraft, but he did regard Göring's tactical incompetence as a decisive factor in the denial of the palm of victory to his airmen.

There were still flurries of activity in the skies of southern Britain, and though the scale and frequency of enemy raids were noticeably diminishing, a few bomber formations with fighter escorts periodically continued to try to penetrate to London. When one such raid was attempted we were scrambled from Biggin Hill, with myself leading 92 Squadron. We successfully intercepted the raiders over Maidstone in mid-Kent, broke up their formation and turned them back after a fairly brisk encounter. It was a run-of-the-mill operation, and since it had used up all my ammunition I thought I would head for home. I looked around and found myself alone in the skies, apart from three

Spitfires in the far distance. This was a not uncommon phenomenon for Second World War fighter pilots. One moment they
were in a sky full of swooping aircraft, tracer bullets, smoke and
flying debris, occasionally a parachute, more rarely a human body
in free fall. The next moment the sky would be miraculously
empty

It was around noon, and the October day, as I have said, was
glorious. I could see Biggin Hill in the distance, and began to
think of my uneaten breakfast. This I had missed as a result of
the Germans' sadistic sense of humour, which led them to time
their raids to coincide with meals – especially tea, since they
were clearly aware of the sanctity of this peculiarly English habit.
I put my nose down to head straight for home and lunch, but
then thought I might as well kill two birds with one brick and
decided to throttle back and practice a 'dead stick' forced landing;
that is to say, one with simulated engine failure.

It was breathtakingly stupid behaviour. It was so irresponsible
that it would never even have occurred to me to warn new pilots
against it. The skies of Kent were at all times a hostile environment,
whatever the illusion of emptiness, yet here was I, as operationally
experienced as anyone, casually putting at risk my aircraft and my
life – a vital, valuable piece of equipment and a trained pilot, each
disproportionately crucial, with supplies of both dwindling fast.
I can only put the action down to an over-confidence fostered
by constant exposure to the dawn-to-dusk rotation of 'take off,
climb, engage, land, refuel, rearm, take off, climb, engage…' two,
three or sometimes four times a day, familiarity reducing what had
begun as exciting, adrenaline-pumping action to mere routine. In
other words, I had grown blasé.

And here I was, a lamb for the slaughter, oblivious to danger,
admiring the view, enjoying the sensation of speed as I pushed
the nose down towards distant Biggin Hill, forgetting the fighter
pilot's golden rule to watch his tail however safe he thought he
might be – always to watch his tail. I was sailing in a dream when
my reveries were rudely shattered by an almighty thump to the

back of the right leg. It came as a bit of shock to one who believed himself alone with 20,000 clear feet between himself and other human company. Worse was to follow: a rattling clatter as if some one were violently shaking a giant bucket full of pebbles close to my ear. Still it took me a further moment or two to realise that this sound was the jarring impact of bullets striking in and around my cockpit. Glancing down at my leg, I saw blood welling out of the top of my flying-boot, and knew that what had felt like a thump from a blunt instrument had also been a bullet. I felt no pain. With bullet wounds the pain comes later.

I jerked myself around, but could see no sign of anything except the three Spitfires I had noticed before. They drew along side, peered at me briefly, then peeled away. Whether they had mistaken me for a German, or whether they were white knights who had shot someone else off my tail, was something I was never to know. The point had been rendered academic. I was left with blood flowing out of the top of my flying-boot and my ailerons gone suddenly sluggish.

Here was just the sort of situation I had often mentally rehearsed, behaving with dignity, competence and calm, emulating those phlegmatic First World War movie heroes of *The Dawn Patrol* and *Hell's Angels*, sitting imperturbably in smoke-filled cockpits, nonchalantly saluting their opponents as, engulfed in flames, they began a long spiral to a fiery death. I regret to say I failed dismally to match the image of the Errol Flynn prototype. I was panic-stricken, gripped in a blind, paralysing terror. This could not be happening to me. This only happened to the other chap! For what felt like a century, though it could only have been a few moments, I sat rigid and disbelieving, my stomach churning. Here was the real thing. This was what it felt like. All at once I had become the other chap for whom I had always felt sorry, though I had never lost any sleep about it.

The effect was devastating: one minute relaxed and carefree, in total control with nothing more dramatic in mind than a simulated forced landing and the day's lunch menu; the next, inhabiting a doomed aircraft at 20,000ft, losing blood at a rate that suggested consciousness might slip away at any moment with death following within minutes. Death: so far I had managed to keep him discreetly imprisoned in the back of my mind, vague and ill-defined, a subject fit for black humour, not to be taken too seriously. Now he became a terrifying reality so close I could smell him. Or was this simply the smell of my own fear, unlocking feelings I thought I had defused and put safely aside?

Then, through no conscious effort, the wave of blind panic seemed to wash right over me and pass on. Sanity returned: I became curiously calm and rational, almost detached. Fear remained, but now it was of the right sort, urging survival, keeping the adrenaline flowing fast and giving speed and decisiveness to thought and movement. The upper brain took over from the emotions and began to assess my chances of living. I had two options. Either I could stay with the aircraft, accepting the risk of a last-minute parting of control cables when I was too low and too late to jump; or else I could cut the psychological umbilical cord that tied me to the cockpit (which suddenly seemed more of a home from home than ever) and step into space.

For the second option, the hope was that I would have time to open my parachute before passing out – and, having done that, would manage not to bleed to death on the way down. Running out of blood was a hazard common to both options, of course, so speed of descent became the ruling factor. The thought of launching myself into a hostile, freezing, airless void sent the butterflies in my stomach into paroxysms of fluttering, but there was no dodging the fact that by this point jumping offered the best odds, provided I delayed opening the chute until the last moment.

Did pilots receive any parachute training? It was a question I was often asked at the time. The answer was no, the official reason being that it was unnecessary. This may have been a hangover from the First World War, when parachutes were withheld from aircrew in case they bailed out at the first sign of the enemy. Only the unfortunate artillery spotters in their tethered balloons were allowed them. At least we were allowed parachutes in the Second World War, but my own instincts felt that the officials were right on the question of training. Fear is a great activator, and if your behind is on fire, then merely sitting on it will bring you nothing but blisters in awkward places. In my case the motivation was not so strong as this — quite the reverse. My Spitfire, far from being on fire, was still relatively stable and offered me a sense of security, however false. If it had not been for the obvious continuing loss of blood I do not think anything could have tempted me out of that cockpit.

There were various theories about the safest method of leaving a Spitfire in mid-flight, though the obvious way, over the side, was not highly recommended because of the risk of being blown back on to the tailplane and cut in half. It had happened. A better technique was said to be to roll on to your back, jettison the canopy, unfasten your straps and let gravity do the rest. Maybe this had worked for others; I doubted it would for me. I was travelling far too fast and my suspect ailerons made rolling a dubious exercise. I therefore decided to compromise, get rid of the canopy, undo the straps and give the stick an almighty shove forward. With luck I would then be catapulted out by centrifugal force. The trick might well have worked, but I never got as far as testing it. No sooner had I undone the straps than I was plucked violently out of the cockpit as if by a giant hand, hurled into a furious maelstrom of wind and storm and raging elements that whirled me head over heels, arms and legs windmilling uncontrollably, helpless as a rag doll in a clamouring hurricane.

The brutal blast of air assaulted me with all the sold physical force of a jackhammer, blacking my eyes and bruising my face with a ferocity of which I had never dreamed air to be capable. Fortunately the onslaught was short-lived. The terminal velocity of a human body in free fall averages about 119mph, slightly faster at altitude. Since the aircraft must have been doing between 350 and 400mph as I left it, this must have been my speed also as I first hit the air. But air resistance put on the brakes surprisingly quickly and slowed me down to a natural speed. The difference was profound, and as the gale abated, so did my mood. Replacing the howling chaos was a deep, dream-like lethargy that enveloped me. There was no sensation of falling, nor even of movement. Reality retreated and I found myself cocooned in a silent world, all tension departed, comfortable and relaxed, occupying the centre of the universe as sky and earth slowly revolved about me. A combined lack of oxygen and blood was insulating me from all fear and all emotion.

It so happened that on this particular morning my own parachute had been away on routine inspection. Before taking off I had therefore grabbed the nearest spare to hand. This one, too, I was warned, was overdue for a check-up, and I ought to find another, but I could not be bothered. I was not expecting to have to use the thing, after all, since I was invulnerable, wasn't I? And now, as I revolved in space, cradled by my cushion of air and seemingly motionless – no rush of wind, no sense of falling – I dreamily imagined that I had left both chutes behind, that I was not wearing one at all. The thought left me totally unconcerned. It was a matter of complete indifference to me. Glancing down I saw that the suspect parachute was in fact in place, though the knowledge brought me no sense of relief. I would as casually have accepted its absence.

Time lost meaning and nature stood still until, as I dropped from the thin air of altitude into a denser atmosphere, reality gradually returned with an increased oxygen level and my brain resumed functioning. There was no way I could know how much blood I was losing, but I did know I needed to get down fast. The flight, on the way up; had climbed through a broken layer of cumulus cloud at around 4,000ft, so I knew I could safely free fall 15,000ft or so before I hit the clouds, and would then have time to open my parachute as I came out through the cloud base. It seemed I had spent a lifetime in the upper atmosphere, though it could only have been a few minutes before I finally entered the damp nothingness of the cloud bank and, seconds later, broke through into the sunlight and saw the glorious patchwork quilt of the Kent countryside spread out below me.

I reached for the ripcord and pulled. There was only a split second in which to wonder whether I had made a bad choice of parachute before, with a satisfying crack, it snapped open and braked my downward rush with a bone-bending jerk. My brain by this stage was functioning well enough for me to remember to pull the ripcord just the inch or two needed to release the canopy while leaving the cord lodged in its housing. It was rare for parachuting pilots to bring back their ripcords. A natural reaction while hurtling through space was to pull this life-saving device far harder than necessary, and most used ripcords were cast to the winds. There was a powerful incentive to keep hold of them, however. We were charged ten shillings if we lost them, and since this represented almost a day's pay and a night out in London, or alternatively four evenings in the local pubs, I had always vowed I would hang on to mine if it came to the crunch.

With my oxygen level returning to normal, the euphoria evaporated and reality began to make a come-back. I dangled in the harness, swaying gently, studying the ground beneath me. What astonished me was not what I could see − I was used to that − but what I could hear: the sounds that rose up to me from the ground. I was accustomed to a noisy cockpit and earphones that cut out all other sound, but now, as I drifted down the last thousand feet or so, the silence was broken by car horns, by cattle lowing, even by human voices, which came up to me with startling clarity.

As I floated down over open farmland I could see below me a small group of agricultural workers armed with pitchforks and other businesslike farm implements heading across to the field towards which I was drifting. For the first time since parting company with my aircraft I began to feel a definite alarm. There had been stories of parachuting Allied airmen being beaten up and, on one occasion, even killed by incensed locals, working on the patriotic assumption that if they had been shot down then they must be the enemy. To complicate matters, I was wearing the German Mae West I had commandeered from the body of the crew member of the Ju 88. Apprehensively I gazed down at the group who gazed up at me, gripping the formidable tools of their trade.

The ground, from which a short time before I had seemed to be irrevocably separated, now rushed up to meet me. My wounded leg meant that I landed heavily, permanently damaging a disc in my back before sprawling over and over, the breath knocked out of me. As quickly as I could I sat up and pulled off the German life-jacket to reveal my British uniform. Nervously I surveyed the ring of faces surrounding me and saw with relief that they were smiling and friendly. Luckily my Spitfire had already crashed quite near by so my identity was never in doubt. Eyeing those pitch-forks I felt very relieved that there was no ambiguity. 'We'd better get you to hospital before you bleed to death,' said one of the beaming faces, peering at my blood-soaked trouser leg. 'Where'd you like to go?'

I was stumped. How on earth should I know? My only other experience of hospitals had been some three years before, after my quite consequential accident in my Clyno car, when I turned it over three times and almost drowned 'Puker' Watson in the ditch.

* * *

Slowly the misty clouds of anaesthesia faded and parted and I looked groggily about me. I was not impressed. It seemed I was in a barren, cheerless, ugly cell of a room. Dimly I recalled the cluster of friendly faces beside the array of pitchforks as I lay in a heap in a Kentish field. It was they who suggested sending me to the Royal Naval Hospital at Chatham, and although I at once had vague reservations, it seemed churlish to express them just then. My past experience of the skills of the current crop of service medics was still strong in my mind, but that had involved plastic surgery. This was only a simple bullet wound. Surely a naval hospital would be more likely to have knowledge of coping with bullet wounds than any civilian one. I was making a fallacious assumption.

Standing by the bed, hand on pulse as she studied my return to consciousness, was an anxious-eyed nursing sister. When she realised I was trying to focus on her, her face broke into a relieved smile. 'Welcome back,' she said. 'I wasn't too sure we were going to see you again.'

Even in my doped-up state I sensed her obvious relief and was puzzled. 'What are you talking about,' I asked quaveringly.

'Well,' she said, 'I suppose I shouldn't be telling you this, but...' – and promptly proceeded to.

Evidently the surgeon who got his hands on me had decided the best way of finding the bullet in my leg would be to probe along its track rather than rely on an X-ray. In the course of his exploration he cut through a blood vessel, whereupon the two ends sprang apart and he lost them. His solution to this dilemma was to slice his way down my leg in search of them, and when he failed to find them he stuffed the wound with dressing, enclosed the leg in plaster, crossed his fingers and made for the bar. As the sister told her sorry tale, memory slowly returned. I remembered how my misgivings had begun to flood back as the ambulance delivered me to that gaunt, forbidding building, and intensified when I was met by the duty surgeon, rheumy of eye and trembling of wrist. By that stage it had been too late to do anything. Not now. I was once again in a position to take action on my own behalf.

I sent word to the station adjutant at Biggin Hill, who mounted an instant rescue operation. Next morning I was transferred to Orpington Hospital, not far from Biggin Hill, where an alert young surgeon located the bullet by X-ray, just under the skin at the front of my leg between the two shin bones. He removed it through a tiny half-inch incision. Six weeks later I was back with the squadron, though still hobbling from the massive damage inflicted by the naval sawbones on the back of my leg.

Perhaps he would have found it easier to cope with a cannon-ball or cutlass wound. A modern high-velocity bullet had clearly been too much for him. He had managed to do far more damage to me than any German, but at least I had escaped with my life. I also felt I had gained fresh insight into how it was that Nelson finished up with only one eye and one arm.

EIGHT

THE CHANNEL DASH

It took me six weeks of hospital and convalescent leave to recover from the bullet wound in my leg and the treatment it had received from the naval surgeon. During that period yet another CO was posted to 92 Squadron. He was a Canadian by the name of Johnny Kent, and he was, we had to concede, a most distinguished aviator. He arrived straight from very successfully commanding one of the Polish fighter squadrons, and before that had won an AFC, the equivalent to a DFC, though it was limited to achievement in such non-operational flying duties as test and experimental work. Johnny Kent's more than well-deserved AFC had been awarded for testing the strength of barrage-balloon cables by flying into them in old Fairey Battles which had been modified with armour-plated wings. Even unmodified, these appalling aircraft resembled a cross between a Hurricane and a banana and possessed the flying characteristics of a pork sausage. Merely taking off in one would have been worthy of an AFC, and to fly them deliberately into balloon cables must have taken rock-solid nerve and courage.

Unfortunately, despite having these unusual heroic exploits to his credit, Johnny did not endear himself to the squadron at the beginning. There was one particular incident that wrong-footed him (with the team) almost immediately after he arrived at Biggin Hill. This had its origins in the fact that, while still recuperating at nearby Orpington Hospital, I had got into the habit of hobbling over on crutches from time to time, to break the monotony and stay in touch. On one of these occasions I met up with Bob Tuck, who was taking time off from commanding his Hurricane squadron in East Anglia and paying a visit to Biggin for old times' sake. It soon came to our attention that 92 Squadron was scheduled to patrol along the south coast later in the afternoon, and, as one man, we thought it might be fun to join in. To borrow a couple of aircraft was no problem. Two pilots standing by for take-off were only too pleased to be allocated an impromptu break. I jettisoned my crutches, was somehow hoisted into the cockpit by the ground crew, and away we went into, the air.

By good fortune the patrol was eventless and everyone landed safely, but I had definitely over-estimated my fitness. Every time I exerted any 'G' I had felt most peculiar, and I should, indeed, have known better, especially in the light of a warning experience that had come my way a few nights earlier when I turned up for a mess party, raring to go. The consequence was that I spent the entire evening in agony on an ante-room sofa with my leg, stuck up in the air, swelling out like one of Kent's barrage balloons. Nature had not yet been given enough time to repair the damage done by the scourge of Chatham Naval Hospital. It was while she was still finishing her work that Johnny Kent arrived as CO.

His first action as soon as I returned to take up my old position as flight commander was to summon all the squadron's pilots together for a pep talk. We were, he declared, a notoriously ill-controlled rabble and 92 Squadron had become a byword for indiscipline. The one thing we should therefore be sure about was that he, Johnny Kent, was about to change all that. We were not going to know what hit us. Kingcome in particular, he continued, had behaved disgracefully. It had been reported to him by the new B Flight commander, who was technically in charge in my absence, that I had overridden his authority in commandeering an aircraft. What was more, I had been in breach of King's Regulations by flying while still officially medically unfit. Make no mistake about it, *he* was *certainly* going to keep an eye on *me*, and one more serious breach of discipline would see Kingcome posted.

The diatribe was greeted in stony silence. One might go even further and describe it as a silence heavy with resentment and antagonism. And, truth to tell, Kent's remarks about 92's lack of discipline were both misinformed and unjust. The squadron's discipline in the air was immaculate. It had proved itself to be the most efficient killing machine in the Battle of Britain: as the air attack unit longest in the firing line, its record of success was unmatched. On the ground an outsider might have thought there was a lax air to be detected amid the general discipline, but the laid-back attitude was superficial, a front: the usual small irregularities and assertions of individualism – silk neck-scarves and longish hair. But 92 Squadron had stronger bonds of loyalty and solidarity, a fiercer pride in itself than existed in any other unit I came across before or after. Outsiders, as they sensed this, may well have felt excluded, but the only way for a new CO or flight commander to penetrate the protective wall of pride was to show he had qualities the squadron could respect. Leadership by example was the best method of winning such regard, rather than nit-picking with a copy of King's Regulations laid open at the elbow.

Alter the war, Johnny went into print to claim that he had transformed 92 Squadron into a disciplined force out of an undisciplined rout. In fact the reverse was true. It was not Johnny who changed the squadron but the squadron that changed Johnny. Almost without being aware of it he absorbed 92's unique spirit and, in a few short weeks, matured from being a chippy colonial into a relaxed, respected commanding officer. In our eyes he had certainly needed to do a little maturing, and, to be fair, he caught on quickly. Those initial unjust criticisms may have rankled down the years, but he and I developed a friendship that lasted long after the war, until his sadly premature death.

His metamorphosis from martinet had unfortunately not yet come about in the early spring of 1941, when 92 Squadron was attached to Manston for a couple of months to cover the eastern corner of Kent and its coastal waters. It was my first time back at the station since my brush with the forces of law and order when I misbehaved in the local theatre. Before long we had another incident involving the law, though this time I found myself on the right side of it, if only marginally.

We divined there would be problems at Manston the moment we encountered its ambitious station commander, fresh to his post, very young to be holding the rank of wing commander and hungry for success. With one eye on the promotion ladder, he kept the other open for people and incidents he could crack down on and so highlight his administrative talents. On the day we arrived he paid a visit to our dispersal hut and delivered a diatribe along the same line as Johnny Kent's, except that mercifully I was not singled out for comment. It had come to his knowledge, he said, that 92 was a squadron that seemed to think it was a law unto itself. He therefore wished to warn us from the start that he was not the kind of chap to tolerate breaches in King's Regulations or lowering of the high standards of comportment he was determined to maintain on his station. Any such breaches would be treated with the utmost severity and offenders held up as an example *pour encourager les autres*.

It so happened that there was, among the thorns in the flesh of authority, a tendency among front-line squadrons to siphon off the odd gallon of aviation fuel as an unofficial donation towards their trips to the local to help eke out the stringent petrol ration. In 92 Squadron we made firm efforts to keep this practice to a minimum, for few were more aware than we were of the risks run by the Merchant Navy in bringing the stuff into the country under their Royal Navy escorts. On the other hand, it was our privilege to give the shipping convoys the best air cover we could when they sailed within our limited range and we never felt they would be likely to begrudge us the odd gallon here or there. Nevertheless the habit was still a fundamental breach of rule and so presented a natural target for any glory-seeking new broom hoping to sweep clean. The eager young station commander saw his big chance one fine morning when the fates decided to have a field day.

Johnny Kent was away on a few days' leave. This meant that once again I became acting squadron commander. Johnny was none too happy with the arrangement, but there was nothing he could do about it as I retained seniority over the opportunist sneak who had done his best to unseat me after taking over the other flight. I walked into the CO's office expecting nothing more exacting to cope with than routine paperwork, but found myself confronting an agitated squadron adjutant. 'Bad news,' he announced. 'I'm afraid Snowy's been arrested. Bloody fool parked after dark last night, on the wrong side of the road without lights, right outside the nick, would you believe it?'

Snowy was my aircraft fitter, a first-class technician who was a most likeable young man. He had for a long time been getting me safely into the air and down again, while also servicing and maintaining my car (which, needless to say, was really sister Pat's). In return he was allowed to borrow the car when I was not using it myself.

I went blank with incredulity. How could Snowy have been such a damned ass? In those days of blackout, with no street lighting and cars' lights reduced to tiny slits by metal covers, emergency laws stipulated that vehicles parked after dark must have their side-lights on at all times and be left next to the left-hand kerb, pointing in the direction of the traffic flow. It was an utterly sensible law, considering the drastically reduced night visibility, and Snowy must have suffered a brainstorm to take such an obvious risk. I could only think some preoccupation with a new girlfriend had hazed his wits.

The adjutant continued: 'The worst of it is they've found a drop or two of the dreaded green 100-octane fuel in the tank and Snowy's been packed off back here under military escort. The station commander's champing at the bit, expecting you to pass him up the line. He's even got the armed escort outside, waiting to wheel him away the moment you put him on remand.'

The path of duty was marked out with disconcerting clarity. Air force law dictated that offenders must be seen in the first instance by their immediate commanding officer, whose powers to punish were limited in accordance with rank. In other words, if the immediate CO deemed the offence too serious to be dealt with summarily, then it fell outside his scope for punishment. His duty was to remand the offender to be dealt with by his immediate superior. And so it went on, a notch at a time, until it arrived with the station commander, who could deal with the matter summarily or recommend the ultimate step of a court martial.

Here, then, was a real dilemma. My immediate superior was Johnny Kent, only as yet half-trained and gunning for me on grounds of indiscipline, but away for the moment. In his absence I could jump a notch and remand the prisoner straight to a station commander with a run-away ego longing to pounce. I had no doubt in my mind that the commander would opt for a court martial, with all the glory this would offer as star prosecution witness and the scourge of an ungodly squadron. There was no time to spare. Snowy was already outside, flanked by his armed escort, who would march him away at the double to the station commander just as soon as I could get through the formality of remanding him. It was taken for granted that this was my one legitimate option.

I did not feel quite so sure myself, and weighed the consequences in the balance. Surrendering Snowy to the station commander would undoubtedly lead to his conviction by court martial and a dishonourable discharge once he had served a month or two of imprisonment in the 'glasshouse'. It would certainly mean the end of his career in the air service, quite apart from seriously jeopardising his chances of finding a civilian job. It troubled me not a jot that I could be considered an accomplice for having turned a blind eye to the fact that he was putting the occasional contraband gallon of fuel in my sister Pat's car. The point which most concerned me was that the RAF was in danger of losing a valuable mechanic who was making a positive contribution to whatever success was coming our way in the conduct of the war.

On a personal level I owed it to Snowy that he had kept my aircraft in superb flying trim and been an important factor in preserving me alive. He was a valued member of the squadron, and the squadron was family; blood was thicker than water and 92 looked after its own. Meanwhile, what of Johnny Kent's position? Being absent would absolve him from all blame, and if I bent the rules it would hand him the ammunition to fire me if he so wished. That ought to please him, I thought. It therefore boiled down to a straightforward choice between Snowy and the station commander. Either I could wreck the career and possibly the livelihood of a first-class mechanic whose skills were a basic resource to the squadron; or else I could deflate the ego of a small-minded senior officer who apparently thought the path to promotion was lined by a set of shiny buttons and topped off with a crisp haircut. 'Call in prisoner and escort,' I said to the adjutant.

The party marched in smartly and clunked to a halt in front of the desk, standing to attention as the charge was read out: 'The prisoner parked his car on the wrong side of the road without lights, contrary to regulation number so and so. Furthermore, on examination of the said vehicle, the petrol tank was found to contain 100-octane aviation spirit, the property of HM Government.'

I put on the most magisterial air I could muster. 'I have given this case much thought,' I said, 'and I'm not entirely satisfied that the charges are based on a sufficiently thorough examination of the facts. I have therefore decided to give the prisoner the benefit of the doubt and to dismiss the case on the grounds of lack of evidence.'

There followed one of those deeply satisfying silences so profound that the sound of a pin dropping on a heavily piled carpet would have reverberated thunderously. Even the adjutant's cynical old eyes briefly glazed over as I concluded: 'All charges against the prisoner are hereby dismissed. He is to be released immediately and returned to his unit to continue with normal duties. Case closed. March out.'

I fully expected my head to roll. It never did. Johnny Kent took it all amazingly in his stride and refrained from using it against me. He was beginning to mellow under 92 Squadron's benign influence and also, I think, to appreciate the loyalties that bound his new command together. As for the station commander, once he had emerged from his state of shocked incredulity, he roared, boomed and foamed, but was powerless to do more. He was free to question my judgement, even my sanity, but never the legality of my action. Once a case is dismissed it can never be reopened. Snowy was safe.

There was rather a sad sequel to this sorry tale. Some years later, in 1946, not long after the end of the war, I was posted as an instructor to the RAF Staff College at Bracknell, near Ascot. Among the students on one of the courses there turned up no less a person than the ex-Station Commander at Manston, still stuck at the level of wing commander, never having managed the promotion he sought so desperately. On this occasion I felt genuinely sorry for him. He had a defeated look. It became even more defeated when the course finished. He failed.

I know he held me responsible, but quite without justification. Students at the college were divided into syndicates of half a dozen or so candidates, each supervised by a member of the teaching staff and rotated every so often between staff members to prevent personality clashes. By pure chance the former station commander was never in my syndicate, so I was never called on to report on him and had no hand in his assessment. In any case, I would never have failed him or anyone else out of personal malice, even if I had felt any, which I did not. The man had never once entered my thoughts after the squadron left Manston, and even there my feelings for him had been merely ones of irritation.

There was one more ironic touch. After the war I married his goddaughter, though I doubt whether he remembered he had one.

★ ★ ★

A third Manston episode occurred before long. This time the connection with the base was more tenuous, but the event was infinitely more dramatic. The story had its beginnings in June 1941, when two of Germany's most up-to-date and powerful 'pocket' battleships, *Scharnhorst* and *Gneisenau*, and the almost equally powerful battle cruiser *Prinz Eugen*, finding the Atlantic on the hot side, had made a dash for temporary shelter in Brest harbour. There they were promptly attacked by Bomber Command and remained bottled up for months, subjected to continuous air assault and blockaded by a round-the-clock submarine patrol at the harbour entrance.

One day, following a particularly heavy raid on the ships, air reconnaissance revealed what appeared to be crippling damage to all three, sufficient to immobilise them until extensive repairs were carried out. This assessment was confirmed by the photographic interpreters after minute examination of the aerial pictures. Accordingly it was decided for the time being to call off regular air reconnaissance cover and submarine patrols.

RAF Kenley, a fighter station about five miles west of Biggin Hill, was commanded at the time by Group Captain Victor Beamish, one of three famous aeronautical brothers, all senior air force officers, all enormous former Irish rugby internationals. On the morning of 12 February, a day or so after the critical raid on Brest, the weather was particularly dreary, and as Victor Beamish looked out of his office window at the low cloud and driving rain, he decided to do a 'rhubarb'. This quaint term indicated an impromptu operation undertaken by two aircraft when weather conditions were too bad to allow for normal fighter offensives. The pair of aircraft would cross the Channel at wave-top height to avoid radar detection and swoop on any opportune targets that presented themselves.

Victor squeezed himself into his Spitfire cockpit and took off, and it remained a perfectly routine 'rhubarb' operation until he and his companion aircraft were halfway back on the home run across the Channel. All at once he found, to his astonishment, that they were flying alongside three massive German battleships escorted by a flotilla of destroyers and a fleet of E-boats – high-speed launches armed with torpedoes and cannon – steaming north off the French coast by Le Touquet.

In a daze, he reported the find over his RT. Like the rest of us, he had made a study of the silhouettes of Germany's most important ships of war and felt certain that those he was seeing were *Scharnhorst*, *Gneisenau* and *Prinz Eugen*. Impossible, came the reply. Those ships were known to be in Brest harbour, too damaged to move. That might be so, he insisted, but the fact remained he was looking at three ships whose profiles exactly matched their descriptions. At the very least they must be major battleships, so where had they originated if they were not the ones from Brest? Presumably they are ours, came the answer. This wouldn't, after all, be the first time it had slipped the navy's mind to keep the air force informed of its movements. The matter would be looked into. Now, if he had nothing further to report, perhaps he would be so good as to return to base.

I had recently finished a short stint as an instructor at an operational training unit (OTU), the function of which was to teach qualified pilots fighter tactics. Bob Tuck, by then wing commander at Biggin Hill, had asked that I should take command of 72 Squadron when the post fell vacant, and this event had come to pass. By that February of 1942, however, we were on a temporary detachment at Gravesend, one of Biggin's satellite airfields, and on the 12th, because of the murky weather, we had been stood down from a state of 'readiness' and put on 'thirty minutes' availability'. This jargon requires a little explanation.

Fighter Command squadrons engaged in the air defence of the United Kingdom were held in various states of availability, depending on the level of enemy air activity and the weather. In those days weather played a far more significant role in aerial activity than it does today. Sophisticated technology has made it of almost secondary importance and the modern pilot can find his target on instruments and release a computer-guided, heat-seeking air-to-air missile while still miles beyond visual range. In the 1940s the fighter pilot could fly blind, but could not as yet fight blind. We needed visual contact with our target, even as the bombers needed visual contact with theirs. Solid cloud therefore brought operations (except for those of the 'rhubarb' type) to a standstill.

First among the normal states of availability came 'readiness': pilots in the dispersal hut, in full flying gear, within a short sprint of their aircraft; their fitters in the cockpits, keeping the engines warm and ready for instant take-off. From a state of 'readiness' we could normally be airborne within three minutes from the order, 'Scramble!' meaning, 'Take off.' The second state was 'thirty minutes' availability', which meant pilots could wait in the mess and grab a meal while they had the chance. Occasionally, if the weather was really poor, the 'thirty' would be relaxed to 'sixty minutes' availability'. Finally, thirty minutes after last light, the squadrons would be 'released', which meant you were free to drift off and do your own thing until thirty minutes before next day's sunrise.

We spent the dreary morning of the 12th in our luxury pad at Cobham Hall, the home of the Earl of Darnley, reading news-papers or snoozing to catch up on a bit of sleep. Shortly before midday the phone went and summoned us to a state of readiness. Our transport was permanently ready to go, and within minutes we were back at dispersal. No sooner had we arrived than we were called to cockpit standby. Hardly had I strapped myself in before I was ordered to report to the control tower and had to unstrap myself again.

There was, it appeared, some as yet undefined surface activity off Dover involving the navy, who were very probably going to need our support. The moment more information was to hand I would be told. Meanwhile it was back to the cockpit to resume strapping myself in before, yet again, being called to the control tower. During the next quarter of an hour I must have been summoned four times between cockpit and control tower, each time fastening and unfastening the straps and each time been given a set of different instructions, each set more confusing than the one preceding it. It became obvious there was not a soul, from Fighter Command downwards, who had a clue as to what was afoot in the English Channel.

Eventually I emerged from this spin of activity with a set of instructions which at least looked positive and clear cut: 72 Squadron was to take off at once and fly flat out towards Manston. There we would find four other Spitfire squadrons already orbiting the airfield, and these were to form up behind 72. Kingcome was to take command of this scratch wing of five squadrons, at which point six naval Swordfish of the Fleet Air Arm, based at Manston, would be scrambled. The task of our wing would be to escort them to the Straits of Dover, where some kind of fracas was in progress between a flotilla of German E-boats and several of our own MTBs (or motor torpedo boats – high-speed launches similar to the E-boats). The Swordfish were to do what they could to break up the E-boat flotilla while the Spitfires provided air cover and, air-cover duties permitting, joined in the attack.

Swordfish were affectionately, and for obvious reasons, nick-named 'Stringbags'. They were certainly a joke of an aircraft, and a testimony to the navy's attachment to the prehistoric: ante-diluvian aeroplanes with fixed undercarriages and three crew members crammed into two open cockpits. They had been designed by the Fairey Aviation Co. to function as torpedo car-riers, and this was a task they could just about manage, though the weight of a torpedo left them a top speed of only between 85 and 90 knots – about or below the stalling speed for most other aircraft of their generation.

The trouble with the Royal Navy was that it was still having difficulty coming to terms with air power, and for some time it continued to treat its air arm as the Cinderella in the family. It was fortunate for the navy, if not for its air crews, that the short comings and vulnerability of such aircraft as the Swordfish were counterbalanced by the dedication and heroism of the Fleet Air Arm personnel. These qualities had been demonstrated at the end of May 1940 in the naval action that culminated in the sinking of the *Bismarck*, another of Germany's most powerful battle ships. She had virtually been chased around the Atlantic by the cream of the British Fleet, but her powerful guns comfortably out-ranged those of the Royal Navy, and this, in combination with her superior speed, enabled her to elude her pursuers. Eventually a lucky strike from the torpedo of a Swordfish from the *Ark Royal* sealed the *Bismarck*'s fate. It hit her in the rudder and put her steering gear out of action. She was unable to do more than steam in helpless circles as the British battleships *King George V*, *Rodney* and *Dorsetshire* finished her with a bombardment.

At least my instructions from the control tower at Gravesend seemed clear at last. I sprinted back to my aircraft to clamber into the cockpit and take off before there could be any more changes of plan. We could muster only ten serviceable Spitfires and pilots, and my nine companions formed up behind me as we high-tailed towards Manston. There the six Swordfish were already airborne and orbiting the airfield, but we could see no more Spitfires anywhere in view. How long the Swordfish had been waiting was impossible to tell, but they were making their impatience obvious. The instant they saw us they straightened up and set course without hanging about for the rest of the escort to show up.

With hindsight I realised that their impatience sprang from the fear that the painfully slow speeds of their 'Stringbags' could allow their targets to get clean beyond range before they could catch them. Yet the most immediate surprise they gave me was that, instead of flying south towards Dover, as I expected, they turned due east and, at zero altitude, headed out across the North Sea, the surface of which was uninviting and threatening beneath a swirling cover of low cloud and rain. Undaunted, I took up station above and behind, deploying the ten aircraft to which the promised five-squadron wing had evidently been reduced. Considering the atrocious weather, this depletion was probably just as well. Five squadrons could easily have become unworkable with visibility fluctuating between zero and a few hundred yards. We also had to maintain a low altitude to avoid losing visual contact. Because the maximum speed of a Swordfish equalled the stalling speed of a Spitfire, the only way to hold them in view without spinning into the sea ourselves was to sweep behind them in large loose figures of eight. Trying to co-ordinate the movements of more than ten aircraft in those conditions might well have got us all into an untimely tangle.

The coast was hardly more than a few minutes behind us before the first attack came from enemy fighters. We managed to thwart them without sustaining casualties. Then, without warning, I found myself gazing at an astonishing sight as it materialised dramatically and magically out of the low cloud and tempestuous rain. I found I was sitting at masthead height above the most magisterial warship you could have imagined. Its sinister beauty and overpowering menace were palpable. Mentally I began to chalk up points of congratulation to the Royal Navy. At last, it seemed, they had made a dramatic move up-market and got themselves a real ship of battle for the present and future. The contrast between our lumbering patrol of Swordfish, wallowing sluggishly over the waves, and this magnificent vast floating fortress cruelly showed up the contrast between struggling museum relics and a sleek, deadly product of the latest technology. Perhaps, I thought, if the Sea Lords of the Admiralty could only be here to witness this scene, then even they might take the decision to scrap those farcical flying machines.

I wasn't given long to ponder the imponderable. In the midst of my reveries the marvellous fighting ship I was circling so admiringly opened up at me with every mighty gun barrel. I moved deftly away from the turmoil of shrapnel, aggrieved if not astounded. The Royal Navy was known among airmen for having this habit of firing first and asking questions afterwards. Then all at once the gunners on the great warship switched attention to the Swordfish, which were by now driving straight towards her in two 'vics' of three in line astern. There was no doubt about it. They were preparing for combat. My confusion intensified by the second. Either we had a case of mistaken identity and the torpedo planes were about to attack one of our own, or else the beautiful ship belonged to a set-up other than the Royal Navy. But if she was not one of ours, then whose could she be? It was impossible to think she might be German. Surely in that case we would have been briefed; and surely a major enemy warship could never have come so close to the English coast without triggering the nation's alarm bells long before this.

The huge ship herself seemed in no doubts. She lowered her big guns and fired salvos into the sea ahead of the approaching Swordfish. As the colossal walls of water and spray rose directly into their paths, I had the impression that one was brought down by the deluge. Somehow the others seemed to survive, however, and then the battleship raised her sights and let fly directly at the Swordfish with a fiery inferno. The brave 'Stringbags' never faltered, but just kept driving steadily on at wave-top height, straight and level as though on a practice run. They made perfect targets as they held back from firing their missiles before closing to torpedo range. They were flying unswerving to certain destruction, and all we as their escort could do was sit helplessly in the air above them and watch them die.

Mercifully our role as inactive spectators came to a dramatic close as, out of the murk and broken cloud, a swarm of German fighters appeared. We had expected nothing less. What we had not expected was that among the Messerschmitt 109s, Germany's front-line, single-engined, single-seat fighter, there would be a strange new radial-engined single-seater never before seen or even mentioned in advance intelligence warnings. As we discovered later, we had made our first contact with the Focke-Wulf 190, a first-class performer destined to supplant the Me 109 as Göring's most deadly answer to the Spitfire, and the air cover had been led by no less a person than Adolf Galland. Meanwhile there was not a split second free for speculation. We turned in towards the attacking fighters and did our utmost to intercept between them and the vulnerable Swordfish. The battle was short, sharp and violent, and it probably lasted only a few minutes before the German fighters melted away. Of the Swordfish no trace remained, apart from floating wreckage and one or two life-rafts.

There had been six aircraft and eighteen crew. Five survivors were later picked out of the water. I never knew how many of the Swordfish were shot down by the ship's guns and how many by the attacking aircraft, but I hoped we had at least managed to protect them from the main brunt of the attack from the air. The rest became history, much of it still shrouded in a fog of obfuscation to the present day. The great ship I had so admired turned out to be the *Prinz Eugen*, the battle cruiser escorting the twin battleships, *Gneisenau* and *Scharnhorst*. It had paused and with almost contemptuous ease swatted six buzzing mechanical insects out of the way before turning to rejoin *Gneisenau* and *Scharnhorst* where they lurked in the mist a few hundred yards distant. The mighty trio, with escorting fleet, then vanished eastward into the gloom of the North Sea, on its way through the minefields to the haven of the north German harbours. Thirteen men had died and six aircraft been lost on a doomed mission. Their effort had had as much impact on the progress of German's mighty battleships as raindrops on the windscreen of a speeding car.

With guns empty, the Spitfires of 72 Squadron made their way back to base together, many shot up but none shot down. We had been in the air little more than an hour since take-off, but it had been time enough to witness the highest heroism and its toll; time enough for lives to be ended and family ties shattered. An epic of sacrifice and tragedy had been squeezed into sixty fleeting minutes, the time you might take over a hurried lunch. Back on the ground at Gravesend we taxied to dispersal and our waiting groups of ground crew, who were eager to hear the news and assess any damage to the aircraft in their charge. It was usual for the eight gun ports along the leading edge of a Spitfire's wings to be covered with fabric patches to protect the guns from dirt and weather. As the guns were fired, these would be blown away, and consequently as they came into land the aircraft emitted rather weird whistling sounds, alerting ground crew to the fact they had been in action.

One other innovation had been present on that historic day. At about this time the new camera guns were being developed and an experimental one had been fitted to my aircraft. They were activated by the gun button and designed to operate automatically every time the guns were fired. During the fracas over the *Prinz Eugen* I had got what I thought must be a number of particularly good shots of the new German fighters. Naturally I was agog to see the results and asked Snowy, my fitter, to do all he could to get the film developed as quickly as possible. Apart from the matter of my own satisfaction, the film could hold valuable information about these new combatants. Away Snowy trotted to unload the camera, only to return crestfallen and red-faced a few minutes later. 'Very sorry, sir,' he said. 'I'm afraid I forgot to remove the lens cover.' The camera gun was taken away a few days later for more experimental work and I never managed to get hold of another.

In war, as in peace, it seems we tend to forget the triumphs and remember the disasters. The Channel Dash stayed in my mind so vividly because it was a failure and a tragic one; it was also entirely man-made. The Germans fooled us totally, and panicked our staff personnel into making ill-considered, off-the-cuff decisions that were never vetted by planners with up-to-date operational experience. Had that happened, we would undoubtedly have thought twice before sending out six absurdly outmoded Swordfish to stop three of the most advanced floating fortresses in the world.

There was a Whitehall cover-up, I hardly need to add. I attended a couple of inquiries, but nothing came out and the operation, a

German naval and propaganda triumph of the highest order, was heavily and correctly exploited to the full in Germany. It passed largely unknown and unremarked in Britain, which was scarcely surprising. For three German battleships to have outwitted our intelligence and sailed unscathed in broad daylight up the English Channel and through the Straits of Dover before escaping into the wilderness of the North Sea was barely credible. It was certainly an event Whitehall preferred to have swept quietly under the carpet then and thereafter.

Later it emerged that the factor which made the feat possible for the Germans was the brilliance of the Brest dockyard workers and their directing genius. The last air attack on the ships in Brest supposedly did so much damage that all air and submarine surveillance could be called off, but in fact it achieved only superficial damage, leaving the ships' main fighting and navigational systems intact. The ingenuity of the Germans was that, after the raid, they managed to strew the ships' decks with debris so cleverly arranged that our photographic interpreters were deceived into thinking the damage far more extensive and invasive than it was. As soon as the surveillance of the British was eased off, all that the Germans needed to do was − literally − clear the decks. The ships were then free to put to sea with operational systems working perfectly, transformed by sleight of hand back into their deadly selves. The Germans completely hoodwinked our intelligence.

It was a pity the cover-up threw an obscuring shadow over the shining exploit of those Swordfish crews. Their leader, Eugene Esmonde, was deservedly awarded a posthumous Victoria Cross, the first in the Fleet Air Arm, but in my view each of the men who took part should have received the highest honour. They were unquestionably launched on a suicide mission. As they took off every crew member must have had it as a certainty at the back of his mind that he was going to his death. The fact that five of the eighteen survived miraculously was a bonus none could have expected or believed possible.

Perhaps their heroism was best and most simply summed up by an eyewitness from the other side, who saw all that happened from the deck of one of the two sister battleships being escorted by *Prinz Eugen*. Helmuth Giessler, who was navigation officer on board *Scharnhorst*, put it in these words: 'Their bravery was devoted and incredible. They knowingly and ungrudgingly gave their all to their country and went to their doom without hesitation.'

29 Brian in 1942 as Wing Commander.

30 Bob Tuck.

31 BK introducing HM King George VI to 92 Squadron pilots. The king is seen here shaking hands with Robbie Robertson, with New Zealander Owen Hardy standing to Robbie's left.

32 The 'Glorious' twins (Moira and Sheila) outside the White Hart.

33 By the White Hart. Left to right: BK, Moira, Sam Saunders, Bill, Roy Dutton, Sheila and Kath Preston.

34 Janet Montague (*née* Aitkin), Paddy Green, Sheila, Bob Holland and Roger Frankland.

35 Opposite above: Some of the 'few' taken later in the war (14 September 1942). Tony Bartley, DFC, Desmond Sheen, DFC, Ian Gleed, DSO, DFC, Max Aitkin, DSO, DFC, 'Sailor' Malan, DSO, DFC, SIL 'Al' Deere, DFC, Air Chief Marshal Sir Hugh Dowding, F/O Henderson, MM, FIL Richard Hillary, Johnny Kent, DFC, AFC, Brian Kingcome, DFC, OSO D. H. Watkins, DFC and R.H. Gretton.

36 92 Squadron, Biggin Hill, 1940/42.

37 Wing Cdr Duncan Smith, Maj. Malcolm Ostler and Group Capt. Brian Kingcome, outside their mobile operations room in Italy. 'Group Capt. Kingcome seems to have recovered from the injuries he received when a jeep turned over recently.' (*Flight*, June 1944)

38, 39, 40 *Above and left:* Photographs of BK in Italy in 1944 showing the injuries he sustained falling out of a jeep when it overturned.

Churchill visiting 244 Wing in Italy. BK (behind) as CO showing the Prime Minister around.

'Cocky' Dundas stands tall on the left, with BK in the middle, in this group shot of 244 Wing in Italy.

43 The Malcolm Club in Italy – where chaps went to drink and relax and be entertained by rather collect young ladies!

44 Left: BK and a friend (possibly Allan Wright) walking the dog on the beach in Italy. The dog, Nelly, was BK's.

45 Below: 324 Wing at RAF Zeltweg in Austria, August 1946, with BK as CO.

46 Lesley Kingcome and Betty Barthropp drawing the raffle tickets to win a car that Paddy annually presented to the RAF Benevolent Fund (early 1960s).

47 BK and Paddy Barthropp in the early 1960s.

48 Battle of Britain reunion. Left to right: Jamie Rankin, Paddy Barthropp, (?), 'Sailor' Malan, Bobby Preston, Brian Kingcome, (?), Tony Bartley and Bob Tuck.

49 Christopher Foxley-Norris (middle foreground), Bob Tuck (eighth from right), Douglas Bader (fifth from right), Paddy Barthropp (fourth) and Brian Kingcome (third).

50 Brian and Paddy standing by a Spitfire (1970s).

51 Battle of Britain personalities at Hendon, 20 November 1978. Douglas Bader is sitting nearest to BK, who stands with hands in pockets.

52 The blackboard in the White Hart, Brasted,

NINE

THE ENIGMA OF THE MORLAIX RAID

It was the summer of 1942, by which time the tide of war, or certainly of the air war, was beginning to flow against the Germans. The crucial date of 7 December 1941 – the day of the Japanese attack on Pearl Harbor – had ended the neutrality of the United States and brought her in on the Allied side. Daylight bombing raids on Britain became almost a thing of the past, except for opportunist sorties by one or two aircraft in bad weather. I had left 72 Squadron and Biggin Hill to take over as Wing Commander Flying at Kenley, a fighter station similar to Biggin Hill but a few miles to the west. The Kenley wing was built up from four Spitfire squadrons based at Kenley and Redhill, the first to arrive that August being No.402 Squadron (Canadian). Towards the end of September it was joined by its sister Canadian squadrons, Nos 401, 412 and 416. From then on we became known as the 'Canadian Wing'. Our Station Commander was Group Captain Richard 'Batchy' Atcherley (later Air Marshal Sir Richard Atcherley). To my mind it was the perfect posting. I could not have asked for better squadrons or a better station commander.

The timing of the war had played cruel tricks on the careers of some of the generation of pre-war pilots. For the Cranwell adjutant it came too soon; this was unusual. For most it arrived too late. The 1930s produced a number of legendary pilots who would have excelled in the Second World War, but they were just that touch too old by the time it broke out. It must have been a bitter pill for them to swallow. Nevertheless they masked their disappointment and, with their warmth and advice, generously welcomed the new wave of young pilots who stepped forward to take their place in the air. The one who fell within this bracket whom I recall most clearly — and with deep affection — was the famous 'Batchy'. He was probably the best known of the handful of larger-than-life pre-war pilots who had brought glamour and excitement to the emerging new world of flying.

Batchy had been a member of the 1929 Schneider RAF High Speed Flight, which won the airspeed record that year, repeating its original triumph of 1927 before going on to complete the hat-trick in 1931. With his equally daredevil identical twin, David, he had achieved legendary fame in aviation circles with a repertoire of crazy though highly skilled exploits. The brothers were illustrious for, among other things, their barnstorming activities at air displays in both Britain and the United States. One of Batchy's party tricks was a variant on the old circus act, when a 'drunk' would stagger into the ring, leap on to one of the performing horses, and proceed to go though a series of amazing equestrian stunts. In Batchy's case he disguised himself as a mad professor dressed in exaggerated civilian clothes, with flowing false beard and locks and pebble spectacles, before making a dash out from the control tower on to the host airfield with the guards in hot pursuit. Meanwhile an aircraft would be taxiing out for take-off, but in a trice Batchy would have hauled its frantically protesting pilot out of the cockpit, have leapt in, pushed the throttle wide and scrambled wildly into the air. Once aloft he would go through a set of the most hair-raising aerobatics, seeming to miss the ground and the gaping crowds by inches before performing an equally hair-raising landing, leaping from the cockpit and escaping into the distance.

It was said that when the twins were serving in the Middle East they were in the habit of signing their names in the desert sands with the wingtips of their aircraft. Whether there was any truth in this tale I cannot personally say, but it seemed entirely in keeping with their characters and skills. Both rose to high rank and the story of their unique careers was celebrated in a book by John Pudney called *A Pride of Unicorns*. David, alas, went missing in a Meteor a few years after the war. In 1952 he was on a tour of inspection in the Middle East and on a flight from Fa'id to Nicosia, when he stopped off to refuel at Cairo. He never reached Cyprus but disappeared somewhere over the eastern Mediterranean. No trace of his aircraft was ever found, despite an extensive search. I always felt that the main suspect was his carefree nature, in the light of which he may well have decided not to hang about to top up with oxygen at Cairo, reasoning it would hardly be necessary for the short final leg of his journey. If my theory is correct, then it is entirely possible that he passed out and plunged into the sea before he had time to radio a warning. It is the only hypothesis that seems to fit with his happy-go-lucky personality and the few known facts.

At Kenley I had two main tasks. The first was to lead my wing of four squadrons in fighter sweeps over France on sabre-rattling expeditions to penetrate as far south and east as fuel allowed in the hope of luring German fighters into combat. The second was to provide bomber escort. As a general rule the RAF bombed by night, the USAAF (the combined command of the United States Army and Air Forces) by day. The fighter cover we provided was therefore usually for the massed formations of American bombers, mostly Flying Fortresses, as they went on daylight raids into northern Europe.

I always felt the highest admiration for the crews of the daylight bombers, and at this time the Americans were particularly vulnerable. The range of the Spitfire was unfortunately too limited for us to be able to cover them for more than the first and least dangerous part of their missions. During the most hazardous part, when they were farthest from home, they had to rely on their own defences. These were formidable in their own way. They were heavily armed and the formations they adopted were designed to allow for the maximum cross-fire. This could be surprisingly effective, but the lack of a fighter escort left them highly vulnerable to air attack and the casualties they took were intimidating. By a later stage of the war the development of long-range fighters would help to redress the balance, but the role of the daylight bomber was always particularly hazardous. In fact the role of all bombers, day or night, was indescribably dangerous, and there was a constant awareness among the fighter pilots that we were incredibly lucky to be facing our own risks with at least the illusion of having a measure of personal control over our destinies.

The Spitfire continued on its evolutionary course throughout the war, a story eloquently told from a personal viewpoint by Jeffrey Quill in his *Spitfire: A Test Pilot's Story*. Not long after I arrived at Kenley the new Mark IX began to be introduced into service. The Germans had gained an edge with the Focke-Wulf 190, and although they could never quite touch the Spitfire for manoeuvrability, they were superior in speed and climb above 20,000ft, a crucial altitude where much fighter activity took place. They were also beginning to introduce their new high-altitude Junkers 86R bombers, which were capable of attacking their targets from altitudes above 40,000ft, where none of the earlier marks of Spitfire could reach them. The Spitfire Mark IX was designed to combat both these threats.

Aero engines, like car engines and human beings, are aspirated. In other words they need to breathe oxygen to stay alive. Internal-combustion engines gulp in air, mix it with vaporised fuel to form a nice explosive mixture, and then squirt this into the cylinders. There it is compressed to give it even more vigour before it is ignited by the spark plugs. The resultant explosions provide the energy to drive the machine. Aero engines, however, have one unique problem which becomes evident if they have to operate in the higher reaches of the atmosphere. The higher they fly, the thinner the air. Less air means weaker explosions, which means less power, which means performance dropping away sharply at the upper reaches.

This effect would have mattered little if fighter pilots could have chosen their operational altitude. Unfortunately the height at which we flew was dictated by other factors, including the task in hand. If you were escorting bombers, for instance, it was essential for you to stay in close contact. It was also important to fly as high as possible to avoid being jumped by the enemy. The bombers normally flew at somewhere around 15,00ft, which automatically nudged the escorting fighters up into the bracket of 20,000ft or over, with performance dropping away noticeably.

Where there were no such restrictions imposed by operational needs, then fighter pilots were free to choose their own altitudes within the parameters of weather and objectives, but a fighter prowling on the hunt for the enemy instinctively tended to fly at the top of its performance range. Height advantage could be crucial. For one thing there was the extra speed you gained as you dived to engage. For another there was the chance it gave you to appear without warning out of the sun, invisible to the enemy till the last moment, as we all knew well from having watched Errol Flynn in *The Dawn Patrol*. Superior performance at altitude had a priceless tactical advantage.

Another gimmick of Mother Nature's to be exploited to the full was the condensation or so-called 'con-trail'. Today the whole world is familiar with the fine white lines drawn across the sky as commercial jetliners ply their aerial routes. These trails occur in certain quite common meteorological conditions when moisture in the engine exhaust gases condenses and turns into a highly visible cloud-like vapour laid down along the aircraft's track. The appropriate conditions normally occur between 20,000 and 30,000ft in bands of around 5,000ft in depth, which are quite invisible until you hit them and 'start smoking'. They give no advance hint of their presence and begin and finish abruptly. In the classic phrase of the conjuror, 'Now you see it, now you don't.' Mysterious or not, they provided a handy alarm system for wartime pilots. As soon as you hit one you could drop to fly just below it, which meant no enemy plane could jump you from above with out giving away its intention. Alternatively, you could climb through the band to the clear air above and prowl in the hope that, if you spotted an enemy aircraft below, you could build up enough speed as you dived back through to retain an element of surprise even with your smoke trail. Either way they were an important tactical factor in the battle craft of the fighter pilot.

The constant modifications to fighter aircraft on both sides were mostly small improvements here and there, which more or less kept them abreast of one another in general increased performance. With the Mark IX, however, the geniuses at Rolls-Royce, who made the Merlin engines that powered our Spitfires – and, indeed, most of our front-line aircraft – came up with a truly significant development: a two-stage supercharger that was to revolutionise performance. In the estimation of Jeffrey Quill himself, it was 'a quantum jump' in design and function.

Most aero engines were supercharged, or 'blown'. That is to say, they were fitted with fans that forced air into the engines faster than it could be drawn out by the normal 'breathing' process. For the Mark IX, Rolls-Royce produced the Merlin 61, an engine that operated in two stages, the first to boost power at sea level in the normal way, the second to come into operation at around 15,000ft, just as the ordinary power level began to fail.

As the new planes began to come off the production line, the first batch was allocated to No.64 Squadron at Hornchurch in June. Other distributions followed, and happily for me it was the turn of the Kenley wing in August, when No.402 Squadron was equipped with Spitfire IXs. Naturally, as Wing Commander Flying, I lost no time in appropriating one of the new aircraft for myself, on the grounds that it was among the perks of the job. 'Wingco's flying' had their own aircraft identified by their initials painted on the side as well as their own call signs. Mine were always identified by the letters 'BK', and for convenience I used my Christian name 'Brian' as call sign. For one thing, it would be unlikely to slip my memory, even in a moment of turmoil.

The first time I flew the Mark IX I could hardly believe the experience. The effect was magical. I had expected an increase in power, but nothing to match the reality. To enhance the dramatic effect, the second stage cut in automatically without warning. One minute there I was, relaxed and peaceful, as I climbed at a leisurely pace towards 15,000ft, anticipating a small surge of extra power as I hit the magic number. The next minute it was as though a giant hand had grabbed hold of me, cradled me in its palm like a shot-putter and given me the most terrific shove forwards and upwards. The shock was so great that I almost bailed out. It literally took my breath away. It was exhilarating, a feeling I could never forget. I yearned at once for a chance to demonstrate this astonishing new tool to the Germans.

It so happened that the arrival of the Mark IXs coincided with the last days of the American Eagle squadrons, whose origins went back to the days when Britain first declared war and a number of adventurous young Americans enlisted in the RAF and were trained as pilots. To begin with they were scattered among the RAF squadrons, alongside the volunteers from the Dominions and Europe, and treated as normal RAF personnel. They wore RAF uniforms with identifying shoulder flashes and were subject to RAF discipline. Later, when the urge for national identification understandably took hold, most young men from the Dominions and the Allied nations were withdrawn and formed into squadrons of their own national identities. The United States had not yet come into the war, however. A compromise therefore needed to be arrived at for the American pilots and they were formed into three new squadrons which took the impressive title of 'Eagle'. No.71 Squadron was stationed at Debden, No.121 was at North Weald and No.133 was at Biggin Hill.

The Eagles continued to wear RAF uniform and to be subject to RAF discipline, but at least they had their own identity, and very dashing it sounded while chatting up the ladies. When, after Pearl Harbor, the United States officially declared war on Germany and Japan, she naturally had a need for these battle-hardened pilots in her own air force. In theory they were given the choice of whether to remain with British units or transfer to the USAAF, and several chose not to transfer, despite the better pay and conditions. Others came under considerable pressure to transfer, among them 'Red' McColpin, the leader of 133 Squadron.

On the morning of the last day before the Eagle squadrons were disbanded, Batchy sent for me. 'Nice cushy number for you today,' he announced. 'A farewell and thank you to the Eagle squadrons.'

Someone had thought up the idea that we should mark the occasion with a gentle, danger-free romp in the air over northern France with an operation that would include the only Eagle squadron to have been re-equipped with the Mark IXs, No.133, by now transferred to Great Sampford in Essex pending its dissolution. Accompanying the Eagles would be No.64 Squadron from Hornchurch and No.401 (Canadian) Squadron from Kenley. And a gentle and carefree jaunt it would have been had fickle Mother Nature not decided to spring one of her desperate surprises.

Our orders were straightforward. The three chosen squadrons were to fly from their respective bases to come together at a temporary landing strip at Bolt Head, the second most southerly point of Devon. There we would be given final details of route and timing. Subject to these, the three squadrons were then to fly as a wing, which I would lead. The general plan was to fly due south to Morlaix, a German fighter airfield on the north coast of the Brest peninsula, where we would meet up with a squadron of American B-17 Flying Fortresses. The heavy bombers would then drop their loads on the Morlaix airfield before heading for home. Unless there were enemy activity, we could bid them goodbye at this stage, call back at Bolt Head to refuel, then return to our respective bases. The operation would give the Eagle pilots a chance to baptise their Spitfire IXs at minimum risk − a fitting farewell gesture.

The first snag occurred when Batchy sent for me just as I was about to take off with No.401 Squadron. I told Keith Hodson, the tall Canadian squadron leader, to make his way to Devon without me, and I would follow as soon as I could. But Batchy held me up for longer than expected, and by the time I was in the air and hot-footing it to Devon the three squadrons were already briefed and waiting to take off from Bolt Head. Tony

Gaze, the leader of the third squadron, No.64 from Hornchurch, was an experienced and competent pilot. I therefore told him that he had better take over from me as wing leader since there was no time left for me to be briefed. I would then take over the leadership of the Canadian squadron to act as 'top cover', with the Eagle squadron in the middle. A British pilot, Gordon Brettell, had been temporarily delegated to lead them when McColpin found himself on the receiving end of a set of heavy orders from the American top brass to go to London to liaise on the transfer, despite making every protest that he wished to stay put with his squadron until it had seen the Morlaix raid through.

As soon as I had fuelled up we took off again and got into formation before heading south in a gradual climb towards Morlaix. We had been flying for hardly more than five or ten minutes before a layer of cloud began to gather below us. It was thick and mountainous and the sea was entirely concealed by the time we were halfway across the Channel. For twenty-five minutes or so we continued climbing steadily until we had reached to around 20,000ft and were, by our calculations, directly above the French coast. We then went into a gentle orbit as we began to scan about us for the Flying Fortresses. At first the skies seemed empty, but then I spotted them a long way to the south, little more than dots on the horizon and evidently forced up by the towering clouds to much the same altitude as the one we were holding. The first thought to occur to us was that it was odd they should be so far from the target area, but even as we watched they wheeled round to the north-east and began to head for home. Evidently the exceptional cloud cover had made them decide to abandon the operation. For a while we kept them under observation to make sure they were safely on their way, and then turned north and homewards ourselves.

We flew due north for thirty-five minutes, by which time we expected to be within spitting distance of the English coast. But something seemed weirdly adrift. Still the towering cumulus cloud stretched below us with no sign of a break. Our flight southwards had included a slow climb to 20,000ft. Returning northwards we were flying straight and level and consequently covering more ground. We should have been finding the sky over the English coast more or less as we had left it an hour before — that is to say, clear.

Another curious aspect was that, try as we might, we could raise no response from ground control. On the way out we had maintained radio silence to avoid alerting enemy monitoring stations to our presence. This was standard procedure. But now we were as good as home and the need for radio silence was long gone. Ground control would be listening out for us. Their failure to respond was baffling.

Yet while ground control's obstinate silence certainly fretted me, it was the clouds that worried me more. The former could conceivably have been caused by a technical hitch or a gremlin in the works; the latter was another question altogether. Weather can be changeable, clouds can build up quickly, but the junction of two weather systems is generally a well-defined, recognisable area. There is a slow change of character from clear skies to wisps of low stratus cloud, and these thicken and build into towering cumulus only gradually. It was just such a junction of weather systems that we had flown through on our outward journey. By now we should have been able to see it again if we were anywhere near the English coast. There was something more to this than a niggling instinct; my reason told me decisively what we ought to have been finding and the home skies should still have been clear. In the hour or so we had been airborne it would have been quite impossible for the weather to change so dramatically in character, or for it to have moved so far.

There was still no response from ground control. My mental alarm bells were beginning to sound insistently when all at once a small break appeared dramatically between the mighty towers of cumulus directly below. Through the gap there showed a small section of rugged south-facing coast with cliffs and headlands, identical in character and appearance to the stretch of Devon

coast around Bolt Head. With whoops of joy the two other squadrons peeled away and dived down through the gap. I was sorely
tempted to follow, but still found myself hesitating. Perhaps I was
being too clever by half. The time element alongside the fact that
the coast was south facing surely confirmed that this could be
nowhere else but Devon. There could not be another south coast
within a hundred miles. Nevertheless the inconsistent weather
pattern and ground control's sphinx-like silence continued to
feed my profound unease. I decided that 401 Squadron ought
to press on.

Fuel conservation was essential by this stage. Hitherto we had
not troubled ourselves, since the operation as planned was a very
short one, but the Spitfire's only shortcoming was its limited fuel
capacity. Depending on how ham-fisted you were with the throttle – and, as the saying went, in action you were either ham-fisted
or dead – your flying range was somewhere between two and a
quarter and two and a half hours. By this time we had been in
the air for over an hour and a half without giving any considera-
tion to fuel conservation. It would be a shrewd move for us to
begin treating our throttles very tenderly. This was easier for me
as formation leader than it was for the others. They had to keep
station, an exercise in which the throttle played a central role.

Mentally I fired off a quick message to St Christopher, invaluable saint of the traveller, and we continued north. A handful
of minutes later a most unholy racket broke out on the RT.
'For God's sake, ground control,' came a cacophony of American
voices, 'for God's sake stop those bloody Pongos' – air force slang
for the army – 'shooting at us! We're trying to land and the stupid
buggers won't stop firing!'

It caused me little concern, apart from thinking that they were
having no more luck with ground control than we were. Like
the navy, the army was deeply suspicious of anything with wings,
and also tended to blast off as a reflex and only afterwards begin
to ask some questions. They seldom did real damage, but they
were capable of putting you through an alarming experience. Still

ground control kept silent, and did nothing to clarify our own situation, or tell us who those Wyatt Earps might be banging away somewhere far below us. Soon the clamour died away.

We continued northwards, remaining above solid cloud, and still the airwaves were empty of sound over the RT. I decided our only option was to go down through the weather and hope the clouds had no hard centres, but just at that moment they started to thin, then began to change slowly back to the low-level stratus we had passed on the way out. The relief was huge, overwhelming. Here was the weather pattern for which I had been watching, the indication that we were at last well on the way home. Expectantly I waited as the cloud slowly melted away, confident that when it finally cleared we would see ahead of us the friendly, beckoning shores of England. And the cloud did clear − yet all that was visible in front of us was an endless expanse of ocean stretching as far as the eye could reach till it merged with a hazy horizon. My mental alarm bells jangled deafeningly.

By now instinct and reason were truly at loggerheads. The south coast I had rejected well over an hour earlier, reason now insisted could only have been Devon. This meant we had over-flown the western peninsula and must be somewhere above the Irish Sea on our way to the Irish Republic. Instinct disagreed, but could produce no logical arguments to say why. Reason therefore pointed out that we had flown south for half an hour, then north for nearly an hour and a half − almost three times as long − and here we were, still over water. *Ergo*, this had to be the Irish Sea. No other location would fit the puzzle. It seemed the time had come to give way to reason before writing off our entire squadron of brand new beautiful Mark IXs.

Clearly the situation was desperate. Within the next half-hour we would begin to drop one by one into the drink − literally, since we would all have to bail out. In the early days I had taken it for granted that a Spitfire could ditch in the sea without difficulty, skim along the surface and come to rest before slowly submerging. During the Battle of Britain I always planned, in a lackadaisical way, that if I ever were shot down over London, I would ditch in the Thames as close to the Embankment entrance of the Savoy as possible. My calculation was that, with fighter pilots briefly being the flavour of the month while the risk of invasion was uppermost in the public mind, someone would then proceed to buy me lunch. This congenial fantasy was brought to an unceremonious close when I got to know Norman Ryder, the only person I ever did meet who survived ditching a Spitfire at sea.

Norman, an experienced pilot, gave a hair-raising account of the incident after he was brought down in the Channel. The impact itself, comparable to hitting a brick wall at 80mph, was enough to daze him even with his seat belts tightly fastened. Then, within seconds of touching the surface, he was shot downwards into water so deep that the light was snuffed out as if a switch had been thrown. He found himself disorientated, semi-conscious and in total darkness. Fortunately he had managed to jettison his cock pit canopy before hitting, and somehow, groping blindly, he managed to undo his belts and other attachments and struggle out of the cockpit with straining lungs. Once he was free, the in-built buoyancy of his Mae West shot him to the surface, where he arrived in a sorry state and lucky to be alive. The fact was that the Spitfire's extremely nose-heavy characteristic meant that, as soon as it hit the water, the nose dug in, the tail shot up and the aircraft dived to the bottom like a gannet on the hunt. Norman's vivid narrative cured me of any inclination to ditch in any circumstances.

Time was meanwhile running out for 401 Squadron; all the odds seemed stacked against instinct. Nevertheless I could not rid myself of the feeling that there was a joker in the pack some where. Since the onset of war I had been flying operationally virtually without a break. Long experience in any field develops a sort of sixth sense, a feeling for when things are right and when they are not. Perhaps it was time, after all, for instinct to defy logic. The gut reaction I now had was not to be denied. With my heart in my mouth I decided to go for broke. We would press on.

At that very moment the earphones started to crackle. Miraculously, from out of the blue, so faint as to be almost inaudible, came the sweetest sound ever: 'Hello, Brian. Hello, Brian. This is ground control. Are you receiving me? Over.'

'Hello, ground control. This is Brian. Where the hell've you been the last two hours?'

'Hello, Brian. You've been off Fighter Command's board most of that time. Where the hell've you been? You're still eighty miles south of base. Fly due north, and for God's sake watch your fuel! Over.'

As if I needed telling! But still eighty miles south! What on earth had been going on here? It was no time for rumination, but at least we knew our direction now. The crucial task was to get everyone home intact if I could. Luckily we still had plenty of altitude, so we throttled back to the minimum revs needed to keep airborne, and in due course let down slowly in long, shallow, powered glides towards Bolt Head. The airfield was laid out at the edge of quite sheer granite cliffs, and an off-shore wind meant we had to land towards them. As I came in on my final approach I expected each second to hear the engine cut and anticipated ending as an ephemeral scar on those impervious granite walls. But as squadron leader I had needed to work my throttle less than the others and in fact still had a few gallons in hand. The engines of two other aircraft stopped as they touched down, and one pilot had to bale out just short of the coast.

In all the circumstances I felt we had come off fairly lightly, though the incident overall was an unmitigated disaster. The two other squadrons had got down safely through that gap in the clouds but then they became separated. It had not taken Tony Glaze too long to realise they were, after all, still over France, and he at once headed north with his squadron and arrived back safely, though he shed several aircraft on the way as a result of fuel shortage.

The real tragedy concerned the Eagle squadron. Believing themselves to be safely back over England, they began to search for somewhere to land. The cacophony of protests we had heard over the RT was caused not by entrepreneurial British gunners having a bash but by German artillery about its legitimate business as the Eagles inadvertently entered the heavily defended air space over Brest.

Those who were not shot down subsequently had to force-land or else to bail out as they ran out of fuel. As a result, a couple or so of our brand-new top-secret Spitfires Mark IX came down intact and handed the German aero-engineers and pilots one of their handsomest free gifts of the war. For the RAF it was a serious blow. It dramatically shortened the margin of time in which we were able to enjoy the huge advantage of our two-stage blowers. Of the twelve Eagle pilots, one had had to turn back with engine trouble soon after take-off. Four were killed and six were taken prisoner, including Gordon Brettell, who was sadly among the fifty Allied prisoners of war shot after the attempted mass escape from Stalag Luft III in 1944. The twelfth pilot crash-landed in France, but managed to evade capture and made it back to Britain.

The post-mortem to this truly sad and tragic tale produced little in the way of concrete explanation. Everybody knew that three Spitfire squadrons and one Flying Fortress squadron had ended up well over a hundred miles south of where they should have been, but no one could say why. When the Spitfires assumed they were over the French coast, they were in reality over the Bay of Biscay; and when we first spotted the Flying Fortresses, they must have been well on their way to Gibraltar. Indeed, as we heard later, one of them landed there, and the rest dumped their bombs somewhere over the Pyrenees before returning home. The coast we had glimpsed through a hole in the cloud on our way back was not the south coast of Devon but the Brest peninsula, and the airfield where the Eagles landed was needless to say a German installation in occupied France. The junction of the two weather systems which I had been watching out for had drifted to the south, increasing the gap between it and the English coast. In terms of flying time it only represented ten or fifteen minutes, but it caused us anxiety with our critical fuel situation. Ground control's failure to respond was simply because we were way beyond their RT range. Everything was thus neatly explained, except for the most important question of all. How had it happened in the first place?

It took some years for any plausible explanation to be forthcoming. After Frank Whittle's jet engine made high altitude the most economic space to fly in, and ultimately the busiest aerial highway for the commercial airliners, a phenomenon was encountered which came to be known as 'jet stream'. This extraordinary meteorological sport of nature is a freak band of air occasionally encountered at altitudes of anything above 20,000ft, and it moves at speeds of well over 100mph. This, it was concluded, must be the answer to what had happened to us on that September day in 1942. With such a freak gale up our tails, and ten-tenths cloud cover below, we could with ease have overflown the Brest peninsula and motored well into the Bay of Biscay without realising it. By another fluke, the gap in the clouds on the way back happened to open up above a strip of coastline that deceptively resembled the coast of south Devon.

As for the Flying Fortresses, they had reached the target area ahead of us and, forced up to the critical altitude by the cloud, must have hit the jet stream before we did. This would have accounted for their being so far to the south of us; also for their being still deep in enemy territory when we believed them to be safely back in friendly skies and left them. Fortunately they were never intercepted by enemy fighters, though even if they had been the dense cloud cover would have provided ample cover for them to escape.

So, to the best of my belief, 'jet stream' was finally officially accepted as the cause of the disaster. It was also believed to be the first recorded encounter with this mysterious force. As a last foot note, it also emerged in time that the transfer of McColpin under protest had rendered No. 133 (Eagle) Squadron demoralised and weakened at the critical moment. The planning of their mission had left a certain amount to be desired and there were gaps in their briefing and communications. It was the fatal combination of a casual approach to discipline and a freak weather condition which no one fully understood that had turned a simple jaunt into a calamity.

There was one interesting sequel to this story. Many years later I was in Washington, one of a small group of RAF and Luftwaffe pilots lecturing at the Smithsonian Museum. At the end of my lecture, while I was still on the platform, an American walked up and called me by name. 'You won't remember me,' he said. 'In fact we never actually met.'

I raised an eyebrow.

'I started out with the Eagle squadron on that Morlaix raid from Bolt Head,' he explained. 'I was the one that took off with the squadron but had to turn back after a few minutes with engine trouble and crash-landed near Kingsbridge. I guess you could say I was lucky.'

I guessed I could.

★ ★ ★

The seven months I spent as wing leader at Kenley were mostly occupied with routine fighter operations over France. Apart from the Morlaix raid, the only one I recall as being in any way a break from routine was the Dieppe landing, scheduled at the time as a dress rehearsal for D-Day. Apart from the importance of the occasion, to us it seemed just another straightforward air-cover job, protecting the ground and sea forces from air attack. On the ground the Dieppe raid was a different matter: another tragic fiasco. The German forces somehow got wind of the operation and were ready and waiting. The Allied troops, mostly Canadian, were met by a pulverising wall of fire as they scrambled ashore from the landing barges. The casualties they took were horrific. It was a disaster for the ground forces, and for us another frustrating occasion when we were in the air above them but almost powerless to help. We could protect them from air attack, we could strafe enemy transport and gun positions provided we could find them. Apart from that the constant movement of skirmishing troops locked in a land battle made intervention as dangerous for our own men as it would have been for the enemy. In the euphemism of this more modern age, they would have been highly vulnerable to 'friendly fire'. It was said that a naval officer who saw the events at first hand called it 'a naval version of the charge of the Light Brigade'.

For some unfathomable reason never explained it was decided that the Kenley wing would, for the Dieppe operation, operate from Lympne, an airfield in the south-east corner of Kent. Kenley would have been as handy as Lympne for reaching Dieppe, but no one moaned since it made a pleasant change. For two or three days we found ourselves billeted at Port Lympne, the country house of the former MP and Under Secretary of State for Air, Sir Philip Sassoon. Any mention of Dieppe has for me always had the effect of mixing up sharply contrasting memories between the action on the beachhead,' the carnage and tragedy, with Sir Philip's spectacular house and its terraced gardens with views across Romney Marsh, and the black marble bathrooms with sunken baths and friezes with black cherubs being chased by black satyrs to what ends one could only guess. Until his death in 1939 Sir Philip had been a dazzling figure on the social scene, and the house was built as a backdrop to his activities as a host to the high and mighty. Herbert Baker, the architect he picked to design it, possessed, in the opinion of the art historian Sir Kenneth Clark, 'a positive genius for errors of design; in his public buildings every proportion, every cornice, every piece of fenestration was (and unfortunately still is) an object lesson in how not to do it'.

One other fond memory of my Kenley days was far removed from aerial activity. It concerned Douglas Watkins, the amiable young commander of one of the squadrons, who became a good friend until he died too soon after the war from a simple operation that went wrong. One evening he and two comrades in arms, Emanuel and Michael, decided to slip into town for a few drinks. To achieve the expedition they borrowed the squadron transport, a small Singer pick-up van such as most squadrons used as general run-arounds – busy little vehicles with canvas tops that rolled back and tail-boards that hinged downwards, leaving a flat platform behind. Douglas drove, with Emanuel and Michael sitting in the back. Leaning in a corner of the van was a single-barrel twelve-bore shotgun and some cartridges, part of the clay-pigeon shooting equipment which fighter squadrons used to keep their eyes in sharp condition while waiting to be scrambled.

As the trio was about to make its way home again, suitably refreshed, it occurred to Emanuel and Michael that their vision and reflexes would be immeasurably improved by a little practice from a moving gun platform, just like the one, for instance, on which they found themselves riding at this moment. And what better targets could there be than the traffic lights so conveniently to hand? Sitting in the back, legs dangling over the tailboard, they began to blast away at each set of traffic lights as they swept passed. It was fortunate that at this stage of the war the streets after dark were pretty well empty. Few people went out for the evenings, because there was nowhere to go, and if you did go out the rationing meant there would very likely be nothing to eat or drink. There were no street lights, virtually no pedestrians or other traffic, and never the smallest chink of light from any building. Even the traffic lights were hooded. The van was travelling through a dark, deserted world.

All went well until they passed a light which seemed unusually low. Nonetheless it was about the right size and the right shade of red, so they let fly. The response was a yell as the light dropped to the ground and shattered on the pavement. In some bemusement they ground to a halt to investigate. Far from being a traffic light, it had been a red warning lamp carried by a night watchman, who was now clutching his groin and expressing pain and indignation in loud and voluble tones. Thoroughly alarmed, they rushed the poor man round to the local hospital before returning to base, chastened and sober.

The next morning Batchy telephoned the hospital for an up dated bulletin before giving orders to convene a meeting of all officers in the officers' mess that evening. Once he had us all gathered together, he told us we had been very lucky indeed — and so had the watchman. He'd been peppered in the unmentionables, as we already knew from Emanuel and Michael, but by sheer good fortune only very lightly. There was no serious or permanent damage. Just the same, Batchy thought we owed the poor chap more than a mere apology. The appropriate gesture, he suggested, would be a whip-around to raise £100 for the inconvenience he had been caused.

There was a bit of a stunned silence. The sum of £100 was enormous at that time, when fully qualified pilots were paid the equivalent of 70p for a twenty-four-hour day. Nobody felt like arguing, however, and especially not Emanuel or Michael, who correctly felt they were getting off extremely lightly. In due course we heard that the night watchman was delighted and almost went so far as to offer himself for target practice any time one of us might be passing. Here was one incident at least that could have ended in disaster and tragedy but which instead arrived at a relatively light-hearted conclusion.

★ ★ ★

Dear Batchy survived the war, in which I served with him not only at Kenley but also in the Desert Air Force (DAF), where he had command of the mobile operations unit that exercised air control of the DAF fighter wings. He was another, however, who died ahead of schedule. His death was another that could easily have been postponed, except that it would have meant him step ping out of character. As a bachelor, living on his own apart from the elderly housekeeper who looked after him, he developed a minor heart ailment. It was nothing serious — something that could easily have been rectified by seeing a doctor. But seeing doctors was not Batchy's style. It was months, even years, before his housekeeper became alarmed and took it on herself to send for one. Batchy was packed off to hospital at once, but very soon, again entirely in character, he felt he was in danger of dying from boredom and discharged himself. Not long afterwards he died from his heart condition.

I visited him once or twice while he was still in hospital, but the last time I saw him was soon after he had asserted his right to end his days in freedom. I had booked Batchy to be a godfather to my daughter Sam before she was even born, and a few days after her first birthday there came a knock one evening, quite late, on the door of our London flat. I opened the door and there stood Batchy. 'Good evening,' he said. 'I hope my goddaughter's at home. I've brought her a belated birthday present.'

And he handed me a gift-wrapped bottle of single-malt whisky. Batchy was one of the Royal Air Force great originals who truly justified the old cliché, 'a legend in his time'. I felt glad he had stayed in character till the end.

TEN

PROSPECTS OF ITALY

At around Christmas 1942 it was decided I was overdue for an operational rest. I had been continually on operations since the onset of war, and all my operations had been in 11 Group, Fighter Command's front line of defence, apart from the short break in Wales between Dunkirk and the Battle of Britain. My duties had included flight commander, then acting commanding officer of 92 Squadron at Biggin Hill during the Battle of Britain (Fighter Command's top-scoring squadron) before becoming CO of 72 Squadron, also at Biggin Hill, and finally wing leader of the Kenley wing.

The scenario was that I be posted in the New Year to the restful role of observer-cum-adviser at the newly founded Fighter Leaders' School at Chedworth in Gloucestershire. It was a new unit and a new concept, set up by Trafford Leigh-Mallory, the C-in-C of Fighter Command, to train operationally experienced pilots in the art of leadership in the air. Initially I had to go through the course myself in the role of 'guinea pig', and after that I looked forward to a lovely non-executive job with no responsibilities. It was not to be. The school's CO, Wing Commander Paddy Woodhouse, promptly went down with an attack of jaundice. Kingcome, the wrong man in the wrong place at the wrong time, was made acting CO on the spot and took over the arduous task of overseeing the early formative courses that would shape the school's policy and format.

In practice it turned out to be a highly enjoyable and worthwhile posting. The work was interesting and rewarding besides being relatively free from the incessant nagging telephone calls of an operational fighter station. A further bonus was that I was ably and entertainingly assisted by two well-known stable-mates, Pete Simpson, a massive, benign young man, and P. B. 'Laddie' Lucas, back from serving in the Mediterranean on a tour of duty that had included notable exploits during the siege of Malta when he commanded the top-scoring 249 Squadron. Laddie had been famous before the war as an amateur schoolboy golfing champion, and became famous during it as a distinguished fighter pilot who rose from the rank of Aircraftman 2nd class. Fame continued to dog his footsteps after the war, first as a Conservative MP, then as chairman of the Greyhound Racing Association, and finally as the successful author of a dozen or so books, including *Malta: the Thorn in Rommel's Side*. It seemed there never was a time when Laddie wasn't famous. He was also the best of companions and his gift for mimicry enlivened many an evening. In this company the health hazards grew to be considerable. Before long the Fighter Leaders' School moved to Charmy Down in Somerset, from where the 'watering hole' of Bath lay within comfortable drinking distance. Thither we repaired on numerous occasions.

The relaxed, enjoyable life at the school was short-lived and soon ended by the inevitable interruption in the shape of a new posting. This time the finger of destiny was pointing me in the direction of the Desert Air Force (DAF), somewhere in the Middle East. It was decided I should travel by sea rather than air, and the voyage was to form part of my operational rest. Since the Mediterranean was considered too high a risk zone for unescorted shipping, we were routed round South Africa, as was usual at the time. A long, leisurely sea voyage was indicated, with plenty of space for contemplation. Our ship as far as Durban was the SS *Orion*, flagship and pride of the P&O, though as a requisitioned troop carrier she had been stripped of most of the refinements of a massive and stately luxury liner to capitalise on space and take the maximum number of bodies.

It turned out that as a wing commander I was the senior officer on board, which meant, in turn, that I found myself in the position of OC Troops. It was just the sort of grind I could have done without during what was supposed to be a 'rest' trip, but it offered me one important advantage that had to do with the purchase of a razor. For some time in England I had taken to shaving with an electric razor, but if I was going to be living under canvas in the middle of the desert, I now reasoned, then convenient supplies of mains electricity were liable to be rarities. It seemed I had better change my shaving habits. Safety-razor blades were also going to be difficult to come by, no doubt. The obvious way to make myself independent of such logistical problems would be to invest in a 'cut-throat' razor as wielded by such masters of the art of barbering as Sweeney Todd.

Unfortunately I had never used one before, and I realised as soon as I bought the implement that this was no toy to be trifled with. After a certain amount of nervous practice I found I could cope with the right-hand side of my face, though it at once became clear that dealing with the left-hand side was going to take a different technique. In the barbers' shops in the old days they used to give apprentices balloons to practice on, but fate had delivered into my hands something even better. On board we had about a dozen young Australian pilots who were also bound for DAF, and now they would be coming under my command for the voyage.

In the RAF the bonds of friendship formed between our personnel and the volunteers from the Commonwealth and Dominions transcended prejudice as the youth of many continents and creeds worked and flew together. I felt at the time that it all boded well for the future, though sadly my optimism that these values would feed through into the post-war world was not born out by history. During the war there was plenty of name-calling between us, but it was all part of the general banter. We did not sulk when the Australians called us 'Pommy bastards', using the American short 'a' to make it sound worse. The nickname, they explained, derived from the pomegranate fruit, whose pink and white flesh, they claimed, matched the 'girlish' complexion of an

Englishman. Nor did they throw tantrums when we called them 'Bisins', a 'bisin' being what an Australian washes his face in – and this, too, was carefully explained, *touché*!

Luckily the heavy-handed sensitivities of modern-day political correctness were something entirely unknown to us, and so I lined up my young 'bisins' and pointed out to them that they were the only pilots on board apart from myself. I assumed that as such, and especially bearing in mind that they might one day wind up in my wing, they would be keen to co-operate in helping me to solve a small problem. Having won their undivided attention I went on to explain my predicament with the cut-throat razor. In the absence of balloons, I said, I looked forward to them volunteering as guinea-pigs.

There was a slightly stunned silence, but I discretely pulled rank a little while suggesting that compliance could be a shrewd career move on their part. They soon saw the force of my argument and for the first two to three weeks of the voyage I had my volunteers reporting every morning at the door of my cabin, ready for me to go to work on them. In this way it did not take me long to master the technique and so far as I remember I never did anyone an injury. In fact, many years after the war I met one of my former victims at a reunion. He was quite unscarred and recalled the episode with surprising good humour. He said they had regarded it as one of their more unusual duties, quite apart from providing an eye-opener into folk customs in the British armed forces.

During the first half of the trip there came a day when my mind was carried inexorably back to the sad demise of my Clyno car when I was a Cranwell cadet in 1936. We had been steaming southwards down the west coast of Africa and passing the Canaries, and conditions for a tropical cruise could hardly have been bettered. The weather was superb, the seas were calm. The flying fish flew and the tropical heat was tempered by the breeze created by our steady cruising speed of between fifteen and twenty knots. We were in a dream world and the grey clouds, rationed food and general shortages of war-torn Britain hardly seemed to be real any longer. Suddenly the dream was shattered. Somewhere off the Canaries there came about an abrupt change of ambience and atmosphere. We could not think what it was, till suddenly the significance hit us. The engines had stopped.

It was nothing more than this, a simple explanation, yet it was enough to send alarm waves through the ship. As any old sailor can tell you, a boat under way is a living creature – it has a vibrant, unique life-force of which its passengers are scarcely aware. The engines, with their gentle, hardly perceptible murmur and steady vibration, become such of part of daily life that their presence enters the area of unconsciousness. They may as well not exist. Yet as soon as the engines stop the ship dies, transmuted instantly into a sluggishly wallowing corpse, dead in the water. And now they had stopped indeed.

The silence was paralysing, almost palpable. It exactly mirrored the sensation of time ceasing that I had felt as I hung upside down in the wreck of my crashed sports car. We stood and waited wherever we happened to be in the ship, nerves on edge and sensing danger but blind to what it could be or from which direction it might come at us. Then, over the klaxon, sounded the duty officer's abrasive orders: 'Boat stations!' The activity of running to stand by our allotted lifeboats came almost as a relief as we realised what the explanation must be: there were U-boats in the area and the engines had been stopped to reduce any risk of detection.

Many more such alarms and silences were to follow before we reached Cape Town. Fortunately no U-boat ever came close enough to unleash a torpedo in our direction and the incidents grew less frequent the farther south we travelled. But the first few moments of each of those literally shocking silences as the engines closed down without warning were unforgettable to me and they always reactivated the feeling of hanging upside down in a limbo of time. These maritime alarms considerably increased my already keen admiration and respect for the Merchant Navy, and the way its incredibly brave and grossly under-appreciated and unsung band of heroes faced up to the dangers of sea warfare.

At Durban the *Orion* put us ashore before preparing to steam on to the Far East. We transhipped to a small Norwegian passenger boat, a beautiful little vessel with a great crew and marvellous food. There was only one drawback. She had been designed and built for the Arctic Circle, and along the walls of all the cabins and living quarters ran pipes to carry scalding-hot steam from the engine room. There was, it seemed, no way of cutting off the heating without shutting down the engines. As an in-built central-heating system it must have been marvellously cosy when cruising in sub-zero temperatures through the arctic wastes, but it made the ship staggeringly unsuitable for use in the tropics. We made our way up the coast of east Africa towards the Red Sea and the Suez Canal in the early summer, enduring heat that was impossible to describe.

All in all, the journey took the best part of three months, and it was thoroughly enjoyable apart from the sauna-bath conditions of the last leg. My initial destination was Cairo, HQ of the Midlle East Air Forces. From there I was to be dispatched to wherever DAF might be at the time. As yet I knew very little about the Desert Air Force other than that it was a completely mobile, utterly self-contained tactical air group whose task was to support the Eighth Army, and that it was having a very busy time as Rommel and Montgomery were slogging it out in north Africa. It was a tough, independent, battle-hardened group, experienced in mobile warfare and capable of moving anywhere at a moment's notice without interruption to its activities. It laid down the model for the Second Tactical Force (2nd TAF) when it was later formed to support the invasion of northern Europe that began on D Day. Thereafter the DAF became officially known as First Tactical Force, though it never lost its affectionate sobriquet of 'Desert Air Force'.

The official label tied to my posting was 'Supernumerary Wing Commander Flying', which, once translated, meant I would be

attached to a fighter wing in a non-executive flying role pending an appropriate vacancy. Heavy casualties were anticipated in
the operations ahead and 'P' Staff (the postings branch) at the
Air Ministry did not want to be caught short on numbers. As it
happened, this was a factor that worked out in my favour.

★ ★ ★

By the time I caught up with DAF it had arrived in Malta and
was preparing for the invasion of Sicily and Italy. Malta was just
beginning to recover from the poundings it had taken from the
Luftwaffe and, although it was still under a state of siege, creature
comforts seemed in reasonable supply. There were, however, a few
unusual features. The bedroom of my billet, for instance, only
had two walls, the other two having been demolished during
the blitz, against which the island's heroic resistance justly earned
a collective George Cross. There was also half a bathroom, in
which I seized the opportunity to take a leisurely bath on my
first night. A severe ticking off followed. No one had thought
to tell me that Malta had no natural water. Every drop needed
to be brought in by blockade-busting tankers in mortal danger
from sea and air attack, and consequently was jealously hoarded.
Commodities of which there was no shortage, it emerged, were
safety razors and safety blades. I swiftly consigned my 'Sweeney
Todd' to the bin. When, years later, I met the Australian 'bisin'
who had been under my command on the voyage out, I never
had the heart to tell him how the shaving exercise which put at
risk the youthful good looks of him and his comrades had been
a total waste of effort.

I did not have long to wait to shed my 'supernumerary' status.
DAF was commanded at the time by Air Vice-Marshal 'Broady'
Broadhurst (later Air Chief Marshal Sir Harry Broadhurst), a legendary air ace and an outstanding senior commander. He was one
of the few at his level of seniority to have personal operational
experience, but he was also notorious for surrounding himself

with his coterie of people whom he already knew. This is an understandable foible, and few are exempt from it to some degree. It was just that Broady had a reputation for taking it to extremes and for an outsider it became a sort of chicken-and-egg situation. You could only be a member of his charmed circle if you had served under him, and you had to be a member of the charmed circle before he would give you a job in the first place. He and I had met several times in the past, but since I had never served under him I was definitely unqualified to be one of his blue-eyed boys.

Shortly before I reached Malta my old friend Ian Gleed, CO of 244 Wing, was shot down and killed. As a result Broady lost no time in sending for me as soon as he knew I had arrived. 'Brian,' he announced, 'I'm over a barrel. I need a replacement for Ian. Given freedom of choice I wouldn't choose you. Nevertheless you qualify, you are here, and I can't afford to wait. It's only fair to warn you that I shall be watching you closely. If you put a single foot wrong you'll be on the next aircraft back to Blighty.'

I thanked him for the warmth of his welcome, saluted and left the office. Poor old Broady. It was clear his guns had been spiked by 'P' Staff. Knowing what a disappointment this must be for him, I could almost feel sorry for him. The rank of commanding officers of mobile wings had just been upped from wing commander to group captain, so Broady had not only been obliged to hand me an appointment for which anyone would have given their eye-teeth, he had also been unable to avoid including a promotion in the package.

Stepping into dead men's shoes may not sound like the happiest way of climbing the promotional ladder, especially where your predecessor was a friend, as in the case of Ian Gleed. It was probably the commonest way, however, in operational units in war time. The world of the operational pilot was a relatively small one and it was more than likely that any shoes you stepped into were going to be those of a friend or acquaintance. But death in war, even of close friends, was strangely different from death in peace. Abnormal circumstances made the normal abnormal. The peace time death of a friend or relative is usually a deeply disturbing event, but in a general war situation hardly a day passes without news of the death of someone you know. As a result, emotions become curiously detached, is if nature has closed some psychological door in the mind to the contemplation of grief. A typical conversation in a bar or a neighbouring RAF mess would have gone something like this:

'Heard about old Bifi?'

'No, what's he up to, then?'

'Bought it yesterday.'

'Really? What happened?'

'Bounced by some 109s over Calais. Came down in flames.'

'Parachute?'

'No. Leastways, no one saw one.'

'Tough luck. Nice chap. Time for another?'

It would be too easy to dismiss the laconic style as yet another case of stiff upper lip. We all had to find our own ways of protecting ourselves and carrying on.

In the event Broady never fired me. In fact I remained with 244 Wing for almost two years, a long time for an operational posting, and he and I developed an extremely good, understanding relationship. Once he had accepted you he was the ideal boss. His loyalty to his staff was a byword. He let them get on with the job with the minimum interference, but supported them through thick and thin if the need ever arose.

The wing consisted of five Spitfire squadrons. Four were RAF and one was South African. The South African airmen were a mix of Boer and British, and all were volunteers. South African government policy forbade any except volunteers to fight for the Allies abroad, though the effect of this was probably to give us the cream of their talent. They were first class in the air and great company on the ground, the British and Boer elements mingling perfectly cheerfully and involving the usual name-calling banter.

They had one asset in particular that made them especially cherished as members of the wing. Their warm-hearted government had ordained an allocation of free brandy for them, perhaps to help them forget they were volunteers. The brandy was known as 'ish', short or 'free issue', and it arrived in huge wooden casks (forty-gallon barrels, if I remember correctly). The fact that the South Africans possessed a natural generosity of character was a source of great comfort to their fellow-airmen, including their commanding officer.

When I took over as CO, the softening-up process in preparation for the landings on Sicily was well under way. Within a few days we were covering the first wave of landings by the Eighth Army's battle-hardened troops, flying out from our old bases in Malta. There was little resistance, either on the ground or in the air, and after only a couple of days the sappers of the Royal Engineers had scraped a landing-strip at Pachino, on the southernmost tip of the island, and 244 Wing had moved in. It was still winter, and one of the first things I wondered about was whoever had coined the slogan, 'Sunny Italy'. The Italian winters were mainly notable for sitting in a waterlogged tent with the rain drumming on the canvas and the duckboards afloat under one's feet.

DAF's leading role was to provide protection and fighter support for the Eighth Army. Since Second World War armies, unlike those of 1914–18, rarely stood still, mobility was the keynote. We needed to be based as close behind the ground forces as possible, which meant a move of base virtually every time the army advanced or retreated. During my time with 244 I recall eighteen such moves, including the two invasions involving sea crossings, first from Africa into Sicily and then on into Italy. For the aircrews the moves presented no problems. They simply took off from their old base on a normal operational sortie and when it was over landed at the new one. All the work and responsibility fell on the shoulders of the administrative staff, who had developed the process into a fine and disciplined art.

The first task was to locate a new site in the right place and level enough to lay a landing strip 1,200 yards long and wide enough for aircraft to land and take off singly, the regulation size for Spitfire wings. The final choice was jointly agreed between DAF HQ and the Eighth Army, at which point the sappers moved in and, almost within hours, had scraped the surface flat, un rolled their secret weapon known as PSP (pierced steel planking) and hey presto, you had an airfield. PSP consisted of steel planks, pierced with innumerable holes to reduce weight and capable of being coupled together with huge detachable hinges. They could be transported easily and, like mammoth carpets, rolled and unrolled to any required lengths. The system was one of the keys to our astonishing mobility.

To achieve the moves we developed a simple leap-frog action. We would divide ourselves in three, the advance parties consisting mainly of skeleton ground crews and airfield control personnel. They would go ahead and carry enough resources to receive, refuel, rearm and dispatch the aircraft and feed the crews. Within an hour or two of the order being given, the wing itself would be ready for take-off and would continue flying operationally throughout, prepared to land at the new base with mission completed. As soon as the last machine was in the air, the main ground party then began to follow on with the heavy transport and equipment.

It sounds simplicity itself, but it was an enormous logistical challenge to get the right people to the right place at the right time with the right spares and equipment and food to operate the incoming squadrons without a break. More than that, we had to ensure that the main party with its heavy equipment and the bulk of the spares and men arrived safely on schedule after a journey that could be hazardous and complex in the extreme. They often had to traverse shell-holed and bomb-blasted roads, along which the bridges over the gorges and ravines of the spectacular Italian landscape had been destroyed by the retreating enemy.

COs like myself were tempted to puff up our chests and take all the credit, but it was really the achievement of the dedicated and resourceful senior administrative officers (Wing S Ad. Os) who worked with the squadron adjutants and administrative personnel to make it all seem effortless and easy. None of it would have been possible, of course, without the advanced landing strips. The mastermind who oversaw the construction of most of 244 Wing's was Freddie Keeble, a major in the Royal Engineers. There is an old adage in the film industry, which happened to be one of my various 'life after the Second World War' reincarnations, that says be careful how you treat colleagues on your way up, you may meet them again on your way down. In another post-war reincarnation I and my wife created and ran a company called Kingcome Design. We specialised in manufacturing individually crafted sofas and chairs to sell to the interior design trade as well as to the public.

It was important for us to become members of the IDDA, the Interior Designers' and Decorators' Association, since we hoped to display our wares at that organisation's annual exhibition. Therefore we braced ourselves for a gruelling interview with its president, reportedly a fierce, acerbic guardian dragon who was determined to prevent inferior fringe operators wheedling their way on to his membership list. This awesome elemental, who vengefully stalked the esoteric jungles of the design world to eject intruders, turned out to be no less a person than my old comrade in arms and sapper, Major Freddie Keeble, RE. In our service days we always got on well, and happily the relationship carried over into the temperamental world of interior design.

It was fortunate for us that it did, for Freddie's support and advice were invaluable in the suspicious, jealous, volatile and temperamental mêlée in which we found ourselves. We later discovered that Keeble & Sons, the interior design and decorating business owned and run by Freddie, had been formed by a direct ancestor in 1686, two years, as he liked to tell us, before Hoare's Bank. They opened an account with the bank, and had been with it ever since, while Keeble & Sons has been owned and run by a direct line of the family down to the present day. There cannot be many enterprises able to boast as much, and Freddie's inherited skills in technology and management had found an outlet in the utterly different context of the Allied Italian campaign.

Our advance across Sicily and into Italy might have seemed a romp had it not been for several tragedies that tore gashes in the blanket impersonality of war. The first was when we were on the hunt for a landing-strip site and came across evidence of the aftermath of a brave but failed landing of glider units by the Airborne Division on the east coast by Catania. Bodies and broken gliders littered the coastal fields and beeches, providing a salutary reminder that war is not all fun. The second was being blitzed by the Luftwaffe one brilliantly moonlit night, when we were bombed and strafed from low level. The attack seemed to last the entire night, but it can only have gone on for twenty to thirty minutes. We lost far too many men and machines, even though our practice of dispersing as widely as possible saved worse casualties.

It was a deeply disquieting experience that brought home to me the astonishing fortitude of the civilian population, always at the receiving end and always helpless to strike back. It was too easy to become detached and complacent when you were sitting in the comparative safety of the cockpit of a single-seater fighter and watching it all happen on the ground far below. You were in real danger of growing aloof from the dreadful human tragedies and the suffocating frustration of the helpless victim that were the daily norm in life for so many. The mini-blitz on our airfield was a comparative flea-bite, but to be jerked back to facing reality was, as always, a timely experience.

I could never understand why the Luftwaffe did not repeat such targeting of airfields more often. The tactic was extremely effective and could have made some significant differences in the tide of war. The Eighth Army would have been hamstrung without its air cover, but the Germans, just as they had during the Battle of Britain, when the savage blows they were dealing against

RAF in their blitz of the airfields came close to being mortal, changed both tactics and targets. This air raid in Sicily was the only time 244 Squadron was attacked on the ground during the whole of the Sicilian and Italian campaign.

Two other incidents during the Sicilian phase were of an even more personal and disturbing kind. The first came when one of my Spitfire pilots crashed just inside the British lines after being shot up in a sweep over the island. He survived the crash, but was trapped in the cockpit of his aircraft, which then caught fire. A group of soldiers did their best to free him until they were driven back by the flames, and the pilot, powerless to escape the agonising death he saw roaring implacably towards him, implored them to shoot him. Faced with the alternative of turning their backs and leaving him to burn, one finally levelled his rifle and fired. It was a terrible responsibility and an act of supreme moral courage. Even for a battle-hardened soldier inured to killing it must have left a lasting scar. It was also a tragic end for a promising young pilot. I have always felt grateful that this mercy-killing sentence was not mine to approve or execute.

The other involved Jackie Darwin, the CO of a neighbouring wing of Kittyhawks, the American-designed and built fighter bombers in use with the DAF. Jackie was granted a few days' leave in London to get married, and went to celebrate with his new wife at the famous night-spot of the Café de Paris in Piccadilly. As they danced slowly to the quiet, romantic tempo of the times, immersed in one another and their happiness, swaying gently to the music of 'Snakehips' Johnson and his band, the air-raid sirens sounded and the Café de Paris received a direct hit.

The carnage was appalling. Many were killed, including Snakehips, but Jackie was unscathed and protectively clutched his wife of a few hours amid the roaring chaos, the debris and the crashing masonry. Suddenly she sagged in his arms. She had been pierced by a flying fragment and died as he held her. Jackie returned to his fighter-bomber wing, to all appearances unchanged, but his will to live had died with his wife.

Meanwhile his urge for revenge was very much alive. He undertook every possible operation, ran more and more risks, went after more and more difficult targets and pressed home his attacks at lower and lower levels. He was brilliantly success-ful and seemed to lead a charmed life. But his immortality was an illusion and the inevitable happened. I always felt that when Johnnie finally saw Old Man Death moving in, his scythe already on the down-swing, he would have stepped into the sweep of the murderous blade with a welcoming smile.

★ ★ ★

The final stage of the three months or so we were in Sicily passed uneventfully. There was still enough enemy air activity to keep the wing on its toes, but my main memories are of flying around the crater of Mount Etna as she grumbled away in her usual style, and peering down her fiery throat at the obscenities she habitually gargled with before spitting them high into the air as red-hot boulders and ash. I also remember a lovely house that lay directly on the beach at Taomina, a beautiful, compact, quiet resort where the slopes of Etna reached steeply down to the sea. After the war I came to know the English owner of the house and was glad to hear he had recovered it and found it still in good shape.

By now, in the summer of 1943, the Germans were definitely on the run. The whole operation took on the feel of a beautifully organised adventure holiday. The heady scent of victory com-bined with the summer heat, the scenery, the local wines and the informality of life under canvas in fields of maize. My personal creature comforts were ministered to by a master prestidigitator in the shape of my batman, Corporal Bottell. He had been a docker in Civvy Street and was a most effective scavenger.

As a rule there was all too little contact between the forces and the locals. It was a fact I regretted, but we were self-equipped and self-supporting and therefore did not need them; while they, as citizens of a recently defeated nation, were understandably wary and suspicious. Corporal Bottell, on the other hand, saw things differently. He was one of the few servicemen in Sicily to learn the local lingo, which he picked up surprisingly quickly, and he was a natural entrepreneur. He would disappear with a tin or two of bully beef and some cigarettes and reappear with chickens, sucking pigs, wine, cameras and various local luxuries. Nor was it in his nature to think small. One day he turned up with the Italian version of a double-decker bus, in which one deck was towed behind the other instead of sitting on top of it.

Where he obtained this vehicle or what he used as a trade-in I never did discover. Knowing him, I doubt whether the bargain would have involved more than a couple of hundred cigarettes. At a calculated guess he probably got it from a neighbourhood scallywag who had stolen it in the first place and made a fat profit, while it no doubt started out in life as the property of the local Fascist administration, keen to have the buses running on time. It looked like fair game, in my view.

I concerned myself no further with the ethics. Meanwhile Corporal Bottell presented me with his prize and the Royal Engineers offered their services. The front of the vehicle was swiftly converted into extremely comfortable sleeping quarters with a ninety-gallon overload Spitfire fuel tank on the roof supplying water for a shower. The rear section of the vehicle was transformed into a half-office, half-bar. Needless to say I became an instant object of envy among the other RAF wings. No more sleeping in waterlogged tents for me.

ELEVEN

WINDING DOWN

After we left Sicily our first stop on the Italian mainland was at Bari, north along the coast from Brindisi. I flew in ahead of our advance party to scout the ground and was met at the landing strip by an old friend, Dudley Honor. He was stationed with DAF's advance HQ and had been asked to collect me in his jeep so I could be briefed. Dudley was an Argentinean of massive personality and appetite who possessed wit and charm, though his skills as a driver were of the kind that defy the laws of nature. Ahead of us across a landscape of flat fields there ran a dead-straight road, or rather track, with a loose surface. Dudley accelerated from a standing start and, as the road worsened, went ever faster. The jeep began to dance on the loose surface, and the more it danced the faster Dudley drove. Jeeps are marvellous little creatures that feel as safe as the mechanised roller-skates they resemble, yet they have a very short wheel-base and can show sudden fits of temperament in conditions they dislike.

Here was a case in point. Faster and faster drove Dudley, higher and higher danced the jeep, till suddenly it had had enough. With no warning it uttered a final screech, leapt high in the air, shot off the road and rolled over several times, having fired me out like a bullet to land on my face in the middle of the bordering field. For a while I lay too dazed to move, which turned out to be a stroke of good fortune. I had been deposited between two rows of mines wired in such a way that if one blew they all blew. I never could remember being extricated, but the Sappers came to my rescue and worked their miracles. My face was badly lacerated, but fortunately no bones were broken, though as I had lain there, trying to recover my wits, my mind had flickered back seven years to make me yet again that Cranwell cadet, lying in a shattered Clyno and listening to the first of these now familiar, deafening silences.

As the Eighth Army's steady advance through Italy continued, we zigzagged dutifully, protectively behind it. Occasionally the top brass used my landing strip for high-level meetings between senior commanders. At these my function was merely to be host. One such meeting included Generals Alexander and Montgomery, with the flamboyant American General Patton in attendance on a fact-finding mission, his famous twin pearl-handled revolvers dangling 'Lone Ranger' style from the holsters on his belt. Patton's exhibitionism went down less well with his peers than it did with the public.

Montgomery, though he also had a flair for publicity, needed to work hard for his authority. In this he was unlike Alexander, to whom authority came naturally. Alexander commanded instinctive respect by his quiet, courteous personality rather than by forcing rank, whereas Montgomery was not the type to form warm personal bonds. His habit of publicly humiliating those he deemed to be overweight or otherwise too self-indulgent to match his Spartan standards is well known. On the other hand, he inspired a ferocious loyalty and affection among the troops he commanded. Once I sat next to him in an RAF Dakota from Italy to Cairo. The flight took several hours, and he occupied the whole time with hand-writing personal letters. I peeped as unobtrusively as possible, and saw they were all to wives or parents of his men. 'Hah! A publicity stunt,' the cynical may say. Perhaps, but whatever the motivation, he spent a great deal of time, and went to a lot of trouble, to give many people pleasure and reassurance. Like Churchill, Montgomery was, despite his many critics, the right man to occupy his moment in history.

After we had crossed the great plains of Foggia to Cassibile, just north of Naples, we found ourselves close to one of Mussolini's winter palaces, from the balcony of which he had delivered many of his histrionic speeches to his captive audiences. Not far to the south Mount Vesuvius chose this moment to put on one of its most bravura performances. Whereas Etna had been a grumbling, spitting virago, her big brother Vesuvius became a berserk monster, raging and hurling himself against the alarmingly yielding bars of his cage, the fragile crust of the earth. He bellowed, he roared, he pounded. Huge manifestations of his anger were sent soaring impossibly high into the upper air. The power unleashed was unspeakable. On a number of occasions I circled above the crater and, from an altitude of over 15,000ft, gazed down into an inferno beyond the dreams of Dante as I dodged red-hot boulders the size of double-decker buses.

There was a surprising number of farmsteads and small settlements on the scarred and shifting slopes of both Vesuvius and Etna, and the inhabitants showed an amazing reluctance to move away, even as the very ground beneath their feet stirred and rumbled. I had always imagined that the huge releases of ash and lava would pour down the slopes in molten torrents. In fact they pushed, shoved and slipped their way irresistibly forward in vast smoking piles, twenty to thirty feet high and varying in colour from white hot to red. Sometimes they parted mysteriously before a homestead and circled safely by; sometimes they parted and passed but then closed over behind; sometimes they simply rolled straight over. They followed no rules.

The Eighth Army had little time to spend on the wonders of nature. It steadily forged its way forward, as relentless and unstoppable as the smoking lava piles of Vesuvius. The one serious pause came at Monte Cassino, the ancient fortified monastery high on a hill that commanded the valley that was the gateway to Rome. The monastery was bombed and shelled till its massive walls, towers and turrets were rubble, yet the resistance put up by the Germans was heroic and extraordinary. The ancient dungeons and cellars were dug so deep that the German guns, safe from air attack and able to fire through openings in the mountain's flank, remained untouched and continued to dominate the valley against all the odds.

Eventually Cassino succumbed, and after that I remember only two minor breaks to our forward momentum. Anzio was one and the other was the invasion of southern France, Churchill's 'soft underbelly of the Axis', at Le Lavendou. Anzio was a disaster, intended as a 'left hook' to establish a bridgehead behind enemy lines and speed the capture of Rome. The operation was badly planned, and it failed, and although it gave us a few exciting moments these were not worth the tragic waste of life and effort. The invasion of southern France, on the other hand, went as smoothly as an exercise. Distance was the only problem. We were based at the time on the west coast, opposite the island of Elba, where the captive Napoleon had successfully planned and executed his escape. To cover the Lavendou landings and return to base our short-range Spitfires needed to carry ninety-gallon over load tanks, unwieldy monsters that virtually doubled the Spitfire's range but bore a heavy penalty. You would certainly be dead unless you succeeded in jettisoning the tank before an engagement. This meant that if you were bounced by the enemy on your way to a target, then you must either abort the rest of the escort and head for home or else resign yourself to passing the point of no return. In the event there was no hostile air activity at Lavendou and, as far as I could see, virtually no resistance on the ground. The landing achieved its objectives and passed peacefully into history.

At one point in 1944 when I was back in London on a short leave I ran into Paddy Byrne, who had finally managed to persuade the German prison authorities that he was mad. After being shot down over Dunkirk he had spent the next three to four years acting erratically, rubbing soap into his eyes and mouth to create an impressive red-eyed foaming effect and generally playing schoolboy tricks that you would have thought too obvious to fool anyone, even the Prussian guards. Some might have said he was a genuine case as a crazy Irishman, but whatever the cause he won his repatriation as part of some obscure Anglo-German agreement on the exchange of prisoners of war.

We spent a few hectic days together as I helped him to adjust to freedom and the availability of alcohol in the bars and clubs that had sprung up in wartime London since his departure. His great frustration was that he had reported to the Air Ministry the moment he hit town, but 'P' Staff had turned him down for a job. 'Sorry, old man,' they said. 'Afraid we can't use you. You're mad, the Germans say so. Look, we've had a letter.'

In vain Paddy protested that his madness had only been a ploy, an act to get himself home, and that in truth he was as sane as anyone. The Air Ministry remained adamant. It never emerged whether their refusal to re-employ him followed from a genuine belief in his madness or was only because of the terms of the Anglo-German agreement on repatriation. Paddy left the RAF, settled down, married and became a property owner after the war. He bought up swathes of Chelsea and let out his houses to the homeless and needy at rents far below the viable market rates. Eventually he died, a strange, loveable, memorable man.

Back with the Eighth Army in Italy, it was possible even to feel a little pity for the Germans at times, especially in the light of the fighting styles of some of the units of many nationalities and races on the Allied side. Among these were the Ghoums from French Morocco, a colourful race of ruthless warriors who travelled behind the front lines with wagonloads of wives, camp followers, children and animals. They preferred to work by night and their interest was mainly financial. They were paid, as it were, by the scalp – or, to be more accurate, by the ear. They were not above the obvious dodge of trying to claim a double payment for two ears from the same head, which meant the paying-out officer needed to keep a sharp check on whether the ears submitted were either left or right ones. The Ghoums became notorious for the rape and pillage they inflicted on the civilian population, who had never done anything to deserve such further suffering.

Even more deadly and feared in the field of battle were the famous Gurkhas, those slight, brown, cheerful people of the mountains and foothills of Nepal. The night was also their special province, as they ghosted silently in the dark, keen to blood their kukri, the terrifying double-edged knife that is to a Gurkha like an extension of his arm. It seemed they had the gift of invisibility, and no one, friend or foe, would be aware of their presence until suddenly an arm came around the throat and mouth to choke off all sound while another hand swiftly felt the shape of the helmet to identify its nationality. Tithe helmet was Allied, then the arm would withdraw and its owner disappear as soundlessly as he had arrived. If it was Axis, then the *kukri* would silently and skilfully remove both head and helmet. They had an unnerving effect on our own troops, so heaven knows what they did to the nerves of the Germans.

The Gurkhas were as famous for their disarming sense of humour as they were for their fighting skills. One incident that they found richly rewarding occurred on a dark and moonless night during the siege of Monte Cassino when a Gurkha patrol came across a German gun emplacement as its crew of eight slept soundly around their weapon. Silently they sliced off the heads of seven of the crew and arranged them in a neat circle around the eighth, whom they spared to continue his peaceful slumber. Then they melted away into the darkness. It is beyond my reach to imagine the reaction of the sleeper or the look on his face when he woke in the morning to find himself the focus of his seven comrades' sightless, unblinking eyes. The experience must have haunted his dreams to the end of his days.

As the beautiful cities, towns and villages of Italy fell one by one to the Allies, it was usually without significant resistance. Happily this also meant there was very little damage. Rome, Florence, Sienna, Assisi, Venice – the very stuff of legend. 'What was more, we had these places to ourselves. No tourists, no visitors, no holidaymakers. The streets, bars and restaurants were quiet and the population was wary but anxious to please.

Italy certainly had moments of overwhelming beauty to offer. In the hot summer sunshine the ancient buildings gave off a golden mellow glow, but even in winter one could take off under a cheerless grey blanket of cloud, climb through its sodden vapours and suddenly break through into dazzling sunshine. The effect was breathtaking as the dazzling white sheet spread out below, hiding the lower ground while ancient fortified castles perched in what seemed impossible situations along the peaks of the mountain range that formed Italy's spinal column. It was so profoundly, so absurdly beautiful that I would sit spell-bound in the cockpit.

All good things have to come to an end, alas. By the run up to Christmas 1944 we were based on a landing strip a mile or two inland from the Adriatic coastal resort of Rimini, close to the Yugoslav border. The Italian campaign was set to rumble on for another six months till VE Day, but it was as good as in the bag. At this point my own participation came to an abrupt end in the wake of an official visit from the Deputy Commander-in-Chief of the Mediterranean and Allied Air Forces (MAAF), Air Chief Marshal Sir John Slessor. He took me aside. 'Kingcome,' he said, 'I've been looking at your record. I see that your entire service career has been spent with operational single-seater fighters. Your horizon is obviously limited. I don't even know if you can write. I intend to find out. I'm sending you to Palestine, to the RAF Staff College at Haifa, and we'll see what they have to say about you.'

I had heard a lot about Jack Slessor, all of it good, but this first meeting with him left me stunned and full of thoughts that were uncharitable in the extreme. Yet with hindsight Slessor was right and it was high time I moved on. In any job in the hot seat – and especially in war – it is possible to stay put too long. You lose your edge without being aware of it. Most certainly I had grown stale. The campaign had degenerated into an enjoyable way of life so far as I was concerned, the job had become routine, all its excitement and challenge dissipated. The wing ran itself on well oiled wheels, thanks to the dedication and skills of the administrative staff, while the flying was equally well organised by Hugh 'Cocky' Dundas, my Wing Commander flying. I had brought the fine art of delegation to the point where I was little more than a figurehead. I doubt whether these were precisely the thoughts that prompted Jack Slessor, but his decision was the right one both for me and 244 Wing.

I had no hesitation in lending my weight to supporting the proposal that Hugh Dundas be my successor, or indeed to recommending him for another decoration to add to his collection. He had made a first-class wing commander flying, and, as the enemy air effort diminished and all but disappeared, was largely responsible for the introduction of a fighter-bomber role to augment our original unvarnished fighter duties. Nearly six and half feet tall, with a deceptively laid-back charm, Cocky also combined an iron-willed ambition with courage and humour. The nickname 'Cocky', he explained, had been acquired when he joined 616 Squadron as a pupil pilot in 1939. It was bestowed on him by another legend among fighter pilots, Teddy St Aubyn, because he looked like 'a bloody great Rhode Island Red'.

Cocky's qualities helped him to carve out a distinguished civilian career after the war, though he got off to a false start working on the *Daily Express*. The paper was still under the iron control of the first Lord Beaverbrook with his elder son, Max Aitken, being groomed as successor. Max and Cocky had shared one or two fairly outrageous adventures during the war, so Cocky was delighted, as he told me, to find himself doing a stint, first in the paper's Edinburgh office and then in Fleet Street as Ephraim Hardcastle, the gossip columnist. All was going well, it seemed, till one day he happened to pass Beaverbrook in a corridor and said, 'Good morning, sir.' The great man ignored him and Cocky, somewhat disconcerted, went to see Max.

'Don't worry,' said Max. 'You know what the old man's like. He'll have been thinking of something else – probably didn't even see you.' Reassured, Cocky returned to his column. A week or so later he passed Max Aitken in the same corridor and said, 'Good morning, Max.' Max ignored him. The next week Cocky was fired.

This setback made a good dinner-table story over the years, but ultimately it accelerated Cocky's progress since he went into television and in time became chairman of the BET (British Electric Traction) Group and Thames Television and finally received a knighthood for services to industry.

★ ★ ★

The tale of the rest of my own service career can quite soon be told. It was an astonishing experience at the RAF Staff College in Haifa to find myself living where there was no rationing of food or petrol and no black-out. I was there till January 1945, when Slessor interviewed me again and said how gratified he was to find I could indeed write, but as I had never held a staff appointment, he continued, he now proposed to make me senior air staff officer to a bomber group. How did I like the sound of that?

Frankly, in my innermost thoughts, the answer was not at all, and my innermost instincts turned out to be correct. The posting to 205 Bomber Group at Foggia, in southern Italy, proved to be a shattering experience. For one thing, the bomber crews and I did not even speak the same language in airmen's terms. In an attempt to find out what it was all about I went on a couple of trips as an air gunner, and each time wished I hadn't. It was quite beyond me to know how the boys in the bombers had stood it and I came to appreciate my luck in having been in fighter aircraft. The war of the fighter pilot was a truly lovely experience compared with theirs, which struck me as suicidally dangerous.

I was just getting the hang of the bombing scene at last when the war in Europe ended and our Lancasters and Liberators were converted into troop carriers to repatriate troops from the Allied armies to their homes all over the world. We were transferred to Egypt to operate from three airfields close to the Suez Canal and the Great Bitter Lake. It represented a return to the lotus life, swimming in the lake and generally lazing between visits to the flesh-pots of Cairo, Heliopolis and Alexandria.

Those of us who had been overseas for several years were subject to powerful pregnant urges for an occasional home comfort, and high on my list came the humble kipper. It should have been a happy day when a girlfriend sent me out a box of kippers from England, but alas, the kippers themselves did not enjoy their long hot journey through the Middle East. We were sure we had been able to smell them even when the carrier aircraft was still circling the airfield at 2,00ft. It was a tragedy. We gave the fish a decent funeral after the briefest period of mourning.

Also included in the parcel had been a bottle of hair shampoo, which somebody later spotted in my room. The fact took a lot of living down that I was using, or even contemplating using, a special soap for my hair instead of the standard block of regulation issue with its unforgettable emery-board text and pungent anti-septic smell. The generation of young men who came to the fore in the 1960s, with their peacock styles — earrings and medallions, shirts open to the naval at the dinner table, hair teased and patted into shape in public — never ceased to fill me with wonder. I realised how they were, in their own way, a return to the Regency bucks of the 1800s, but the speed and extent of the change from our no-nonsense haircuts and sober suits of the 1940s and 1950s was bewildering. For myself, the old habits died hard. I never could bring myself even to look in the mirror in a barber's shop, and have always waved away the hand-mirror he holds to the back of my head to show off his handiwork. In the later era there was no mistaking the culture gap.

In the spring of 1946 I was posted to Zeltweg in Austria to take command of 324 Wing, and so found myself back with the Desert Air Force and Spitfires. Zeltweg was a comfortable, permanent airfield, built by the Austrians before the war and enhanced and modernised during it by the Germans, who used Allied prisoners of war in the work of laying down the new runways. As I discovered after the war, these forced labourers had included my local fishmonger, and I was able to congratulate him on his workman ship from personal knowledge. I lived at Zeltweg in the greatest comfort in the former quarters of the Luftwaffe commandant, and for the enhancement of my leisure hours had access to a stable of a dozen horses and unbelievable fishing in the lakes and rivers of the surrounding mountains. Vienna was twenty minutes' flying in one direction, Venice not much more in the other, and it seemed there was nothing that could not be bought for a packet of cigarettes.

Yet again it was too good to last, of course. Just as the snows were beginning to fall at Zeltweg and I was looking forward to a few months of skiing, my nemesis Sir John Slessor stepped in once more and I was posted back to England. For the next two years I became an instructor ('Directing Staff' was the official title) at the RAF Staff College at Bracknell. The duties involved bouts of intensely hard work, and there was a lot that was of interest in the lecture programmes, which made it enjoyable in a masochistic sort of way.

One entertaining interlude came when I renewed my acquaintance with the Anson aircraft, by then close to being totally obsolete. I borrowed one of the machines from the college's communications flight to get to a lunch party at an RAF base somewhere or other, and took along with me an American pilot, Colonel Montgomery, who was a student on the course and had become a good friend. After the lunch, at which we over-indulged ourselves shamelessly, we set course for home in a convivial frame of mind that anticipated no cause for alarm. But no sooner had we reached normal cruising height and begun to sail serenely than both engines stopped without warning. I looked around below for a suitable field to land in and was gliding down on a final approach when both engines started up again with equal suddenness. Counting my blessings I climbed laboriously back to cruising height and set course, only to have exactly the same thing happen again. Both engines cut out completely and down we sailed, but both magically restarted as I was about to touch down. We must have gone through this routine another three or four times before the penny finally dropped. Monty was sitting in the second pilot's chair with the two fuel cocks just beside his knee farthest away from me. While my attention was engaged else where he had been shutting them down and reopening them at the last moment. Once we had that little bit of horseplay sorted out the rest of the journey passed uneventfully.

At no time did the transition from active to peacetime service present an easy adjustment. There was a stage when I tried to resign my commission, but this was turned down on the grounds that, as an ex-Cranwell cadet, I still owed my country a return on the investment it had made in training me. After Bracknell there followed a further two years at the Air Ministry itself, working in the Air Staff Policy branch, which was concerned with a range of tasks that included briefing the Chiefs of Staff. As such appointments went it was not a bad one, and it brought with it insights about what goes on in the corridors of power. It came to an end in September 1950 when I contracted tuberculosis, a consequence of my bachelor life in London, drinking but seldom eating, never observing a sensible bedtime, never doing any of the things one ought to do to assure a healthy life.

When I was finally discharged from hospital in June 1953 I was short of a lung and had engraved on my brain the name of a young doctor whose incompetence had ensured my stay in the sanatorium was many months longer than it need have been. The RAF granted me indefinite leave to decide whether to stay on or to opt out. At least as a result of my 'attributable' disease I now had such an entitlement if I wished to exercise my freedom of choice. But after three years in hospital, with every decision being made for me, I had grown incapable of making up my mind, and so I dithered for six months while compensating for lost time in the pubs and clubs.

One day, as I was drinking in Les Ambassadeurs, I was hailed by an American voice. It turned out to belong to Sy Bartlett, whom I had met in England during the war when he was an aide to General Spaatz. Sy had recently written with Bernie Lay Jnr the script, based on their novel, for an extremely successful movie, *Twelve O'Clock High*. Produced by Darryl F. Zanuck and directed by Henry King, it starred Gregory Peck and told the story of a

US bomber group operating under severe psychological pressure. Now Sy had been sent to England by 20th Century Fox to get together the script for another. Several drinks later I had agreed to be his assistant, and on the same afternoon I went to the Air Ministry to hand in my resignation. The film that emerged was a disaster, but the decision was one I never regretted.

* * *

My father had been due to retire when the war started, but at the request of his firm he stayed on till it ended, finally arriving home in the late 1940s. All his home leaves had been taken in the summer months and so, for the first time in forty years, he experienced an English winter. Remarkably he came through a series of winters unscathed, but then the inevitable happened and he caught pneumonia. His first bout of illness left him with severely damaged lungs, and the second bout was even worse. The wonder drug penicillin was by now in general use, but as luck would have it he was allergic to it.

I was with him the evening he died in 1957, and remember with shame my lack of compassion, my feeling almost of impatience at what seemed his passive acceptance of approaching death. I could not understand how he could lie there quietly and allow his life to ebb away without resistance, apparently resigned to the final curtain. What was it I expected? Visible evidence of a fight against the odds? Certainly it was something more than this stoical acceptance of what to me was the unacceptable.

It is difficult for the young and healthy to understand how, if suffering is prolonged and deep enough, then a point is reached where the instinctive urge to survive is sapped and drained. Despite having lived with death as a close companion for so long, I never paused to ponder the miserable quality of life left him by his ruined lungs or to ask myself whether, in his position, I would have felt it worth while to hang on to the sorry shreds of existence that remained to him. I kept urging him to fight and not to give in, forgetting I was talking to a man who had been a fighter all his life, who had never given in, who was far stronger and more courageous than I could ever be − a family man with the fortitude to deny himself a family life and to live separated from wile and children for forty years in the belief that it was in his children's best interests.

I also forgot the enormous courage he had shown during the last few years of his retirement as he stubbornly fought the exhausting and diminishing disability of his destroyed lungs. Every move he made, even getting up from a chair, had been an ordeal for which he had needed to steel himself beforehand, knowing that the tiniest physical effort could take him to the brink of suffocation. Through it all he never complained, all the while trying to pretend that nothing untoward was happening as he clutched at the back of a chair and apologised for being a bore, desperately anxious not to be a nuisance. Even on his deathbed he continued to try to smile encouragement at me while apologising yet again for causing so much trouble. Yet the smile was a smile of farewell, twisted and almost a grimace, an expression I could never forget.

During the years that followed his death I came to realise the immense stoicism and courage he had shown all his life. I also knew how much more support and strength I might have given him towards the end. I failed him when he most needed me, and my failure had diminished me. But in the event it was Father who had the last laugh.

We decided that his body should be cremated in London and the ashes sent to the family grave at Noss Mayo, the tiny south Devon village with its harbour on the upper reaches of the river Yealm and its church whose graveyard overflows with Kingcomes. It came about that the day most convenient for all members of the family to attend the internment fell during the annual holiday of the vicar of Noss Mayo. No problem, said that worthy cleric. His place would be taken by a locum who was familiar with the parish and who would conduct the simple service on his behalf.

Accordingly I arranged for the ashes to be delivered to Noss Mayo in good time and turned my mind to other matters.

The day arrived, and the family assembled in the church in Devon at the appointed time, and waited... and waited. I was about to go in search of the stand-in vicar when he appeared, a flustered young man in a high state of nervous tension, and beckoned me to join him outside. 'Do you have the ashes?' he asked.

I looked at him in astonishment. No, of course not. They were not something one carried about with one after all. The London undertakers had delivered them to Noss Mayo a week ago at least. 'Well,' he said, 'I've searched high and low and can't find them anywhere. Could you check with the undertakers and make sure there's been no error?'

Noss Mayo church is perched high above the village and a steep flight of steps cut into the hillside leads down to the harbour. At the harbour there is a public phone box. The day was a broiling hot Saturday in June which happened to coincide with the Noss Mayo annual regatta – the reason, no doubt, for the wily old incumbent clergyman to choose that time for his holidays. Duty bound I descended the steps and breasted my way through the en fête village throngs – the visiting yachtsman and holidaymakers whose festive spirits and carnival clothes contrasted utterly with my sombre funeral garb. Long-distance telephoning in those days was still an adventure in itself, but eventually I managed to get through to the undertakers' office and was relieved to find there was still someone there, despite it being a Saturday afternoon. Undertaking is a round-the-clock business, after all.

They went away to check and discovered yes, there was no doubt about it, the ashes had been dispatched on a date leaving ample time for them to have arrived. They should have been there some days ago. Tell the vicar to take another look. Back up the precipitous steps I toiled, sweat pouring down my body. At the top I found the agitated locum still fluttering helplessly. There was no point in having another look, he said exasperatedly. He had searched everywhere. How had the ashes been sent?

This was a question I had never thought to ask. I had simply assumed that there must be some appropriately reverential method of transporting human remains, even in the form of ashes. Beyond that I had given the matter no thought at all. Down the cliff steps I went once more, and through the cavorting crowds I battled my way, an incongruous figure feeling like a carrion crow that had accidentally strayed into a sanctuary for exotic tropical birds. The undertakers seemed surprised by my question. 'They went by post, of course,' they said. 'How else?'

I was staggered. Human remains by post? 'Were they registered?' I asked.

'Of course not,' came the reply. 'Never found it necessary. 'Who's going to want to steal someone's ashes?'

The thought was mind-numbing: the human remains of one's nearest and dearest done up in brown paper and string and sent off through the Royal Mail in a sack with a mundane jumble of other parcels. Then, having got over the initial shock, I found I began to like the idea. It seemed to bring death down to a manageable, earthy, common-sense level, altogether more friendly and natural. It sent a breath of fresh air into the artificial, uncomforting ritual of disposing of earthly remains and even relieved some of the pain by its very matter-of-factness. I gasped my way back up the steps, my funeral rig stained and crumpled with sweat. This time the vicar threw in the towel. There was nowhere else he could look, he declared. The matter would just have to await the return of the resident priest. The funeral party members would have to disperse to their various homes and await the solution to the mystery.

The first thing the incumbent vicar of Noss Mayo had to deal with on his return from holiday was a phone call from me. He was astonished. 'But didn't he look in the top left-hand drawer of my desk?' he asked. 'It's where I always keep the ashes of the departed. He should have known that. Hold on a moment while I take a peek myself.'

And there, it goes without saying, they were. A new date was set, the family gathering was reconvened, and this time the ceremony went off without a hitch. But the predominant impression of my old man's internment will for me always be the visions I had of him, freed at last from the agony of his oxygen-starved lungs, clutching his celestial sides and heaving with heavenly mirth at the spectacle of his son toiling up and down that wretched cliff in a heatwave. It is a thought I have always found strangely comforting.

TWELVE

HEADLINES

Over the years my mind had often gone back to 1940 and an image of myself dangling from a parachute as, escaped from my shot-up Spitfire, I descended towards the fields of southern England. Always this sets me wondering again about the three Spitfires that had pulled up beside me before I bailed out. Could they have been the ones who shot me down? Certainly I had seen no sign of any other air activity in the vicinity, but this was not beyond doubt in itself. Even if it had been conclusive, I harboured no grudge and blamed myself for my idiocy in letting myself go into a reverie while someone crept up on my tail and opened fire. There were no excuses and I deserved what I got. Yet if it had been those Spitfires it would have been unusually careless and lackadaisical of them, to say the least. They were alone in the sky and would have had ample time to identify me.

Identifying friend from foe was very different and a very real problem in the chaotic action of an all-out dogfight. Spitfires, Hurricanes and the Messerschmitt 109 all shared various similarities of design when viewed from certain angles. This was especially the case between the Hurricane and the Messerschmitt, and when a target presented itself for no more than a fleeting second in the heat of conflict it was all too easy to let off a quick burst at the wrong aircraft. At that time we did not yet have the grotesque euphemism of 'friendly fire' to try to explain away unfortunate accidents of this kind. Moreover, such things were not always done accidentally. I knew of one case where an unpopular Spitfire pilot had been shot down deliberately by members of his own squadron. More than twenty years after the war an indiscretion with this knowledge landed me in hot water.

In 1969, at about the time of man's first landing on the moon, the film called *The Battle of Britain* received its premiere. It emerged as more or less a dramatised documentary of that phase of the air war, and if it was never the success it might have been, then this was because it tried too hard to offend nobody. Fences were still being mended between the United Kingdom and Western Germany and many bereaved parents of pilots killed in the battle were still alive. The producers had an almost impossible task. As a result of their efforts not to tread on any toes, the film became too impersonal and the emotion and excitement essential to creating high drama were both missing. Other than depictions of the top brass, no convincing characters were portrayed, and the individual pilots, ground crews and operational staff were represented by actors playing composite roles.

As the night of the London premiere drew near it was realised that public interest was barely honing up to lukewarm. To try to boost the situation it was decided to mount a PR exercise during the run-up. Each day for a week one of the actors playing a symbolic aircrew would be linked to a surviving *Battle of Britain* pilot, with whose role he could be identified. The respective actor and role model would then lunch together at a restaurant in company with a reporter from the *Evening News*, and the scintillating conversation that emerged would be featured in the following day's edition.

It was decided that I should be linked with Michael Caine, who played a squadron leader and was then on his way to the peak of his profession as a film actor. The lunch was duly set up and we met over a very good meal at Stone's restaurant in Leicester Square in the company of the reporter and a tape recorder. The lunch lasted for over three hours and the wine flowed, and towards the end there came the inevitable question from the reporter: in the heat of battle surely it must have been very easy to confuse friend and foe and even accidentally shoot down one of your own aircraft.

Indeed it was, I agreed. I quoted my own case and described the farce of the 'Battle of Barking Creek', which turned to tragedy when a highly strung Spitfire squadron shot down two Hurricanes and killed one of the pilots. Expanding on the theme of mistaken identity, and basking in the convivial glow of the film company's hospitality, I went on to say – in the strictest confidence, of course, and only on the understanding that none of this would get into print – how there had been at least one occasion when a pilot was deliberately shot down by his own squadron. It happened not at the time of the Battle of Britain but in the fighter sweeps over France that followed later.

Naturally I could mention no names, and all I could say was that it involved the CO of a fighter squadron whose pilots were driven to desperation by what they perceived as his appallingly bad leadership. The squadron had been suffering unusually high casualties in combination with a minimal success rate, and the blame for this was placed by the pilots squarely at the door of their leader. They had tried to have him removed through all normal means, but the higher authorities had been unresponsive. Finally, in sheer self-defence, they decided to take the ultimate positive way out. They waited till they were next involved in enemy action and shot him down.

In the context of wartime there was nothing especially novel about such situations. This particular story had been an open secret in Fighter Command at the time; certainly it was common knowledge in 11 Group, Fighter Command's spearhead. Similar stories came from all branches of the active services and 'it ill behoved anyone to pass judgement who had never shared the experience of daily confronting death and of knowing that lives in battle depended on a leader's skill and competence; of seeing friends and colleagues die, and opportunities to strike at the enemy wasted, because of one person's incompetence; and of having all pleas for help to higher authority met by a blanket of inertia. Such acts might seem barbaric in the cold light of peace, but clinical, objective judgements, based on peacetime standards and delivered by armchair theorists, had little place in the reality of the battlefield. I was simply being honest when I said that, as one of the pilots in that particular squadron, I might well have taken a decision to side with the assassins.

Having said my piece I gave the matter no further thought. After all, none of this was newsworthy in my eyes and I had the solemn word of the reporter that not a word of it would be printed. With hindsight, of course, my naïveté was breathtaking. In today's more cynical times we are far less likely to think that integrity is more important than the chequebook or that a promise to keep a confidentiality is more than a device to extract a scoop. I had been excessively foolish and the next day I paid the price when I saw the huge headlines in the *Evening News*: 'ONE OF THE FEW ALLEGES MURDER'.

The order of the next few days was bedlam. Every national newspaper came hounding after the grisly details, and most especially they wanted the name of the pilot who had been shot down and the identity of his squadron. The telephone never stopped as reporters clamoured for interviews, friends rang to wonder what all the fuss was about and a few senior officers – all desk wallahs with no operational experience who did not like to see the waters muddied to tarnish their reflected glory – came on the line to wonder rather stiffly whether I had considered how I was bringing the service into disrepute.

In all of this a notable exception was Lord Dowding, who as Air Chief Marshal Sir Hugh 'Stuffy' Dowding was Commander-in-Chief of Fighter Command before and during the Battle of Britain. There had been a vague public awareness that he was Fighter Command's boss, but I never felt this amounted to a real understanding of how much the nation owed to him. He was always more concerned with the welfare of his air and ground crews than he was in seeking popularity, and this, combined with a scratchy temperament that spoke its mind irrespective of rank, made him a maverick who never fitted smoothly into the internal politics that plague every large organisation.

Dowding's achievements were as often as not accomplished in the teeth of opposition from both politicians and fellow senior officers. From the beginning he understood the immense significance of the revolutionary RDF system (which came to be known as radar under American development), and he was the driving force that ensured it was somehow in place in time for the Battle of Britain. He also won what was said to be a unique victory for a service officer when he locked horns with Churchill over the Prime Minister's proposal to deplete London's defensive Spitfire squadrons and send them to help France before its fall. Without Dowding's intervention in appealing to the War Cabinet, as well as his championing of radar, the out come of the Battle of Britain might have been a very different story. The historian A.J.P. Taylor put it in a nutshell: 'When argument failed, Dowding laid down his pencil on the Cabinet table. The gentle gesture was a warning of immeasurable significance. The War Cabinet cringed, and Dowding's pencil won the Battle of Britain.'

It was therefore a great boost to my morale to receive a wise and charming letter from Dowding in the midst of my troubles. 'Don't worry,' he wrote, 'don't let the press get you down. They were always after me and you just have to learn to ignore them. If you don't react, they'll soon get fed up and move on.'

Nevertheless it was more easily said than done to stop the constant phone calls and knocks on the door getting me down. I began to feel like the perpetrator of a monstrous crime against the state, but the thing everyone wanted – the name of the victim and his squadron – was something I refused to divulge. Eventually, in despair, I phoned Max Aitken at *Express Newspapers*. I had known him during his fighter-pilot days and saw him as a good if not a close friend. 'Max,' I pleaded, 'you're a big wheel in the newspaper business. For God's sake call off the hounds. I'm being crucified.'

'Tell you what, Brian,' he replied. 'You just let me know who it was that got shot down and I'll see what I can do.'

'You bastard,' I said, and hung up.

But then, as Dowding predicted, the storm abated as suddenly as it had blown up. There were no more telephone calls, no more knocks on the door, no friends or foes to accost me at the Air Force Club for an update, no more senior officers wittering on about situations of which they could have no conception. A whisper went round that the Ministry of Defence had, in the end, clamped a 'D notice' on the affair, so banning all further publicity. Whatever the cause the relief to me was absolute.

With hindsight the extent to which I allowed this incident to get me down surprises me. Later on I would have been far more confident in the way I dealt with critics and two-liming reporters. I can only put it down to the muddle I was in over coming to terms with the civilian commercial world. It seemed to be a jungle in which I understood few of the rules and where the other inmates apparently enjoyed exploiting my vulnerability. I had commuted half my tiny disability pension (the maximum permitted) to pay for a honeymoon, and by now was striving to keep myself and a young family alive. The successful assault on commerce that I imagined for myself had simply failed to happen.

From the viewpoint of industry my CV hardly existed. I had gone straight from school to the RAF College at Cranwell, then to a peacetime fighter squadron followed by five years of war as a fighter pilot. My RAF career had ended with two years each as college instructor and administrator in the Air Ministry, finally to be rounded off by three years in a TB sanatorium.

Yet surely there must also have been a positively beneficial side to all of this. During my service career I had been one of the youngest group captains (equivalent to a full colonel in the army) in the RAF. I had commanded two mobile Spitfire wings in the DAF, both during the war and afterwards in Austria. Each wing had comprised five Spitfire squadrons and was self-contained and able to operate independently, having its own operations room and intelligence, maintenance, signals, medical, catering and transport teams. I had been responsible for the lives, morale and welfare of fifteen hundred men who lived and worked under canvas in often appalling conditions, not to mention the service-ability and operational efficiency of ninety front-line aircraft. Both the wings had been capable of moving to anywhere on the globe at a moment's notice without an interruption of operational flying.

It seemed to me that this accumulation of experience might suggest at least a few management skills at middle or even senior management level. The business mind disagreed. In industry and commerce there was a feeling of superiority towards the services that forgot the latter had been in business for centuries with an outstanding record of success – an achievement commerce could never hope to match. There was also a certain amount of resentment towards professional service people, arising from the fact that few senior or middle managers called up during the war achieved significant promotion. An element of tit-for-tat existed in post-war business attitudes.

My biggest mistake was to assume that the ethical standards and codes I had been brought up with at home, at school and in the RAF would apply equally in commercial life. Not a bit of it. In the services it was normal to do someone a favour as an automatic response and to expect nothing in return; in commerce nothing is done for nothing and the wheels are oiled by backhanders under various euphemisms. In the services when you gave someone your word, then it was also your bond and irrevocable; in commerce a verbal assurance unbacked by a written contract is good only so long as it suits the giver. There is no comparison between the principles and moral standards of the services and commerce, and it took me a long time to realise this and it cost me a lot of money.

My first business venture had come about when I decided I was unemployable and ought to start something on my own. At this point an old friend, Paddy Barthropp (ex-Wing Commander RAF, DFC, AFC), invited me to join him as a junior partner in a Rolls-Royce hire business he had started with his 'golden bowler'.

The enterprise was struggling hard, but it contained the seeds of success, and I jumped at the chance. Among all the personalities I came across in a life packed with vivid characters, Paddy was among the most extraordinary. He was an original blueprint for contradictions and eccentricity although in his case, because he possessed an extraordinarily endearing streak, everyone forgave and loved him. If Paddy fell dead drunk into his soup as guest of honour at an important dinner function, then, because it was Paddy, everybody blamed the soup. The secret of this astonishing ability to be loved in spite of all was simple: underneath a façade of eccentric inanity there lurked one of the kindest, most generous and warm-hearted of men, and everyone sensed it.

Barthropp and I worked together for two or three enjoyable years, but it then became evident that there was not really enough activity to keep us both fully occupied. We therefore agreed that I would start up a small garage group to complement the hire business. All began well with the group, which grew from one to seven garages, till the cash flow suddenly slowed for no good reason. Too late I discovered that the general manager had been running a scam with our group accountant and the manager of the most successful garage − all men I had trusted totally. The immediate outcome was that I had to wind up the garages and became dead broke with virtually no income.

Fortunately we owned a particularly attractive flat in South Kensington, and this became our saviour with tedious frequency during our early years of married life. Whenever I was jobless and our income dried, we let the flat and moved into digs till something turned up to relieve the pressure. In this way we managed to raise and educate three small children in the company of a golden retriever at which I occasionally found myself looking with speculative hunger. It was a hair-raising existence, and the press story erupted into the middle of it with depressing effect on my morale. Once again I had failed to learn the basic lesson: trust nobody and nothing in commerce unless you have it in writing.

There was one other occasion when I was the subject of headlines I could have done without, though how it came to be regarded as a news item I will never understand. It happened when I embarked on married life, though the origins of the story were to be traced back over the years to the days at Biggin Hill in Kent in 1940. About seven miles from the airfield was the White Hart at Brasted, the pub known by 92 Squadron as 'our pub', and not far up the road from the pub there lived a pair of identical female twins, the daughters of Sir Hector Macneal, in the Red House. They were tall, elegant, sophisticated and beautiful young women, and as if that were not enough in itself, they were also rich. They exuded the indefinable quality that comes from impeccable taste and the money to indulge it, and although it does not follow that to have money is to have style, the twins had style in abundance. The elder, by ten minutes or so, was Moira. She had two children, a boy of five or six and a girl of one or two. Her husband was an air commodore who was then doing a stint in the Middle East. The younger twin was Sheila, who had been married to Squadron Leader Freddie Shute, a fighter pilot killed earlier that year, in February, but whose death had been avoidable.

Freddie Shute had commanded a fighter squadron of Gladiators, based at an airfield near the Yorkshire east coast. Those outmoded biplanes were well on their way to honourable retirement, but in the early hours of a bleak winter's morning, long before dawn, a telephone call came through to request help for a Wellington bomber returning from a leaflet-dropping raid over France and now lost somewhere over the North Sea. Would Freddie please send out an aircraft to try to find it and lead it home. It was an order of the same calibre as the one that kept us circling overhead in the 'Battle of Barking Creek', and it should never have been given. A few months later such an order would have been counted out by the accumulation of experience. In this case there was not even a faint hope of success to justify the order, as Freddie was well aware. The night was a pitch black with driving rain, the clouds were down to wave-top level, and the idea of locating a Wellington bomber with no aid except the naked eye was an absurdity. Freddie was not prepared to order one of his pilots to go on such a mission of certain death and decided to go himself. He took off into a blinding snowstorm and, of course, was never seen or heard from again.

Regrettably I never met Freddie personally, but he was a well-known respected figure in flying and amateur car-racing circles and I found no one who failed to speak of him in the highest terms. His death was the tragic waste of a gallant man. After Freddie's death Sheila moved with their small daughter, Lesley, then not much more than a toddler, to join Moira in the Red House. There the twins, with their good looks, lavish generosity and captivating personalities, became the centre of an élite coterie of fighter pilots, of which 92 Squadron inevitably formed the core. After the White Hart had reluctantly shut its doors at closing time, as often as not we decamped en bloc to round off the evening at the twins'

There was another bonus from this friendship in that it became possible for me to cover the seven miles of winding road between Biggin and the White Hart at Brasted in seven minutes with the help of a specially modified and tuned Jaguar SS100. This outstandingly beautiful car had belonged to Freddie Shute, who used to race it at Brooklands, and his widow, Sheila, let me have the loan of it. The squadron was not stood down in the evenings until thirty minutes past last light, which could be alarmingly close to 'last orders'. Every minute saved on the journey between airfield and pub was therefore vital and the car a godsend.

92 Squadron could not claim exclusivity at the White Hart, of course, but we did regard the pub as our personal territory and grew pretty stuffy if lesser squadrons – to us – tried to gatecrash. It was run by Teddy and Kath Preston, an ideal couple for the job. Teddy was an archetypal host, ruddy of complexion and genial in manner, equally popular with locals and passing trade and a friend to the Biggin Hill pilots. He was on the

Royal Navy reserve list, and in due time was called up to join the 'wavy navy', the nickname for the reserve since the reserve rank stripes on their officers' uniforms went in zigzags to distinguish them from the straight stripes of the regulars. After that we only saw him occasionally on leave, but Kath continued to run the pub with her daughter, Valerie, and its popularity was maintained.

In time the pub became quite famous in wartime legend, in part because of a blackout screen which stood by the dart-board just inside the main door into the bar from the road. The screen was intended to prevent light spilling outside when the door was opened, in accordance with wartime regulations, and its fame came from a tradition of pilots writing their signatures on it. The reason for the start of this custom was eventually lost in the mists of time, but it had its origins in about the early autumn of 1940 when 92 Squadron threw a farewell party in honour of Group Captain Dickie Grice.

Dickie, the much loved commanding officer at Biggin Hill, had blotted his copybook that September. Biggin Hill, like most other airfields in the south-east, received a pasting from the Luftwaffe in a wave of attacks that, many pundits believed, would have lost us the battle if they had been pressed home. As it happened they were not continued, and the battle was won, and perhaps Dickie Grice's action had been one of the reasons. The German attack badly cratered the airfield and destroyed many surrounding buildings, but it left one hangar intact. Dickie at once reasoned that if German reconnaissance revealed one of the main buildings still standing, then they would soon be back to finish the job. He therefore requisitioned some dynamite and blew it up.

The Germans never came back and Biggin Hill remained operating through the crucial stage of the bombing; many lives were undoubtedly saved and a lot of further damage was avoided. But Dickie had committed the cardinal sin: he had ignored the bureaucracy and acted on initiative. The pen pushers at the Air Ministry took a dim view. In their eyes his crime was to fail to fill in the correct forms (in triplicate) outlining his proposal, before waiting for the request to be studied and a proper reply returned (in triplicate again, naturally). And now, to have destroyed Air Ministry property without the necessary paperwork (in triplicate) was a heinous crime indeed. It was irrelevant that the Germans would have been unlikely to wait for the formalities to be completed, that hangars were never used anyway in wartime, and that Biggin Hill's squadrons could have been grounded for days. Paperwork was paperwork and the administrators might start finding themselves out of a job if people took to carrying on in this way.

None of this, of course, was ever given as the official reason for his removal to another post, but all of us were in no doubt that his action with the dynamite was the real cause. In our eyes he was a first-class CO who showed the style of leadership the RAF needed. 92 Squadron therefore gave him a rousing send-off at the White Hart, and during the course of the evening someone made him sign the blackout screen. Then someone else signed, and some one else, till in the end most of the squadron had followed suit. Regrettably it later became the habit of any itinerant pilot passing through to add his signature until the board became overcrowded, though oddly enough, even today, it is possible to pick out the few signatures from the original gathering. They are bigger and bolder than the rest, and slightly different in colour. Perhaps we used different chalk, or maybe ours was the better party.

I became very close to the twins at the Red House, till my posting to DAF in 1943, when I lost contact. I had also met their father several times at Biggin Hill. Sir Hector Macneal, a man of infinite charm, known affectionately as the 'Black Knight', was a friend of Beaverbrook, who was given the task of overseeing aircraft production by Churchill. With Beaverbrook's blessing Hector was at work attempting to produce a fireproof flying overall to protect pilots when they were shot down in flames and prevent some of the horrendous burns being suffered. It was a brave effort, and had it worked it could have saved many lives and appalling disfigurements. He showed a stubborn unwillingness to be defeated in this project, and thus at Biggin Hill we spent many agreeable hours squirting petrol over his son Lorne, a resigned and less than enthusiastic guinea pig, as we did our best to set him alight.

After the war was over Sir Hector moved into a flat in Piccadilly close to the Air Force Club and he and I started seeing quite a lot of each other as neighbours. Catching up on the news since our Biggin days, I discovered that Moira had divorced her first husband and married back into the RAF. Sheila had embarked on one more marriage, though it turned out to be a disaster which hardly survived beyond the wedding reception. It was a tremendous pleasure to me to meet and come to know the whole family again, and to catch up on the news of what had happened to them all in the meantime.

One evening Hector threw a party in his Mayfair flat, which finally came to an end in the small hours. The indefatigable 'Black Knight', by then in his mid-eighties, moved on to some night spot or other with the bulk of his guests, though I stayed behind, no doubt because I was too broke to go. Also staying behind to help with the clearing up was Sheila's now grown-up daughter, Lesley, and as I sat there idly, glass of whisky in hand, I watched her restoring things to some sort of order. I had to admit I was staggered by the transformation in the interval of what seemed only a few short years. The toddler of just the other day had grown into a bewitching young woman capable of stopping London's traffic. And my heart.

Unplanned, unrehearsed, with no conscious volition on my part and no feeling of reality, I suddenly heard my disembodied voice asking her whether, by any remote chance, she would consider the possibility of marrying me. It was like eavesdropping on a conversation between strangers as, equally unreal, I heard her voice reply in a totally matter-of-fact way, as she hardly paused in her tidying or bothered to look up, yes, she supposed so. Why not?

Had I planned it cold, then my courage would have failed me before I started. The thought had previously flickered through my mind briefly on the odd occasion, only to be dismissed as an old man's foolish fantasy. Here was I, pushing forty, a confirmed bachelor and layabout glorying in my lack of responsibilities, with a comfortable pad in Sloane Avenue and my headquarters at the Air Force Club in Piccadilly. There was Lesley, a string of hungry young men jostling for her favours, not to mention the teetering sugar daddies on the fringe. I had proposed to a gorgeous young woman half my age and found her agreeing in a clinically calm way to marry an ageing wreck with no career and no prospects.

Thirty-six years later I am still at a loss to know what motivated her. I can only think she did it out of politeness, or that she was brought up to be kind to the old and helpless. Kind she has certainly been, with a compassion that knows no bounds. Without Lesley I would have been up there with my sparrow and my granite block in no time. Where the war never succeeded in killing me, the peace undoubtedly would have without Lesley.

For the few weeks after proposing I was on the greatest high of my life. As my feet hardly touched the ground my RAF mates were taking odds that the marriage would not last six months. Their worldly speculations worried me not a jot, though I did wonder whether I might come in for a drubbing from Sir Hector for cradle-snatching his beloved granddaughter. On the contrary, he was generosity and kindness itself and went out of his way to encourage us. He at once took charge of the arrangements. To follow the wedding in St Peter's, Eaton Square, he laid on a reception at Londonderry House, a beautiful old building in Park Lane soon to be demolished by the planning vandals. There were six hundred guests, many of them RAF cronies whom I happened to bump into and at once invited, seizing on the chance to repay past hospitalities. The occasion was a huge success, and we stayed the night at a hotel on Monkey Island in the Thames near Bray, before leaving early next morning for Heathrow, en route for Germany.

As we relaxed in our seats in the aircraft, waiting for take-off, we casually glanced at the morning papers which the stewardess was distributing. The press had done it again: turned the facts upside down for the sake of a good story. The headlines screamed at us: 'THEY SAID HE'D MARRY MOTHER BUT LESLEY IS THE BRIDE.'

EPILOGUE

BIGGIN HILL, 1940–42

What did you do in the war, Daddy?'

'Get drunk in the White Hart at Brasted, my son.'

Not all the time, perhaps, but it was certainly not unknown. And in the early 1940s, long before plastic rusticity became the vogue, the White Hart at Brasted, our 'local' during my days at Biggin Hill, was as congenial a place as any to do it in.

No doubt about it, of all the members of the fighting forces during the last war, the fighter pilot, and especially the Spitfire pilot, had the most enviable of jobs. Not for him the endless tension and terror endured by the convoy patrols in the Atlantic and the North Sea, of the bomber pilot deep into enemy territory and at the mercy of any half-trained Bavarian peasant at the end of an anti-aircraft gun, of the sub-mariner listening for the depth charges crouched in his claustrophobic hole, and of the countless other fighting men who faced acute danger and discomfort over long periods of time. The Spitfire pilot in 1940, charged with the defence of his homeland, faced a longish day, of course – from half an hour before dawn to an hour after dusk – but he flew from a warm and comfortable base with the most versatile of all fighter aircraft, and it being a single-seater he was more or less master of his own fate.

I suppose at the height of the Battle of Britain we averaged three, sometimes four, sorties a day, but a sortie seldom lasted more than an hour, and we had the immense moral advantage of fighting over our own territory. It's surprising how fierce one's protective instincts become at the sight of an enemy violating one's homeland, and how comforting the knowledge that if one is shot down one at least has a chance of living to fight another day. Contrast this with the wretched German pilot, flying at the extreme end of his range, over hostile territory, and for the first time in his hitherto all-conquering operational life up against a fighter aircraft comparable, if not superior, to his own. No wonder the poor chaps couldn't wait for winter and a break in the weather.

Of all the places from which to operate, as I did from August 1940 to June 1942, Biggin Hill was way out in front. It was superbly placed, both operationally and socially. Operationally we were just far enough inland from the main German approach lanes to give us time to climb flat out due north to the enemy's altitude before turning south to hit him head on, by far the most effective and damaging form of attack, usually somewhere over mid-Kent.

The social aspects of Biggin Hill exhausts me just thinking about them. When we were stood down half an hour after dusk there was the choice of either scooting up to London, where ten shillings (the bulk of our day's pay of fourteen shillings) would cover an evening at Shepherds and the Bag of Nails (or the Four Hundred if we could raise a quid!), or the White Hart at Brasted, where five shillings kept us in beer until the local bobby moved us on at closing time. Then, with a few girlfriends, on to our billets, a comfortable local country house where we were dispersed at night against the possibility of an air raid on the airfield (all that money that had gone into our training couldn't be put at risk) where one of our pilots, a pianist who could hold his own against any night club musician – and often did, would play into the small hours, and we would finally snatch an hour or two's sleep in arm chairs, fully dressed to save time and effort getting up for dawn readiness. Then to the dispersal hut with the unforgettable sound of Merlin engines warming up in the grey half-light, the squadron doctor dispensing his miracle cure (would that I had kept the recipe) from a tin bucket, occasionally a pilot, suffering more than the usual, climbing into his cockpit for a quick rejuvenating whiff of neat oxygen.

And then the inevitable stomach-churning ring of the telephone and the voice from Ops: '92 Squadron, scramble. One hundred plus bandits approaching Dungeness at angels fifteen.'

The surge of adrenaline, the half dozen or so pilots, that were all we could normally muster, sprinting to their aircraft, the tiredness and the hangovers disappearing as though they had never been, the flat-out climb to 20,000ft, the mud on our flying boots freezing fast to our rudder bars in our unheated and unpressurised cockpits, the long shallow tension-building dive south to meet the enemy, sometimes seeing the sun lift over the horizon from 20,000ft and again, after landing, on the still darkened earth. The day only just begun and already behind us the savage, lethal action, death for some, and for those safely back on the ground the memory of two sunrises in one morning and thoughts quickly suppressed of friends not yet accounted for. And life, at least until the next telephone call. Adrenaline-filled life. One sustained electrifying high.

I remember Biggin Hill with enormous affection. The strange double life, each one curiously detached from the other. One moment high above the earth, watching a sunrise not yet visible below, killing and avoiding being killed; and the next chatting with the locals over a pint of beer in a cosy country pub as casually as though we had just stopped off the six o'clock from Waterloo after a day in the City. Occasionally a local commenting critically on the aerial activity he had witnessed that day as though he were discussing his local football team. And the next morning back to the unreal world and the twisting smoke trails at angels two-five. This could only happen to a fighter pilot.

Of course there were intensely sad moments as well as intensely exciting ones. I lost many old friends as well as making new ones, and the worst part was watching them die, spiralling down with a smudge of smoke, or breaking up, watching for the parachute to blossom, the relief when it did, the sick feeling when it didn't. I walk with ghosts when I revisit my old station, but they are friendly ones. I mourn them, but they had counted the cost and they died with regret but without surprise. They were typical of their generation, and their generation was typical of all others. The young of all generations are the same. They may dress differently and have different rites and rituals, but give them a crisis and they are all the same.

I salute them.

APPENDIX ONE

A BRIEF SUMMARY OF
BRIAN KINGCOME'S SERVICE RECORD

In January 1936 Brian Kingcome entered RAF College, Cranwell. Graduating at the end of July 1938, he was posted to No.65 Squadron, which was at that time commanded by Squadron Leader Cooke and based at Hornchurch. The squadron was equipped with the Gloster Gladiator Mk I, but in March 1939 it received some of the first Mk I Spitfires, and it was with this aircraft that the squadron went into action over France prior to the Dunkirk evacuation. On 27 May 1940 Brian was posted as a flight commander to No.92 Squadron, which, having recently moved from Northolt, was based at Duxford and, again, flying the Spitfire I. The squadron had been re-equipped with the Spitfire, earlier in May 1940, replacing the Bristol Blenheim 1(f) that had been in service since the squadron was reformed in October 1939. The acting commanding officer at the time of Brian's posting was Bob Stanford Tuck, who had also, at the beginning of May, transferred from 65 Squadron as a flight commander. No.92 Squadron, until a few days prior, had been commanded by Squadron Leader Roger Bushell. A South African, Bushell had been shot down on 23 May 1940 and become a prisoner of war — he will be remembered as one of the chief organisers of the 'Great Escape' from Stalag Luft III and one of the fifty escapers to be summarily executed by the Gestapo.

Brian was posted to Biggin Hill from August 1940 to June 1942. On 15 October 1940, at Biggin Hill, towards the closing days of the Battle of Britain, Brian was shot down by an Me Bf

109 (according to the official record though he always harboured his own doubts). Though wounded in the leg, he managed to bail out of his aircraft. The wound caused him to be hospitalised for some six weeks and so he missed the final days of the air battle. It was during this period in hospital that he received notification that he had been awarded the Distinguished Flying Cross (DFC) for his actions during the Battle of Britain. On recovering from his wound he returned to 92 Squadron, but in August 1941 was posted to No.61 OTU as an instructor – at the same time he was also awarded a bar to his DFC. In February 1942 he resumed operational flying and became CO of No.72 Squadron, which at that time was based at Gravesend and flying the Spitfire Vb. Over the next few weeks the squadron was relocated to Biggin Hill, but Brian only remained with the squadron until June 1942 as he was promoted to the rank of Wing Commander and became Wing Leader at Kenley. Later that year the newly formed Fighter Leaders' School moved from Chedworth to Charmy Down, with Brian in command. On 15 December 1942 he was awarded the Distinguished Service Order (DSO).

Posted to the Mediterranean in May 1943, Brian led No.244 Wing during the Allied invasion of Sicily. He was promoted to Group Captain and confirmed as commander of the Wing in September 1943, with Hugh 'Cocky' Dundas taking over as his Wing Commander (Flying). Towards the end of 1944 Brian was sent to the RAF Staff College at Haifa in Palestine, and in January 1945, on completion of his assessment course, he was posted as the Senior Air Staff Officer (SASO) with No.205 Bomber Group at Foggia, Italy.

In the spring of 1946 he was back with a fighter unit when he was given command of No.324 Wing based at Zeitweg, Austria, but, by the winter of that year, he had returned to the UK after being posted to the RAF Staff College, Bracknell. He remained at Bracknell as Director (Staff) for two years, following which he was seconded to the Air Ministry as Air Staff Plans (1).

In September 1950, while still at the Air Ministry, Brian contracted tuberculosis and spent over two and a half years in hospital
and a sanatorium. He was finally discharged in June 1953, and
although the RAF had put him on indefinite leave, he decided
to resign his commission and was retired from the service in
January 1954.

APPENDIX TWO

SUMMARY OF AERIAL VICTORIES

DATE	SQUADRON	A/C FLOWN	ENEMY A/C	CLAIM	LOCATION
1940					
2 June	92 Sqn	Spitfire I	Heinkel III	D-c (1)	Dunkirk
"	"	"	"	D-c (1)	"
"	"	"	"	Dam.	"
10 July	"	"	Junkers 88	D-u (⅓)	Llanelli
24 July	"	"	"	D-c (⅓)	Ilfracombe
9 Sep	"	"	Me Bf 109E	D-p	Canterbury
11 Sep	"	"	Heinkel III	D-c (1)	Dungeness
14 Sep	"	"	Me Bf 109E	Dam.	Canterbury
"	"	"	"	Dam.	"
15 Sep	"	"	Dornier 17	Dam.	Hornchurch
18 Sep	"	"	Junkers 88	D-c (½)	Isle of Sheppey
"	"	"	Heinkel III	D-p	Southend
"	"	"	"	Dam.	"
24 Sep	"	"	Junkers 88	Dam.	Maidstone
"	"	"	Me Bf 109E	Dam.	Dover
27 Sep	"	"	Dornier 17	D-p	Maidstone
"	"	"	"	Dam.	"
"	"	"	Junkers 88	Dam.	Sevenoaks
"	"	"	"	Dam.	"
"	"	"	"	D-c (⅓)	Redhill
11 Oct	"	"	Me Bf 109E	D-c (1)	Dungeness
12 Oct	"	"	"	D-c (1)	English Channel
"	"	"	"	Dam.	Margate
"	"	"	"	D-c (1)	Cap Gris Nez
13 Oct	"	"	"	D-c (1)	Ashford
1941					
16 June	"	Spitfire Vb	Me Bf 109F	D-p	Le Touquet
24 July	"	"	"	D-c (1)	Le Havre
1942					
15 April	72 Sqn	Spitfire Vb	Focke-Wulf 190	Dam.	Boulogne
27 May	"	"	Me Bf 109F	D-p	St-Valery-en-Caux
27 Aug	Kenley Wing	Spitfire IX	Focke-Wulf 190	Dam.	Boulogne

D = Destroyed : Dam. = Damaged : c = Confirmed : u = Unconfirmed : p = Probable
The number or fraction given in brackets denotes the confirmed score

APPENDIX THREE

LETTER FROM TONY BRUCE

Tel   01255 425607

59 Gorse Way
Jaywick
Nr Clacton
CO15 2HU
21·3·99

My dear Leslie.

I simply couldn't believe it when someone told me Brian had arrived in the Desert. Sand, sweat, flys, beards. The precious pint of tea for breakfast with scum on it, the water being brackish, ship's biscuits it needed a hammer to break, ten pound tins of yellow candle grease alleged to be butter etc etc — there was obviously some mistake — It was grotesque — The super sophisticated, debonair wit "Appears to be entering the company of Wing Commander Rougecoare DSO DFC—" (Tatler) — who was; you? (me too young!) Mona? Stella?

Anyway I was forced to believe it when unwashed, unshaved, dirty, smelling, (we did our laundry in 100 octane petrol!) I was about to throw my parachute into the mess Tent ("Pilot's Mess" no 'Officers" or "Sergeants"?!) but on pulling open the flap. I saw nothing familiar.

There was a huge carpet spread out on the bare sand. There were tables and chairs, and the crowning glory a bar tended by a white Jacketed airman (a cloth draped over the bar disguised its origin as an ME 110's tail plane!)

The amateur barman asked me what I'd like (he seemed to have everything under the sun) and it was only when he or someone told me that Brian had come to command 244 wing that I wondered whether instead of dreaming I was in the world of Mohammed. If the "West End" had little of the desert about it, then it was time the desert was given a bit of the West End!!

Anyway I rang wing headquarters and was invited by that quite unmistakeable voice to come over. Palatial as our Pilot's Mess had become to desert eyes the scales of course had now fallen and Brian's own "office" made our transformed Mess seem almost drab.

I think there was a Persian carpet on the sand cocktail cabinet, luxourious furniture and of course most important of all the best of hosts.

After coming all the way from Egypt Spitfire Squadrons were at a very low ebb. I think the policy was to panic the Germans and Italians into an "Even the Spitfires have caught up" little knowing at what cost.

An "aerodrome" was any reasonably level sand with a white pin :: 40 gallon oil drum at the four corners of a square. Ammunition fuel officers telephone lines hangars hospital tents all appeared and disappeared in only days as the 8th army followed us. Water was flown to us in bombers!

When Brian took over we were all on snarling terms with each other and within 48 hours at the most the whole wing had been metamorphosised into hundreds of really happy men. It was really uncanny.

I am sorry about the writing Leslie. Sometimes I can't understand what I've written myself so I don't blame you if you can't!

Yours aye,
Tony Bruce.

My dear Leslie,

I simply couldn't believe it when someone told me Brian had arrived in the desert. Sand, sweat, flys, beards, the precious pint of tea for breakfast with scum on it… ships biscuits it needed a hammer to break, ten pound tins of yellow candle grease alleged to be butter…

… anyway I was forced to believe it when unwashed, unshaved, dirty… (we did our own laundry in 100 Octane Petrol!) I was about to throw my parachute into the Mess tent… but on pulling open the flap I saw nothing familiar.

There was a huge carpet spread out on the bare sand. There were tables and chairs, and the crowing glory a <u>bar</u> tended by a white jacketed airman (a cloth draped over the bar disguised its origin as an ME110's tail plane!)

The amateur barman asked me what I'd like (he seemed to have everything under the sun) and it was only when someone told me that Brian had come to command 244 Wing that I wondered whether instead of dreaming I was in the world of Mohammed. If the West End had little of the desert about it, then it was time the desert was given a bit of the West End!

Anyway I rang up headquarters and was invited by that quite unmistakable voice to come over. Palatial as our Pilot's Mess had become to desert eyes the scales of course had now fallen and Brian's own 'office' made our transformed Mess seem almost drab.

I think there was a Persian carpet on the sand, cocktail cabinet, luxurious furniture and of course most important of all the <u>best</u> of hosts.

… When Brian took over we were all on snarling terms with each other and within 48 hours at the most the whole wing had been metamorphosised into hundreds of really happy men. It was really uncanny.

… yours aye
Tony Bruce

APPENDIX FOUR

EULOGY FOR BRIAN KINGCOME

By Group Captain Sir Hugh Dundas CBE, DSO, DFC

Words. What difficult, even dangerous, instruments they can be. And never more so, I dare say, than for one standing where I do now and seeking to conjure up the spirit and character of an old and dear friend.

But they are all I have. Words like brave/true and determined/like courteous, amusing, intelligent, well-read. Expressions like a born leader/a loyal friend/a wonderful husband and father. They all fit. But, much as most of us might like to have them applied to ourselves, they are quite inadequate in remembering Brian Kingcome.

Let us start by considering his truly astonishing record as a wartime fighter pilot and leader. He was undoubtedly one of the greats; but he was not at all one of your run-of-the-mill, made-to-measure war heroes or air aces. And he most certainly would not, ever, have wished to be so regarded. Indeed he went out of his way to avoid it. The nearest he would ever have come to talking about the number of planes he shot down might have been to say, with a chuckle, that he did not really know but that he was sure he had frightened a few. And he carried this modest, self-deprecatory attitude with him in relation to all his achievements, which were many.

There were, I think, four key attributes which made him the man he was and enabled him to do the things he did. They were courage, determination, a total lack of pomposity or self-importance and an everlasting lightness of heart and of touch. Those were his hallmarks.

The first major test of his courage and determination came soon after he had gone to Cranwell, when he was involved in a motor accident and very seriously injured. He was told that he would never be able to resume his care as a pilot. He was in hospital for a long time. But, and not for the last time, as we all well know, he refused to accept the verdict of the authorities and, by sheer, dogged determination got himself back into the sky.

Then came 1940, that terrible year when Hitler took over Europe. That spring Brian was posted to command 'A' Flight of 92 Squadron, which was, almost immediately thereafter, in action over Dunkirk, where his plane was hit and he was slightly wounded. There was really no respite from then on. In a few more weeks 92 was in the thick of the Battle of Britain. It was there and then that Brian's extraordinary leadership qualities blazed forth like a beacon, showing the way to every member of the squadron, in the air and on the ground. People who were there, fifty three and a half years ago, remember it and describe it as though it was yesterday. One of them said to me last week: 'He really *was* 92 Squadron and all its spirit.' Those of us who remember 92 Squadron's reputation in those days understand how much those words signify.

What became very apparent as the weeks and months and eventually the years of fighting went by were the other key hallmarks I mentioned – Brian's total lack of self-importance or self-glorification and his constant lightness of heart and of touch. He adopted and projected always, whether speaking to his pilots in the heat of battle, or briefing them on the ground, or roistering with them at night, an almost mocking attitude towards the deadly and actually terrifying business they were all engaged in. And in doing so he bouyed up and sustained all those who lacked his inner strength and fire, keeping their fears at bay.

Paddy Barthropp provides, in his splendid autobiography, a good example of Brian's unflapability and lightness of touch. He describes how, when commanding 72 Squadron, Brian was leading it through foul weather over the Channel on the day when the pride of Hitler's navy – the *Scharnhorst*, *Gneisenau* et al. – were making their dash for the North Sea ports, the squadron suddenly found itself right overhead of those lethal vessels.

'Oh good gracious,' called out Brian on the R/T, 'there are three beautiful battle boats. Do you suppose they belong to the enemy?'

With that his question was answered, as an ack ack shell blew a large hole in his port wing – making, no doubt, a beautiful loud bang.

With only a couple of short breaks, Brian spent almost the whole war leading from the cockpit. He finished up in Malta, Sicily and Italy, which is where and when he ceased to be, for me, a passing acquaintance and became a lifelong friend. For the last six months of that period he was my CO, as Group Captain commanding 244 Wing, where I was his Wing Commander Flying. During those six months in the summer and autumn of 1944, as we fighter-bombed and straffed our way up the Appenines giving close support to the Eighth Army, our association was a very close one and we got to know and understand each other well. That process was certainly helped not only by the fact that the going was quite tough, but also by the more mundane fact that we were sharing sleeping quarters which consisted of two bunks built into the back of a three ton lorry. A friendship which could survive that could survive anything.

Well, the war ended at last. But for him another hard battle lay just ahead. In 1947 he contracted TB – a very much more serious matter in those days than it is today, when a few well-chosen drugs will soon knock it on the head. For Brian it meant a two-year stay at Midhurst Sanatorium. And when he came out one of his lungs had been taken away completely.

And so, inevitably, his career in the Royal Air Force was taken away too. I do not know what his ambitions had been. He never talked of it. But I do know that he had the intellectual and leadership qualities which could have taken him to the very top of the Service. Instead he had to retire, in his very early thirties. It must have been a most bitter blow to his spirit.

He began his new life working with his old and colourful friend Paddy Barthropp, who had started a car hire business in London, specialising in transportation by Rolls Royce. Evidently Brian applied the same insouciance to the business of hiring cars as he had to the business of waging war. He was once overheard by Paddy talking the Duke of Beaufort, a regular customer, who was asking for a car to meet him at Paddington station and added that he would have with him a particularly long fishing rod. 'What a lucky Duke you are,' Brian was heard to say, 'we have a particularly long motor car for you.'

Sadly, that car hire venture failed in the mid-fifties. Paddy had to pick himself up and start all over again, but on his own and on a shoe string. Brian was out of a job. It was a low point. But it did not last for long. Just over the hill there was a future, a wonderful future. For in 1957 he married Lesley. And they never looked back.

Kingcome Sofas, the business they ran together, was in the truest sense a husband and wife, wife and husband affair, a fact which was emphasised by Geoffrey Cridland, who was first retained by them as a consultant but later became managing director. In writing to me about the partnership he said: 'Brian would never have been mistaken for a roving disciple of the Business School of Management. His approach was very much his and Lesley's own. You could not really separate them in this unique enterprise.'

And so for more than thirty years they lived and worked and raised their family together in total harmony and with much success until at last, as Brian grew frailer, they had to move on, down to Devonshire where they had had a country home for many years. And there, in the end, last week, his heart gave up.

His was indeed a life and a friendship which we can celebrate and remember with much gratitude for its strong and often joyous impact on our own lives. And how deeply and how truly we feel today for Lesley and the family.

I am going to end with someone else's words. I certainly cannot better them. They were written by Geoffrey Cridland in his letter to me. They show very clearly the constant and unchanging nature of Brian's character and behaviour, how the impression which he made, in the evening of his life, on a business colleague was precisely that which he had made on the men who flew and fought with him fifty years earlier. 'Working with Brian,' Cridland wrote, 'was never dull. It was always enjoyable because he believed in and acted in ways which so many people have abandoned. He had courage; he was kind; he was amusing; he was supportive; he was loyal; he was polite; he was true. He had no need to go back to basics, because he had never abandoned them.'

If you are interested in purchasing other books published by The History Press, or in case you have difficulty finding any of our books in your local bookshop, you can also place orders directly through our website

www.thehistorypress.co.uk